Testing and the Paradoxes of Fairness

How can admissions officers, employers, and scholarship committees maximize the accuracy of prediction of individual performance while minimizing adverse impact due to group differences? Testing offers a straightforward solution to the first half of this problem. Tests are the best way to predict how someone will perform in school, in the military, in medicine, or while controlling airline traffic and flying a plane. Tests are also useful beyond personnel selection, such as for selection of a college major or courses. However, the other side of this problem is more complex. The use of test scores is usually accompanied by group differences that could result in continued systemic discrimination by limiting opportunities for those who are marginalized. *Testing and the Paradoxes of Fairness* charts an approach to using tests that incorporates evidence, transparency, and societal values to maximize efficiency and fairness.

HOWARD WAINER is an award-winning American statistician and research scientist. His areas of work include testing, graphical methods for data analysis and communication, and robust statistical methodology. He has served on the faculty of the University of Chicago, at the Bureau of Social Science Research during the Carter Administration, and as Principal Research Scientist in the Research Statistics Group at Educational Testing Service for 21 years. In 2016, he retired after 15 years as Distinguished Research Scientist at the National Board of Medical Examiners. This is his twenty-sixth book.

DANIEL H. ROBINSON is the K-16 Mind, Brain, and Education Endowed Chair at the University of Texas at Arlington. He received his Ph.D. in Educational Psychology in 1993 from the University of Nebraska where he majored in both learning/cognition and statistics/research. He previously taught at Mississippi State University, the University of South Dakota, the University of Louisville, the University of Texas at Austin, and Colorado State University. He has served as department chair, director, and associate dean of research.

'There is not a more pragmatically effective, yet maligned field in the behavioral sciences than the measurement of human abilities. It has been effective precisely because it has been built around measurement, and yet it is maligned precisely because it has been so effective in addressing real world issues. In *Testing and the Paradoxes of Fairness* Howard Wainer and Daniel Robinson masterfully describe how and why this has occurred.'

- David Lubinski, *Intelligence*

'One of the best books I ever read on the place of testing in our culture.'

- David C. Berliner, *Arizona State University*

'Wainer and Robinson present an unblinking, data-based look at the discriminatory effects of both standardized testing—and the absence of standardized testing—on admissions, selection, licensing and other personnel decisions. The results for individuals, groups, institutions and society make clear the substantial costs of ignoring evidence in these decisions.'

- Arthur E. Wise, *Education Author, Advocate and Policymaker*

Testing and the Paradoxes of Fairness

HOWARD WAINER

Statistician and Research Scientist

DANIEL H. ROBINSON

University of Texas, Arlington

CAMBRIDGE
UNIVERSITY PRESS

Shaftesbury Road, Cambridge CB2 8EA, United Kingdom

One Liberty Plaza, 20th Floor, New York, NY 10006, USA

477 Williamstown Road, Port Melbourne, VIC 3207, Australia

314–321, 3rd Floor, Plot 3, Splendor Forum, Jasola District Centre, New Delhi – 110025, India

103 Penang Road, #05–06/07, Visioncrest Commercial, Singapore 238467

Cambridge University Press is part of Cambridge University Press & Assessment, a department of the University of Cambridge.

We share the University's mission to contribute to society through the pursuit of education, learning and research at the highest international levels of excellence.

www.cambridge.org
Information on this title: www.cambridge.org/9781009576871

DOI: 10.1017/9781009576857

© Howard Wainer and Daniel H. Robinson 2026

This publication is in copyright. Subject to statutory exception and to the provisions of relevant collective licensing agreements, no reproduction of any part may take place without the written permission of Cambridge University Press & Assessment.

When citing this work, please include a reference to the DOI 10.1017/9781009576857

First published 2026

The image of the scale in the background credit: CSA Images/ CSA Images/ Getty Images

A catalogue record for this publication is available from the British Library

A Cataloging-in-Publication data record for this book is available from the Library of Congress

ISBN 978-1-009-57687-1 Hardback
ISBN 978-1-009-57682-6 Paperback

Cambridge University Press & Assessment has no responsibility for the persistence or accuracy of URLs for external or third-party internet websites referred to in this publication and does not guarantee that any content on such websites is, or will remain, accurate or appropriate.

For EU product safety concerns, contact us at Calle de José Abascal, 56, 1°, 28003 Madrid, Spain, or email eugpsr@cambridge.org

To our colleagues, past and present, whose ideas and data provided evidence for a safe passage through the dangerous shoals bordered by the Scylla of social values and the Charybdis of the inefficient use of human potential. Without you there would be nothing.

Annotated Table of Contents

Preface – How this book came into being, and what you should expect to find within it. You will also learn of the threats posed by Hitchcockian bombs under the table. *page* xi

Acknowledgments xvi

1. **A Brief Recounting of the First Four Millennia of Testing** In this chapter we trace the origins of testing to its civil service roots in Xia Dynasty China and its growth thereafter including IQ testing and U.S. Army placement testing in the early twentieth century. 1

2. **Why Tests Are so Widely Disliked** Although the use of testing has been of remarkable value for millennia, and has improved steadily over the past century, it is now experiencing heightened public dissatisfaction due partly to concerns regarding fairness and equity. In this chapter, we discuss some plausible causes for this apparent change in public attitudes. 11

3. **The Origins and Consequences of Mental Testing in the U.S. Military** Armed services tests have existed for centuries. In this chapter, we focus on the U.S. Armed Services and how the tests used have adapted to changed claims associated with changing needs and purposes of the tests. Military testing was the first program to explicitly move from very specialized tests for specific purposes to testing generalized underlying ability. This made such tests suitable for situations not even initially considered. The practice was both widely followed and just as widely disparaged. 24

4. **Testing in Grades K-12** Since the 1850's, K–12 students in the U.S. have been tested as a way to evaluate schools. Using student test scores for school accountability and to drive educational reform efforts is one of the oldest and continuous misuses of testing in modern history.   35

5. **Licensing Examinations: Physicians, Pilots, and Teachers as Examples** Many professions (e.g., teachers, pilots, lawyers, physicians) require applicants to pass a licensing exam, whose principal purpose is to protect the public from incompetent practitioners. These exams also sometimes show the same sorts of race and sex differences observed in other test scores. Thus, they too are susceptible to equity criticisms. We discuss the implications of getting rid of such tests or even just lowering cutoff scores.   48

6. **Admission Testing for Higher Education** Many colleges that required SAT or ACT scores before the pandemic suspended them during it. Although the dangers of the pandemic have subsided, many have not yet resumed their use. The arguments supporting their continued suspension are based primarily on the fact that such tests, like most other tests, show differences among subgroups (e.g., races). We discuss the costs and benefits of no longer using such test scores in admission decisions.   72

7. **Tests Used for Merit-Based Scholarships** In both K-12 and higher education, it is common to use test scores in deciding which students receive scholarships and other awards. As with placement decisions, this practice is also controversial due to issues of equity. We discuss the evidence supporting test scores as an aid in making such decisions including the costs of finding suitable winners, the costs of false positives, and the costs of false negatives.   82

8. **Using Student Test Scores to Evaluate Teachers: An Assessment of Value-Added Models** Tests are now often used to evaluate schools, school personnel (e.g., teachers, principals, superintendents) or programs. In this chapter we focus on one highly touted methodology, value-added models

(VAMs), that have been advocated as a rigorous scientific solution to what was previously an area rife with subjectivity. We discuss both the technical and logical flaws of these models. 90

9. **Dividing Test Scores into Subcomponents** It is often desired to extract more information from a test score than is available in a single number. The almost universal response to such desires is to divide the overall test score into subcomponents/subscores. In this chapter we summarize the rules governing the legitimate use of subscores and report on the frequency, in modern practice, that it is done correctly. 97

10. **On Cost Functions in Testing** When decisions are made there is a cost to making a mistake. This cost is often different for an erroneous positive decision than it is for an erroneous negative one. Decisions based on test scores are no different. In this chapter we discuss this issue and provide several evocative examples. 111

11. **Evidence in Science: Should We Use Data and What Data Can We Trust?** The use of test scores as evidence to support the claims made for them requires an understanding of causal inference. In this chapter we provide a careful discussion of the modern theory of causal inferences with numerous evocative illustrations. We show how evidence drawn from test scores is comparable to credible evidence of other widely accepted sources. 121

12. **Three Cautionary Tales of Zombie Ideas about Testing** There are awful ideas, which ought to be dead, but which keep getting revivified and so are still walking among us. Three prominent zombies that we discuss are:

    1. making tests optional;
    2. strivers (kids from lower socioeconomic status (SES) groups get a boost to their scores);
    3. coaching gives a large unfair advantage. 159

13. Coda How far we have come? What strategies will most likely aid in achieving our goals? What evidence must be gathered to go further? 176

References 188
Index 203

Preface

Few wish to assess others,
Fewer still wish to be assessed,
But everyone wants to see the scores!

Paul Holland, 2023b

Throughout the preparation of this book, we were acutely aware of John McPhee's sage advice that "When you are trying to decide what to leave out, begin with the author. If you see yourself prancing around between the subject and the reader, get lost." But in the Preface, it is customary for the authors to appear face-to-face with the reader and explain why the book was written and, more to the point, why the reader should spend time digesting it. Let us begin that explanation with Charles Dickens' famous observation opening his *Tale of Two Cities*:

> It was the best of times, it was the worst of times, it was the age of wisdom, it was the age of foolishness, it was the epoch of belief, it was the epoch of incredulity, it was the season of light, it was the season of darkness, it was the spring of hope, it was the winter of despair.

Dickens' observation encapsulated precisely what we felt about the state of the world in the summer of 2023. We had only just emerged from the challenges of a pandemic in which modern science had conjured up the miracle of an effective vaccine and pharmaceutical companies quickly geared up to produce billions of doses that would save us from a re-visitation of the flu catastrophe that had occurred a century earlier (the best of times). But, unbelievably, there also arose a group of people who refused to be vaccinated, claiming, without evidentiary support, that the dangers of vaccination exceeded its benefits (the worst of times).

But regard for evidence (or its lack) was not confined to public health. Millions of people in the U.S. falsely claimed that the presidential election of 2020 had been "stolen" despite the refutation of all evidence put forward in support of this claim. And, indeed, the very notion of what is a fact came under question as the terms "alternative facts" and "my truth" were added to our lexicon.

It is common for there to be some distance between what evidence suggests is true and what many wished were true. But making decisions on the basis of one's hopes instead of what you know rarely leads to a happy conclusion. Suhail Doshi, the CEO of the Silicon Valley company *Mixpanel*, observed that "Most of the world will make decisions by either guessing or using their gut. They will either be lucky or wrong."

In the area of selection for human training, it is not surprising that there was sometimes a divergence between what was true and what was hoped to be true. Testing emerged as an important tool to aid in making wise selection decisions over 3,000 years ago. The use of testing has been polished over millennia. Tests have proven repeatedly to substantially improve the efficient utilization of both human resources and the physical resources to which humans are to be assigned. Today, a highly selective college may use admission tests such as the ACT or SAT to identify the best students it can get. A less selective college may (i) use them for guidance to aid in identifying students it can successfully train, as well as (ii) help potential students understand their likelihood of success at that college, and how that likelihood might vary depending on the discipline they choose.

As social values have changed over time, so too have the criteria by which the quality of tests have been judged. The importance of predictive accuracy, though still usually primary, has been softened by issues of fairness and equal representation. We are still learning how we can use tests to harvest increased efficiency of resource allocation while treating all involved fairly. But there is often a conflict between efficient resource allocation and apparent fairness – what some have characterized as a conflict between the classic goal of **The Truth** and the romantic goal of **The Good**. The resolution of this conflict has too often resulted in strategies that have yielded neither.

Indeed, it isn't hard to find historical incidents of those who avoid using tests because having objective scores gets in the way of their pernicious goals. In the early 1930s a young Henry Chauncey was working in the admissions office at Harvard shortly after his own graduation. Excited by the positive results the use of admissions tests was yielding at Columbia, he became enthusiastic about the idea of using entrance exams at Harvard to open its enrollment to a far broader range of students. Harvard's president Abbott

Lawrence Lowell rejected his idea because using tests would not exclude enough Jews – he preferred quotas instead.[1]

It was this history of the value of test scores in providing objective evidence to improve the quality of personnel decisions that led us to write this book.

Alfred Hitchcock explained the nature of cinematic terror with a story about the bomb under the table. People are sitting around a table having an otherwise banal conversation about baseball when – boom! – a bomb goes off killing everyone. The audience is surprised and shocked.

But what if, Hitchcock asked, we are shown the bomb beforehand? "In these conditions the same innocuous conversation becomes fascinating because the audience is participating in the secret." While everyone is just sitting around chatting, the viewer wants to shout: "Don't sit there talking about baseball! There's a bomb!"

We wrote this book because evidence kept accumulating that there was a bomb under the table.

A small, but characteristic, piece of evidence emerges from the experience at the Law School of St. Mary's University of San Antonio; a fully accredited and well-respected law school. In 1989 the university hired Barbara Aldave as dean of their law school. At the time 88 percent of their graduates passed the Texas bar exam after graduation. Soon after taking office, in an effort to increase enrollment of a more diverse student population, Dean Aldave directed the admissions office of St. Mary's University Law School to lower its objective standards for admission.[2] By 1996 the passing rate of their students on the bar exam had fallen to 71 percent. In the July 1996 administration of the bar exam 50 of the 170 St. Mary's graduates failed the exam. Failing students have to wait six months to retake the exam. A large number had taken and failed the bar exam several times. Of course, without passing the bar, students' earning power was vastly diminished and repayment of the (substantial) costs of their legal education became for most essentially insurmountable.[3]

---

[1] Lowell was successful at implementing his policy, for Harvard reduced the percentage of Jewish freshmen at Harvard from almost 28 percent in 1925 to less than 15 percent when he retired in 1933. Chauncey left Harvard to found the Educational Testing Service. Lowell's successor as Harvard's president was James Bryant Conant, who reversed Lowell's policies. The administration building at the Educational Testing Service is named Conant Hall.

[2] StMU professor and Senior District Court Judge Robert Barton concluded that "we are accepting students who have inferior credentials" who are selected "principally by economic and racial considerations" with little consideration for standardized test scores (Associated Press, 1997).

[3] Dean Aldave's solution to the problem was to strongly recommend that students take a $490 bar review course; she negotiated with a private company that offered such a course which thence lowered its price to $250.

In the Spring of 2023, as this book was beginning to take shape, a friend on the faculty at an elite university told us, in confidence, that over the past few years the admission process at some departments was forbidden to use the Graduate Record Exam (GRE). So, the admissions committees soldiered on and used the other data they had available to them (undergraduate institution, courses taken and grades) to admit new classes of graduate students. Two years later, the first bomb exploded. For it was after two years of study that each student was required to take qualifying exams before being permitted to continue on to write a thesis and receive a Ph.D. They found that the failure rate on qualifying exams quadrupled (from 8 to 32 percent) from earlier (with GRE) times. The following year the same trend continued. It meant that a substantial proportion of students had spent two years in graduate school with no degree to show for it. It also meant that, because of the increased failure rate, the cost to the department of producing a Ph.D. had increased by 20 percent. Faced with these disappointing outcomes, the university realized that they had to take prompt and dramatic action. And so some departments decided to eliminate the qualifying exam as part of the requirements to be admitted to candidacy.

It seems clear to us that any solution must recognize the validity of the goals of both **The Truth** and **The Good**. We must, therefore, try to devise an approach that satisfies both goals simultaneously. Happily, we are not the first to try to solve this difficult problem. Almost fifty years ago statisticians Mel Novick and Nancy Petersen proposed a solution that we endorse (echoed by Lee Cronbach in the same year). Their proposal is based on two key components: transparency and evidence. They (and we too) believe that the importance of some societal goals associated with equity may, to some extent, overwhelm those associated with efficacy. So, the first step is that representatives of all of the relevant viewpoints get together and argue in public, each explaining why their goals are important. As part of this argument evidence is presented showing the costs and benefits of what they propose. And the arguments continue until they reach at least a tentative agreement. So, for example, they might decide that the admitted class ought to be 50 percent female (or 50% $\pm$ 10%), 12% African American (or 12% $\pm$ 2%), and so on. Or to avoid the legal issues that come with race and sex groupings, SES could be used where, if 20 percent of the population makes less than $20K per year, then 20 percent of admitted students come from that group.[4]

---

[4] We recognize that this approach may need some adjudication because of the current rules about affirmative action, but it seems wise to at least start with a plan that covers the logical bases.

Arguing in public, with evidence, is how a democracy should work. To pave the way for a politically acceptable resolution of contending forces, the courts and the public should hear advocates (Cronbach, 1976, p. 31).

The second step is to use all available information (test scores, grades, recommendations, ...) to predict future performance of each applicant as accurately as they can with the information available. Next, rank order the applicants within their various subclassifications and then select from the top down in each. That allows institutions to do as well as possible on their performance criteria within the constraints of societal fairness.

Obviously, the character of the solution will vary with the kind of selection task; the rules for college admission are not likely to be the same as those for the licensing of physicians or airline pilots. The margin for error varies with the task.

We will discuss this approach in fuller detail in Chapter 13.

It was the repeated reports of actions taken by otherwise sensible users of tests that led us to conclude that the bombs under these academic tables were not unique events. While it is easy and almost irresistible to stand on the sidelines and shout, "What are you doing? There is a bomb under the table," we hope we might be able to induce others to defuse at least some of those bombs if we carefully explain the issues involved and provided evidence-based solutions.

Thus, was born the book you now hold in your hand.

Testing is a topic that is widely disliked, but even more widely misunderstood. Our cautious optimism grew from the hope that an improved understanding can rid us of at least some of those ticking bombs.

Acknowledgments

Writing a book is generally not thought of as a team sport. But the ancient image of an asocial author sitting alone at a desk crouched over a messy manuscript illuminated by a bare bulb is no longer accurate – indeed it is unlikely that it ever was. Pixels and screens have long replaced yellow pads and ink; and sharing intermediate results with one's collaborators with periodic transmissions by post has been replaced by electronic multiple back-and-forth versions each day. Revisions and corrections involve matters factual, issues stylistic, and all things grammatical. But more than these usual issues, the preparation of this book required attitude and focus.

Exploring a topic as old and broad as testing, with a special focus on the interaction between scientific truths and social desires, is different than the usual scientific exploration. Scientific advancement has traditionally been thought to be akin to climbing a mountain (to borrow Julian Jaynes' evocative metaphor), in which the goal of increasing elevation is always clear; rope on, test the pitons, follow the leader, look out for the better lay backs. This straightforward? Perhaps not, but confusion is on the ledges and not the overall direction.

How different is our topic! It is less like a mountain than a huge entangled forest in full shining summer, in which there are multiple crisscrossing paths, some wide with fashion, others overgrown with disuse. Most paths are encumbered by adherents shouting, "follow me, this is the way." Blinders and earplugs replace ropes and pitons. What is needed for wise exploration is not so much aid in gaining altitude as guidance in choosing direction and support in clearing away undergrowth.

This metaphor makes it clear why this exercise in scientific authorship is not a strictly two-person partnership, even if it is so suggested by the cover of this book. We had a lot of help in finding direction and sweeping away pious nonsense. It is our pleasure to now be able to acknowledge it.

There were many colleagues who gave generously of their time, writing at length about the topic, referring us to important references, and providing helpful suggestions and directions, all of whom would have aced any test we might have used to select advisors. Of special note are:

Long-term friends and colleagues RJ Andrews, William J. Berg, Joseph Bernstein, Kenneth Lerman, Sam Savage, and Arthur Wise whose expertise and good sense provided both general and specific guidance.

Geoscientists and neighbors Isaac Held and Allan Rubin gave expert guidance about fracking and the role the reinsertion of wastewater played as the principal cause of Oklahoma's recent spate of earthquakes. Without their help Chapter 11 would have indeed been a more barren causal landscape.

We have been fortunate to have among our friends and colleagues a group of scholars whose past focus in various areas of educational testing and policy provided a rich lode of knowledge and wisdom that we were able to mine. Prominent among these are David Berliner, Rob Bligh, Derek Briggs, Richard Feinberg, David Lubinski, and David Thissen. And there is no one with deeper or wider knowledge of military testing than Malcolm Ree, who has been kind enough to share his wisdom with us whenever we required it.

Most of the arguments we have made lean heavily on data and their correct analysis. We are delighted to have this opportunity to thank five old friends who rank high on anyone's list of the finest statisticians in the world: David Donoho, Andrew Gelman, Shelby Haberman, David Hoaglin and Bob Mislevy.

To all of these worthy scholars we offer a hearty but wholly inadequate thank you for adding the beauty of their minds to the labor of ours.

We also owe a debt of gratitude to two anonymous reviewers who provided feedback on the completed version. Of course, most factual errors or fuzziness of thought that remain in this book must be laid at our doorstep, but some of them are surely due to too gentle early readers of the manuscript.

A special thank-you goes to Cambridge University Press, and in particular, our editor, Lauren Cowles. Lauren is simply the best editor to emerge in the business since Maxwell Perkins. She shares with Perkins an infallible sense of structure, which has markedly improved every aspect of the book.

Thanks go to Louise Attwood for her copy editing – her sharp eye helped us say more nearly what we meant; Arman Chowdhury for help with permissions; Lucy Edwards the content manager who kept everything together.

Finally, specific thanks from each of us goes to our employers and families.

Howard Wainer

At the beginning of December in 2016, at age 73, I entered my post-employment career. Prior to that date I spent 21 years working for the Educational Testing Service. I was there during that remarkable institution's halcyon days when extraordinary scholars world-wide competed for an opportunity for an extended visit: Sweden's Karl Joreskog spent a few years, it was Michael Browne's first stop after leaving South Africa, Fumiko Samejima and Jim Ramsay visited from Japan and Canada, respectively. We also hosted many U.S. scholars – from Chicago came Darrell Bock and David Thissen from Kansas, to name just a very small fraction. But these visitors were but the cherry on the top of the sundae of the wonderfully talented research staff at ETS. I also had immediate access to the resources of Princeton University, which for me meant being able to meet regularly with John Tukey. Tukey was a perfect model for how a really first-class mind worked; from him I learned much that could not have been learned elsewhere.

But ETS was not my only stop in the testing industry – after leaving there in 2001 I spent 15 productive years in the employ of the National Board of Medical Examiners; which is to medical licensing what ETS was for collegiate admissions testing. During my tenure there I absorbed a great deal while accumulating many debts to my colleagues at the Board as well as those in the statistics department of the University of Pennsylvania. In the former I should single out Peter Baldwin, Brian Clauser, Steve Clyman, Richard Feinberg, Bob Galbraith, Irina Grabovsky, and Peter Scoles. Of special note was the too rare enlightened management of Don Melnick and Ron Neugester. At Penn I benefited from regular contact with Eric Bradlow and Paul Rosenbaum, not to mention the terrific graduate students who made my teaching there such a pleasure.

But the most special benefit from working at a testing organization is derived from association with the test development and production staffs at both ETS and the National Board – the folks who actually built, administered, and scored the tests. From them I learned what was not in any books – and because the problems they faced in the daily transactions of their work were real and important, it was from them I developed good taste in choosing problems to work on. I thank you all.

To my wife Linda for substantive help in preparing and sharpening the arguments in this book while avoiding nonsense and excessive semicolons. My thanks to Sam, Laurent, Lyn, Koa, and Sophie for general inspiration.

Dan Robinson

Writing a book is a full-time job. Trying to do it while actually holding down another full-time job means foregoing many activities, mostly sleep, but also cutting short other responsibilities. I would like to thank the University of Texas at Arlington for providing the resources that made my work on this book possible. Special thanks are due to Stephen Palko whose generous donation to endow the chair that I currently hold opened the final door to allow me to squeeze enough time for the scholarly activities represented by this book. I am also grateful to Teresa Taber-Doughty for awarding the chair to me in 2020.

To my wife Sheri, daughter Kylie, and son Austin, thanks for your many sacrifices and for providing inspiration. Living with and being around someone who is writing a book is not easy. You are my every reason for what I do professionally.

Chapter 1
A Brief Recounting of the First Four Millennia of Testing

In this chapter, and in others to follow, we begin with a discussion of history.[1] We do this for two reasons. First, because we agree with Maya Angelou, that "history, despite its wrenching pain, cannot be unlived, but if faced with courage, need not be lived again." And second, to convey some of the validity of the theory and methods of testing that derives simply by virtue of the weight of experience. Tests were not devised last week. No, they have been actively under development for *thousands* of years and used to solve the very real problems that are associated with the fair and efficient utilization of human resources. These problems, in complex combinations, persist to this day. In the many years of testing's existence, there were uncounted numbers of issues that arose and had to be thoughtfully dealt with. Had their solutions not been successfully managed, testing could not have survived. Four of these issues remain particularly relevant today.

1. Questions of generalizability – what bearing do the results of this test taken today have on a somewhat different problem at a somewhat different time?
2. Questions of reliability – how similar are the results generated by the test this morning to those generated this afternoon? Tomorrow? Next week? (See Section 2.4 for an expanded discussion of these issues.)
3. Questions of validity – is the test generating evidence related to the claims we want to make?
4. Questions of fairness – are the decisions made from the test's results influenced by factors (e.g., race, ethnicity, age, gender) unrelated to the competencies of relevance?

---

[1] We do this despite Andrew Moravcik's (2017) warning of the futility of this task "Those who write history are doomed to watch others repeat it." Hope springs eternal.

Some of the pathways around these issues have become overgrown with disuse, others have been broadened with fashion, but all have been carefully examined. We do not claim that new problems cannot arise, because, for example, of new technologies or modern sensitivities borne of our increasingly heterogeneous society; nor do we claim that the solutions of the past cannot be improved upon. We only claim that a knowledge of history can reduce the necessity of revisiting old problems that have long been resolved.

> *There is nothing new in the world except the history you do not know.*
> Harry S. Truman (Rushay, 2009)

1.1 The Fundamental Tenet of Testing

Serendipitously, as we sat down to write this book in 2023, we noted that, exactly 4,000 years ago (on Wu Yue Wu Hao in the 93rd year of the Xia Dynasty – August 5, 1977 BCE) the signal event occurred that marked the beginning of testing.[2] It was on this date that an anonymous functionary, tasked by his emperor to find a path to improve the way that government officials were chosen, was struck by what has since been recognized as

> **the fundamental tenet of testing:**
> *A small sample of behavior, measured under controlled circumstances, could be predictive of a broader set of behaviors in uncontrolled circumstances.*

This was the intellectual beginning of a program of testing in China that has continued, with only one minor interruption[3] until the present day. The Chinese testing program imagined by that functionary, his very bones now long dust, was essentially a civil service examination program and many of its performance-based components and procedures bore a remarkable resemblance to most examination programs that have been developed since. The Chinese tests were designed to cull candidates for public office; job-sample tests were used, with proficiency in archery, arithmetic, horsemanship, music, writing, and skill in the rites and ceremonies of public and social life. Moreover, because they required objectivity, candidates' names were concealed to ensure anonymity; they sometimes went so far as to have the answers redrafted by a scribe to hide the handwriting. Tests were often read by two independent examiners, with a third brought in to adjudicate differences. Test

---

[2] This recounting tells of a place faraway and a time long ago; before there was reliable written Chinese history. Some of the details are not fully documented.

[3] During the 1911 revolution that overthrew the Qing Dynasty and its Emperor, the national testing program was temporarily suspended. It was resumed as soon as peace was restored.

conditions were as uniform as could be managed – proctors watched over the exams given in special examination halls that were large, permanent structures consisting of hundreds of small cells. The examination procedures were so rigorous that candidates sometimes died during the course of the exam (Teng, 1943).

The pathway connecting ancient China to the twenty-first century is remarkably direct. The Chinese testing program became the model that the British used in their design of the Indian Civil Service Exam system, installed in 1833 during the Raj. This, in turn, was the template that Senator Charles Sumner and Representative Thomas Jenckes used in designing the Civil Service Act passed by the U.S. Congress in January 1883.

1.2 Tracing the Shibboleth

Despite this clear historical pathway, testing did not jump directly from China to India. There is overwhelming evidence that this fundamental idea spread throughout the known world. About 600 years after the Chinese testing program began, we know that it had spread at least as far as the Middle East.

In the Bible, *Judges 12:4–6*, during the time of David, we are told how, after the Gileadites captured the fords of the Jordan leading to Ephraim, they developed a one-item test to determine the tribe to which the survivors of the battle belonged. "If a survivor of Ephraim said, 'Let me cross over,' the men of Gilead would ask him, 'Are you an Ephraimite?' If he replied, 'No,' they said, 'All right, say "Shibboleth"'. If he said, 'Sibboleth,' because he could not pronounce the word correctly, they seized and killed him."

Forty-two thousand Ephraimites were killed at that time. This total might have included some Gileadites with a lisp, but we will never know, for there is no record of any validity study being performed.

There have, however, been two fundamental changes in testing, especially over the past century or so. The first grew from the realization that the subjectivity involved in scoring answers that were constructed by examinees yielded enormous error. And so gradually there has been a shift toward constructing items that could be scored objectively. A little of the evidence supporting this shift was evident in ancient China. The second shift was in test construction paradigms that went from considering the test as a single entity (where the examinee's score was usually represented as the proportion of the presented items that were answered correctly), to a much more flexible form in which the test is drawn from a large pool of components – some of which are selected as needed to estimate the examinee's ability in some optimal fashion.

Thus, the individual test item, or sometimes a fixed combination of items – a testlet – became the fungible unit of the test.

This shift in test structure was captured by three signal events in the four decades between 1950 and 1990. The first was the 1950 publication of Harold Gulliksen's *Theory of Mental Tests*, which provided the machinery necessary for rigorous scoring of tests using what has become known as True Score Theory. The unit of measure was the test itself, and so the proportion of the test that was answered correctly characterized performance. Different forms of the test were equated so that the scores on different forms could be compared.

The second breakthrough was the 1968 publication of Fred Lord and Mel Novick's *Statistical Theories of Mental Test Scores*. This signaled a new era in which tests could be built that were customized for each examinee and yet still be standardized. It put a capstone on true score theory while simultaneously providing a rigorous statement of a new approach in which the test item becomes the fungible unit of measurement – item response theory (IRT). IRT was crucial if the goal of efficiently creating individualized tests for each examinee was to be realized. Such a dream was instigated by the third event, the growing power and availability of high-speed computing. A combination of individually calibrated test items, a statistical theory that allowed us to calculate comparable scores for tests that might be made up of wildly different mixtures of items, and a computer that could construct such tests on-the-fly has yielded the most modern realization of what was begun 4,000 years ago by that anonymous Chinese functionary. IRT made it possible to use a large pool of items from which one could sample to make up any particular individual's test. This portended a major improvement in test security.

The revolutionary character of the third breakthrough, which ironically took place in 1917 in Vineland, New Jersey, was only recognized much later. It was at that meeting that the focus of exams shifted abruptly from testing knowledge of specific topics to testing the cognitive ability of the examinee. This remarkable change is explored in greater detail in Chapter 3.

1.3 The Need for a Second Watch

The expression "A man with one watch knows what time it is, but a man with two watches is never sure" helps us understand the evolution of testing. Newton gave the world its first watch, and for a while we knew the time; but eventually Einstein and Heisenberg gave us a second watch, and we haven't been sure since. Sometimes this is interpreted as an argument for ignorance, which is quite the opposite of our point, for science advances when we have some notion of our own uncertainty. And it is only when we have multiple measures of the same thing that we are made aware of our own uncertainty, and these multiple measures enable us to assess that uncertainty.

Written exams required an expert grader to assess the quality of the answer, and the examinees' scores were typically a summary of those assessments. We can only imagine the chain of events that led the West to revert to the Chinese practice of having multiple graders. Perhaps some examinees complained about their scores and when they were rescored a different result ensued; or accidentally some exams were scored twice, and it was discovered that the results were not the same. We don't know what the key motivating events were, but certainly it was clear by the beginning of the twentieth century that fair scoring of exams required a second watch.

One of the instigators of this movement was the work of Albert Binet and Theodore Simon who, in 1905, published their eponymous test to measure the intelligence of children. Though the individually administered test was cumbersome, it was wildly successful. A decade later this success led Stanford University's Lewis Terman to develop a less cumbersome version that could be both mass-administered and objectively scored.

Terman's success, coupled with the need for the efficient classification of soldiers for the First World War, drove the formation of Robert Yerkes' Vineland Committee in 1917, which, within just a week, developed the modern multi-part multiple-choice exam. Its eight sections were designed to be administered in about an hour and among those eight were such familiar item types as arithmetic reasoning, synonym–antonyms, and verbal analogies. The test forms they prepared, then called "the Army Alpha" (to distinguish it from "Army Beta," the nonverbal version for illiterate and non-English speaking examinees) was a testing model followed widely, with only modest differences, ever since. The exam could be administered quickly and scored objectively and automatically using a stencil.

In 1909 the College Board, through its fledgling college entrance exams, made a remarkable discovery. It found that the variation observed in the scoring of a single essay over many graders was about the same as the variation in scores of the same essay over many examinees. It concluded that this was unacceptably inaccurate and that graders needed to be trained better. Almost a century later, in a study of licensing exam results for California teachers, the renowned psychometrician Darrell Bock (1991) reported, "the variance component due to raters was equal to the variance component due to examinees." It may be that this century-old problem is still due to insufficient training of graders, but more likely it is the subjectivity inherent in the task of grading itself.

As testing became more widespread, and with experience, our eyes became accustomed to the Byzantine dimness surrounding its use, the necessity of multiple graders added costs to testing. But balanced against these costs was the savings derived from the improved manpower utilization due to testing. The spreading belief that expanding testing beyond its relatively narrow confines would improve industrial efficiency led to attempts to streamline the practices of testing without compromising its efficacy. Twentieth-century psychometrics realized that fair scoring of exams required a second watch.

1.4 The Critical Importance of Objective Scoring

The lessons learned from the variability always present in human scoring led to a shift away from traditional test items like essays, which required a constructed response on the part of the examinee, to item formats sharing the objective nature of the multiple-choice item.

The need for economically practical mass administration of tests that faced the U.S. military during the First World War gave rise to a huge increase in the development of multiple-choice items. Then, as now, there was concern that such a format was incapable of testing certain proficiencies that were crucial. Sometimes these concerns were well founded, but surprisingly often it turned out that the multiple-choice option worked better than even its most ardent supporters could have hoped. Why?

The answer draws on the psychometric/statistical developments described in Gulliksen's foundational book and stems from the basic fact that scores derived from any test format are imperfect. They contain errors. These errors fall principally into two broad categories.

(i) The estimates fluctuate symmetrically around their true values, due to variations in the examinee and the scorer. On some days we perform better than on others. As mentioned earlier, variation among raters of essays has always been substantial and seems relatively insensitive to improved rater training. In addition, scores also fluctuate due to the specific realization of the test item; if we want to study writing and so ask for an essay on Kant's epistemology, we are likely to get less fluid responses than if we asked for one on 'My Summer Vacation.'

(ii) The estimate can also contain some bias if the item used is measuring a proficiency that is not exactly what we are specifically concerned about. Suppose, for example, we are interested in measuring writing ability and instead of testing it in the obvious way, by asking the examinee to write an

1.4 The Critical Importance of Objective Scoring

essay, we use multiple-choice items designed to measure general verbal ability (e.g., items involving verbal analogies, antonym/synonym interpretation, sentence completion). We are measuring something related to writing ability, but not writing ability specifically.

The test that is most predictive of future behavior is one that minimizes the sum of both kinds of errors. What the experience gained in the first half of the twentieth century (and reconfirmed many times since) was that for a remarkably wide range of proficiencies, multiple-choice items were superior to their much older cousin, the essay. This surprising result is because the bias that multiple-choice items might introduce was much smaller than the errors introduced by subjective scoring and the limitations in breadth of subject matter coverage that are the unavoidable concomitants of essay style exams. In one study (Wainer et al., 1994), examinees were given a test made up of three half hour sections. Two of the sections required the writing of an essay; the third comprised forty multiple-choice verbal ability items. The essays were each scored with two raters (and sometimes a third to adjudicate any large disagreements), and the multiple-choice section was scored automatically. It was found that the score on the multiple-choice section was more highly correlated with either essay score than the two essay scores were with one another. What this means practically is that if we want to predict performance on a future essay test, we could do so more accurately with a multiple-choice test than we could with a parallel essay test. Some argued that 30 minutes is too short for a valid essay test – perhaps, but if the essays were allocated an hour, the one-hour multiple-choice test would also improve, probably more than the essays.[4]

It is worth emphasizing that for any fixed amount of testing time there is an advantage to asking many small questions over asking very few large ones. In the latter case an unfortunate choice of question can yield an equally unfortunate outcome ("I knew just about everything in that subject except that one small topic"). In the former case, there is still the possibility of such unfortunate choices, but through the larger sampling of topics, the effect of such bad luck is ameliorated considerably.

The shift from an essay to a multiple-choice format yielded enormous benefits; the material covered by the test could be vastly expanded, the test forms were scored much more accurately, and thus the inferences made from

---

[4] The unreliability of judges is widespread, but not universal. It is certainly true for rating such outcomes as essays, but for very narrowly defined tasks, expert judgment can be workable. For example, in judging the severity of hip fractures by orthopedic surgeons it was found that only 5 percent of the variability of responses was due to differences in opinion among raters, while 95 percent was due to variability among X-rays (Baldwin et al., 2009).

tests' scores became more valid, the scores themselves were more reliable, and simultaneously the exams were much cheaper to administer.

Military testing, which had played such an important role in shifting the testing paradigm to the multiple-choice format in 1917, made possible another breakthrough 50 years later, which developed from the possibility of computerizing the test administration. The principal test that the U.S. military gives to sort recruits into various training programs is the Armed Services Vocational Aptitude Battery (the ASVAB). It was a long test with ten parts and required two days to administer. In 1960s and 1970s, in an effort to reduce this time and to help control other problems, the Office of Naval Research funded research first by Educational Testing Service (ETS)'s Fred Lord and later Minnesota's David Weiss. What they came up with was a way to meld the strengths of individualized assessment and the standardization and reliability of modern multiple-choice tests.

The aim was to construct a practical and standardized equivalent of a wise-old examiner who would sit with a candidate for an extended period of time and tap into all aspects of the candidate's skills and knowledge, asking neither more nor fewer questions than required for the accuracy of the inferences planned. This is especially important for tests used for diagnostic purposes. This remarkable goal was, in fact, accomplished by presenting previously calibrated individual test items to the examinees on a computer. After each item was presented, it was scored instantaneously and the computer selected another item. If the earlier item was answered incorrectly, an easier one was presented; if it was answered correctly, it was followed by a more difficult one. In this way the test would focus quickly on the ability level of the examinee. This allowed the test to yield the same precision as a typical fixed format test, while using only about half the items. It can also cycle through various subtopics as required for diagnostic testing. Such tests are called computerized adaptive tests or CATs for short.

The shift was formally chronicled by the 1990 publication of the definitive text *Computerized Adaptive Testing* (Wainer, 1990), which laid out and illustrated how a test could be individually constructed to suit each examinee while also being standardized. Now scores obtained from exams that were very different in the items from which they were constituted could be compared directly.

Because Wainer's book also laid out in detail how such exams could be built and scored, it motivated several testing organizations to try out this new technology. What many discovered was that building a CAT requires a great deal of work. Huge banks of items must be constructed, pre-tested, and calibrated so that the item administration algorithm can select them

1.4 The Critical Importance of Objective Scoring

appropriately. In the first rush of enthusiasm, a fair number of large-scale tests had been successfully converted into CAT format (e.g., the ASVAB) and remain so to this day. Others (e.g., the Graduate Record Exam (GRE)) were transformed into CATs only to be changed back after it was found that the extra expense involved was not justified.[5]

CAT remains an attractive option if the use of the test includes instructional diagnosis. For this purpose, the ability to efficiently isolate precisely those areas that need remediation is likely invaluable. But the evolution of testing is not done yet, for as technology yields new challenges to security, it also provides us with new tools to meet them.

One vexing problem associated with computerized administration is the practical requirement that tests be administered continuously. It was just too expensive to utilize the old tactic of gathering hundreds of examinees in a gymnasium three or four times a year and passing out #2 pencils; while #2 pencils are cheap, laptop computers are not. So instead, testing centers are set up and examinees are scheduled to come to them a few at a time. Such an approach has substantial extra costs: maintaining testing centers is expensive, and the continuous testing required by computerized testing yields security challenges. Giving a test continuously means that the items used on the tests must be changed very often; consequently, there must be a lot of them. But there is no going back: modern tests that are computer administered have many item types that cannot be administered in a paper and pencil format (e.g., ones where an examinee listens to a recorded heartbeat and must make a diagnosis). Technology may again provide a solution. Tablet computers have become both capable and relatively inexpensive. We may soon be able to return to the old style of a few mass administrations in which the twenty-first century #2 pencil is a specially made tablet. This is but one of the likely future possibilities of exams. But what is critical is an orienting attitude of questioning the status quo to power the drive toward improvement through change. This attitude melds perfectly with the tenets of modern quality control (Deming, 2012). Whenever

---

[5] The two competing costs are those associated with building and administering the test: the costs of writing, pretesting, and calibrating a large number of items that span all of the subject areas and all of the difficulty levels; and the costs of individual administration. Balanced against these costs are the savings in examinee time, since an adaptive test takes roughly half the time as a fixed-format test of equal accuracy. For the military it meant that the test would shift from being a two-day affair, with all of the housing and other costs associated with an overnight stay, to a one-day test. In addition, there was the saving of the opportunity costs for the second day. In the end it was determined that the personnel savings offset the testing costs. Conversely, the examinee costs for the GRE were not borne by the testing organization that administered it and so the little savings achieved did not justify the expenses incurred. It is likely that, if the CAT-GRE could have been mass administered, rather than administered continuously, the financial calculus would have been different.

we have a complex system, whether it is a manufacturing process or the licensing of physicians, it is well established that the worst way to improve matters is to convene a blue-ribbon panel to lay out the character of the future of exams. This doesn't work reliably because the task is too difficult.[6] What does work is the institutionalization of a constant process of experimentation in which small changes are made and evaluated. If the change improves matters, make a bigger change in the same direction. If it makes matters worse, reverse field and try something else. In this way the process gradually moves toward optimization and so when the future arrives the testing process of the future is waiting for it.

---

[6] In this obscure footnote we record for posterity a wonderful story to tell about this. Around 1990 a large, blue-ribbon, committee was formed at ETS for a project called "TOEFL 2000" whose goal was to design a future language test that would accommodate both the recent developments in psycholinguistics and the likely technological tools that would be available a decade hence. The committee's budget was several million dollars because it was anticipated that the planning process would use many hours of many expensive professionals. At the initial meeting a fair amount of time was spent going around the (large) table soliciting advice as to how they should proceed to make best use of the money. Bob Mislevy, one of the world's leading psychometricians suggested that, "we should buy a helicopter." This provoked nervous laughter, but Bob wasn't laughing – he was deadly serious. He explained that if they continued trying to ascertain from current knowledge the test of the future, they would continue meeting until the money ran out and, when the year 2000 arrived, they would have nothing to show for it. But, if they followed his advice, at least they would have a helicopter. For a long time thereafter whenever someone suggested a blue-ribbon panel to solve some difficult problem it was greeted with "better to buy a helicopter."

Chapter 2
Why Tests Are so Widely Disliked

2.1 Introduction

Now is the winter of our discontent

William Shakespeare,
Richard III, Act 1, Scene 1

In Chapter 1 we learned how testing has for millennia been a practical solution to many common problems. It has proved repeatedly to be a simple way to improve profoundly the efficiency of hiring and selection decisions. Over the last century testing has been an integral part of the admissions process to colleges and professional schools, for placement in classes or occupations, for finding especially talented individuals for scholarships, for licensing professionals in such disparate occupations as physicians and lifeguards, fire fighters and pilots, veterinarians and real estate brokers, the selection of athletes for sports teams, and the list goes on. Additionally, the science and methodology of testing has proved invaluable for medical diagnoses and (through DNA testing) even for determining culpability in crimes.

Yet despite its continued success over an enormous breadth of situations for literally thousands of years, testing has now fallen under attack from those who argue against the validity of the scores. Why? In this chapter we will try to understand why we seem to have entered this winter of discontent. Over the last decade or so we have found that:

1. There has been a huge decline in the number of colleges that require applicants to submit their scores of an entrance exam (either ACT or SAT[1]). In 2022–2023, 43 percent of college applicants included entrance

---

[1] The SAT and ACT are the two principal college entrance exams that are used in the United States.

exam scores, compared to 75 percent in 2019–2020 (Bauer-Wolf, 2023). In California 273,000 students took the SAT in 2019, but by 2022 this had declined to 102,000.
2. Twenty-one states have modified their testing requirements that had previously been employed to measure student progress. The number of states using nationally normed assessments of student achievement decreased from 31 in 1999–2000 to fewer than 10 by 2007–2008 (Council of Chief State School Officers and State Departments of Education, 2008; Goertz et al., 2001)
3. Nineteen states have modified or eliminated a test score requirement for high school graduation. As of 2023, only eight states have such a requirement for high school compared to twenty-seven in the mid-1990s (Schwartz, 2023).
4. Numerous legal efforts have been filed challenging the legitimacy of licensing tests for various professions. In 2021, New York City paid $1.8 billion to teachers and once-aspiring educators affected by "discriminatory" New York State teachers' exam (Calder et al., 2023).

There have long been critics of testing, who have, despite slender supporting evidence, donned the mantle of John the Baptist and wandered in the wilderness crying out their complaints. But recently their shrieks of "Follow me – mine is the way" has found a receptive audience that has begun to clamor for an end to long-established and successful testing programs.

What are the sources of these complaints?

Throughout their long history, the chief complaint against tests is that they divide people:

- in admission they divide those who get in from those who don't;
- in hiring they divide those who get the job from those who don't;
- in licensing they divide those who get to practice their trade from those who do not;
- in the granting of scholarships, they divide those who win the prize from those who do not.

There are winners and losers, and so it is natural that some of those who lost blame the test. And, in a very real sense, they are right. Often, if there had been no test, the selections would have been done less accurately, thus there would have been a greater chance that those who were not chosen would have been selected. But there are costs associated with an approach whose natural endpoint is random selection: the costs of less efficient utilization of both human and physical resources.

2.1 Introduction

In the modern world a nation that makes inefficient use of its human capital cannot effectively compete with others. The realization of this inexorable and fundamental truth has provoked some societies that previously excluded large portions of their population from even participating in the workforce to change. As one profound example, in 1970 Saudi Arabia opened *Princess Nourah Bint Abdulrahman University*. It was that country's first institution of post-secondary education for women. It was quickly followed by thirty-five more institutions that enrolled women. It is hard to judge what will be the long-term effects of enfranchising women in the Saudi workforce, but we see that over the 30 years from 1974 to 2004 the number of Saudi women enrolled in post-secondary education increased by a factor of eight (from 272,054 to 2,121,893) and the literacy rate among Saudi women over the past 25 years has risen from 57 to 99 percent.

It has not escaped our attention that to make optimal use of their limited facilities, the Saudis use a competitive entrance exam to their universities (for both men and women) that is patterned after the SAT.[2]

Countering the movement toward increasing the efficient utilization of educational resources, we are waiting for data on graduation rates to become available that reflect the effects of the reduced use of college entrance tests for the selection of students.

Shifting our gaze for a moment to medical testing, would anyone suggest that we stop using vision tests and instead dispense eyeglasses at random? Or forget about cancer test results and instead assign potential patients to chemotherapy on some arbitrary basis? And who would advocate that tailors ignore their tape measures and just dispense garments willy-nilly?

These are such obviously silly ideas that even someone on the fringe of the anti-testers would not advocate for their adoption. Yet there is a loud movement afoot whose apparent goal is to vastly reduce the use of mental tests regardless of the resulting costs in the efficient utilization of both human and material resources. Why?

The short answer to this is that no one knows and, as we will learn in Chapter 11, trying to determine the cause of an effect is a task of insuperable difficulty.

If we have data, let's look at data.
If all we have are opinions, let's go with mine.
      (commonly attributed to Jim Barksdale, former CEO of Netscape)

---

[2] Actually, it was patterned after the Arabic form of Israel's PET (Psychometric Entrance Test), which itself was modeled after the SAT.

But with that caveat, let us nevertheless now consider, sequentially, just two possibilities.

Possibility 1. Concern that tests prevent improvement through inclusion Identity politics has, ironically, as one of its goals, the increased efficiency of the use of human capital through the inclusion of segments of the population which heretofore had a more difficult path. The irony arises because testing is often cited as the opponent of such efficiency. The evidence of testing's culpability that is often cited are the differences in average performance on tests by race or gender or language group.

Possibility 2. Fear that tests are not a mirror of reality, but instead reflect the biases of their construction Tests and their associated scores can have profound consequences on not just immediate goals but also for long-term dreams. We join with the multitudes in agreeing that anything that has the potential to be the assassin of dreams must first survive the most rigorous examination of its ethical, moral and scientific validity. In sections to follow we will elaborate on what are the hurdles that a professionally prepared test routinely clears and suggest that subjective alternatives (e.g., interviews, letters of support, and even course grades of uncertain provenance) usually don't come close to well-prepared tests.

2.2 Improvement Through Inclusion – Running and Musical Proficiency as Examples

"Virtuosos are becoming a dime a dozen," exclaimed Anthony Tommasini, chief music critic of the *New York Times* in his column in the arts section of that newspaper on Sunday August 14, 2011. Tommasini described, with some awe, the remarkable increase in the number of young musicians whose technical proficiency on the piano allows them to play anything. He contrasts this with some virtuosos of the past – he singles out Rudolf Serkin as an example – who had only the technique he needed to play the music that was meaningful to him. Serkin did not perform pieces like "Prokofiev's finger twisting Third Piano Concerto or the mighty Liszt Sonata," although such pieces are well within the capacity of most modern virtuosos.[3]

---

[3] *The overall level of technical proficiency in instrumental playing, especially on the piano, has increased steadily over time. Many have noted the phenomenon, which is not unlike what happens in sports. The four-minute mile seemed an impossibility until Roger Bannister made the breakthrough in 1954. Since then, runners have knocked nearly 17 seconds off Bannister's time.*

Something similar has long been occurring with pianists. And in the last decade or so the growth of technical proficiency has seemed exponential.

A new level of technical excellence is expected of emerging pianists. I see it not just on the concert circuit but also at conservatories and colleges. In recent years I have repeatedly been struck by the sheer level of instrumental expertise that seems a given.

But why? Why are there so many young pianists that have set "a new level of conquering the piano?" Tommasini doesn't attempt to answer this question (although he does mention Roger Bannister in passing), so let us try.

We see an apparently unending upward spiral in remarkable levels of athletic achievement that provides a context to consider Tommasini's implicit riddle. We don't mean to imply that this increase in musical virtuosity is due to improved diet and exercise, nor even to better coaching, although we would be the last to gainsay their possible contribution. We think a major contributor to this remarkable increase in proficiency is increasing population size through inclusion. Let us elaborate.

The world record for running the mile has steadily improved by almost three-tenths of a second a year for the past century. When the twentieth century began the record was 4:13. It took over 50 years until Roger Bannister collapsed in exhaustion after completing a mile in just under 4 minutes. In a little more than a decade this was being surpassed by high school runners. And, by the end of the twentieth century, Hicham El Guerrouj broke the tape at 3:43. What happened? How could the capacity of humans to run improve so drastically in such a relatively short time? Humans have been running for a very long time, and in the more distant past, the ability to run quickly was far more important for survival than it is today. A clue toward an answer is seen by looking at the names of the record holders. In the early part of the century the record was held by Scandinavians – Paavo Nurmi, Gunder Haag, and Arne Andersson. Then mid-century came the Brits[4]: Roger Bannister, John Landy, Herb Elliot, Peter Snell, and later Steve Ovett and Sebastian Coe. And the twenty-first century arrived with the Africans: first Filbert Bayi, then Noureddine Morceli and Hicham El Guerrouj. As elite competition began to include a wider range of runners, times improved. A runner who wins a race that is the culmination of events that winnowed the competition from a thousand to a single person is likely to be slower than one who is the best of a million.

A simple statistical model was proposed and tested in 2002 by the statistician Scott Berry that captures this idea. It posits that human running ability has

> The pianist Jerome Lowenthal, a long-time faculty member at Juilliard School of Music, observes it in his own studio. When the 1996 movie "Shine," about the mentally ill pianist David Helfgott, raised curiosity about Rachmaninoff's Third Piano Concerto, Mr. Lowenthal was asked by reporters whether this piece was as formidably difficult as the movie had suggested. He said that he had two answers: "One was that this piece truly is terribly hard. Two was that all my 16-year-old students were playing it."
> Anthoni Tommasini, New York Times, August 14, 2011.

---

[4] Brits = British Commonwealth excluding Kenya

not changed over the past century. That in both 1900 and 2000 the distribution of running ability of the human race is well characterized by a normal curve with the same average and the same variability. What has changed is how many people live under that curve. And so, in 1900 the best miler in the world (as far as we know) was the best of a billion; in 2000 he was the best of 6 billion. It turns out that this simple model can accurately describe the improvements in performance of all athletic contests for which there is an objective criterion.[5]

It does not seem far-fetched to believe the same phenomenon is taking place in other areas of human endeavor. Looking over the list of extraordinary young pianists mentioned by Tommasini we see names that are commonplace now, but would have seemed wildly out of place at Carnegie Hall a century ago – Lang Lang, Yundi Li, Yuja Wang. As the reach of classical music extended itself into areas previously untouched, is it any surprise that among the billions of souls who call such places home we would discover some pianists of remarkable virtuosity?

Tommasini illustrates his point with his reaction to 80-year-old recordings of the respected pianist Alfred Cortot. He concludes that Cortot "would probably not be admitted to Julliard now." This should not surprise us any more than noting that Paavo Nurmi, the flying Finn, would have trouble making a division I collegiate track team. The best of a billion is almost surely better than the best of a million.

Such is the power of inclusion.

Arguments for improvements on all important criteria that are based on increased inclusivity are easy to make and support. And we have, and we do. But we take issue with the contention that testing, used properly, is the enemy of inclusion. Quite the opposite.

Historically, fairness was one of the most critical reasons that collegiate admissions testing was implemented in the first place. Henry Chauncey,

---

[5] Of course, social factors – the shrinking and homogenization of the world – have increased the effect still more. Kenya did not compete in the 1900 Games – nor did any other African country. Not only was the global pool smaller, but an entire continent's population was excluded from it. At that time probably none of the long-legged Kalenjin peoples who lived and still live at high altitude 7,000 feet up on the edge of the Rift Valley had ever heard of the Olympics, or even of Paris where they were held that year; and if they had, the practical as well as the conceptual possibility of travelling across a quarter of the world just in order to run a race simply did not exist. Kenya did not compete in the Olympics until 1956; three Games later their athletes picked up three Golds in Mexico City – the famous Kip Keino was only one of those athletes. Since then, Kenyans – the vast majority of them Kalenjin – have gathered 68 Olympic medals in athletics. Noah Beardsley has calculated that in 2005 the Kalenjin made up 0.08 percent of the world's population but won 40 percent of the top international distance running events.

before he founded the ETS, was an admissions officer at Harvard and was an avid fan of tests, one of which had then been in use at Columbia for some time. Chauncey proposed its use to Harvard President Abbott Lawrence Lowell who rejected it because it would not exclude enough Jews. He preferred quotas instead.[6]

Yet, there are group differences in performance on standardized tests, whether for college admission, or fourth-grade reading, or to be licensed as a physician. Why? Test scores are functions of both the ability of the person taking the test and the environment in which that person has been living. When we see such differences, our response should not be to shoot the messenger but rather to focus on the causes. If a bathroom scale says we are too heavy for good health, we do not help matters by blaming the scale. In a similar manner, if a valid test predicts that a particular student is unlikely to do well/graduate at a particular school, we must ask why. And, if possible, try to remediate the potential academic weaknesses of that applicant. Again, consider, by analogy, if the policy of shooting the test messenger was adopted in medical testing. Currently, African Americans are 20 percent more likely to get colorectal cancer than other ethnic groups, and, for several reasons but principally because of less testing, African Americans are 40 percent more likely to die from it.

Eschewing testing is not the answer.

But suppose the test is not valid? Wouldn't we then be excluding some applicants for no good reason?

The truth is rarely pure and never simple.

But the short answer is that there are some measures that provide valid information important for making good decisions, and there are other measures that are less valuable and may be more likely to mislead. Tests usually fall into the former category and such measures as letters of recommendation tend toward the latter. One reason for this is that a test is something like a controlled experiment in that it is under the complete control of those who developed it. Professionally built, high-quality exams are under constant scrutiny for issues of invalidity and are continuously improved and corrected. Something like a letter of recommendation is more like an observational study; we just find it lying on the street with little idea of its validity. Some letter writers may be wonderful truthful descriptors of the subject of their letter, others not so much.

---

[6] This was included in Lowell's correspondence with William Hocking, Professor of Moral Philosophy at Harvard and was reported by Alan Dershowitz on page 67 of his 1992 book *Chutzpah*.

It is almost impossible for an admissions officer, reading at a distance, to be able to know which is which.

In later chapters we will discuss this issue in much greater detail.

2.3 Compared to What?

If tests are not to be used in making choices among people for various purposes what could be used instead? And how well do they work? This topic is too big for just this chapter and we will return to it from various directions throughout this book. What we will do now is to lay out in some detail the rigors that a professional test must go through before it is used, and the limitations of purpose that are typically written in bold letters in its manual of operations. The parallel information and warnings for all other options is conspicuously absent.

Who pays the price for bad decisions? For some decisions (e.g., college admissions) the cost is borne primarily by the applicant: if turned down in error they will temporarily feel bad and then attend someplace else (see Chapter 10 for a list of eminent folks who didn't attend the most competitive schools); if accepted in error[7] they wasted time and family resources that might have been spent more profitably elsewhere. For other decisions (e.g., licensing decisions) the costs of an error are usually much larger and are often borne by the general public: doomed passengers in a plane flown by an unqualified pilot, stricken patients of an unqualified physician, endangered motorists sharing the same road with trucks whose drivers who can't handle their rigs, school children who can't do fractions because their teacher was improperly allowed into the classroom.

Clearly the rigors associated with the professional production of standardized tests are completely justified. The obvious question is why are the other components of such decision making not also subjected to those same rigors?

As we elaborate next on what those rigors are for a prospective test, we leave it as an exercise for the reader to try to imagine what the parallel structure would be to establish the validity of those other measures (e.g., application letter, resume, high school Grade Point Average (GPA), letter of recommendation, etc.), and to wonder about the extent to which such rigors are actually used – or even contemplated. As one example, in the past high school GPA predicted college GPA almost as well as the SAT and ACT but now, due to grade inflation, its value has deteriorated substantially.

---

[7] "accepted in error" we define as someone who was accepted but didn't graduate.

As we will discuss in the coda of this book (Chapter 13) we advocate that not only should all such alternatives be thoroughly evaluated, but that the results of such evaluations must be made public – in much the same way that studies of validity and fairness of tests are public knowledge for all who care to look in the mandated technical support documentation of all professionally built tests.

2.4 How Good Tests are Constructed

We began this book with a succinct statement of the irony of testing from the legendary statistician/testing expert Paul Holland (2023b),

Few wish to assess others,
Fewer still wish to be assessed,
But everyone wants to see the scores!

Before we can effectively explore this irony, it is important to elaborate the range of tests that are available. Tests –like automobiles, plumbers, and strawberries – can vary enormously in their quality. The quality of tests is measured on two separate, but related, characteristics: *validity* and *reliability*.

Validity has been the subject of many, sometimes impenetrable, scholarly treatises (e.g., Messick, 1995) but can be briefly summed up as the extent to which the test is measuring what it is supposed to be measuring. Or, placed within the context of a legal argument, "validity of a test score is the extent to which it is providing evidence in support of the claims that users of the score want to make."

Reliability is a measure of the stability of those test scores. Or, in the legal context, it answers the question 'how much evidence is there?'

Reliability forms an upper bound on validity.[8] So, a test may be measuring just what you want but, if it is not particularly reliable, its usefulness is sharply limited. Again, in legal terms, an unreliable test score might provide evidence in support of your claims, but the amount of evidence it provides may be too limited to be of value.

2.4.1 How the Pros Construct a Test – An Illustrative Outline

We shall not provide all the details here – for that the interested reader is referred to the various authoritative sources (e.g., Almond et al., 2002;

---

[8] Actually, the validity of a test score is bounded by the *square root* of the reliability.

Behrens, et al., 2012; Embretson, 1985; Lord & Novick, 1968; Mislevy, & Levy, 2007; Mislevy et al., 2003; Riconscente et al., 2015; SAT Suite (n.d.); Thissen & Wainer, 2001; Wainer et al., 2007).

> **Step 1.** Gather groups of the prospective users of the test scores and find out from them what claims they want to be able to make about the student that the test score would support (e.g., student can successfully manage a college curriculum, or student can read the *NY Times* with 90 percent comprehension, or ...)
>
> **Step 2.** Find out from those same prospective users what *observable* evidence they would deem sufficient support for their claims.
>
> **Step 3.** Determine how to gather such evidentiary support. Sometimes a test is deemed to be one good way to gather some of the evidence required, in which case go to Step 4.
>
> **Step 4.** Gather subject matter experts to construct such a test and set them to work creating suitable test items.
>
> **Step 5.** Review the test materials generated for suitability in terms of content, level, fairness, and so on; examine the nature of the observable evidence produced by the test items and the scoring algorithms.
>
> **Step 6.** Pretest the test materials on a cohort of individuals who are drawn from the same population for which the test is intended in order to confirm expert judgment as to their suitability.

Typically, a substantial proportion of the prepared test material that survived expert review is eliminated during the pretest.

> **Step 7.** Using the surviving test material, assemble and review draft versions of the test using faculty committees, policy committees, and so on.
>
> **Step 8.** Administer the test and subject the (now large-scale) data results to intense statistical scrutiny, eliminating any items that behave unacceptably/erratically from inclusion in any individual's score as well as equating the score to previous versions so that a score on this test has the same meaning as a score on previous forms. This latter step is crucial if we are not (for example) to infer a decline in a student's performance from what was, instead, an increase in the difficulty of the test form.

And there is much more. But this should be more than enough to illustrate why a classroom quiz, built by a single teacher on their kitchen table is of vastly lower quality – and hence should have much less impact on a student's progress, than a score on a professionally built test.

2.5 Coda (But Only for This Movement)

Thus far we have posed a puzzle. Tests have been of enormous value in helping us improve the quality of difficult decisions. These have ranged from hiring decisions in Xia Dynasty China – 4,000 years ago this past August – and subsequently the awarding of civil service jobs during the British Raj in nineteenth-century India, and improved manpower utilization in the military beginning in the twentieth century. Along the way, the Gileadites used a test to rid themselves of invading Ephraimites. The twentieth century saw the expansion of mental testing into all aspects of life: measuring the progress through primary and high school, an important part of many students' applications to college and to graduate/professional training, and after training often playing a crucial role in licensing. And, most recently, test scores are used to measure success in those professions (e.g., so-called 'value-added models' (VAMs) use changes in student test scores to evaluate their teachers – see Chapter 8).

As the use of test scores increased and with that growth a concomitant increase in their consequences, it is no wonder that they have come under increased scrutiny and criticism. Unsurprisingly, when a test score divides those who win some sort of decision-making process from those who lose, the losers are upset and claim unfairness.[9]

By far the most important current issue about the fairness of tests are the differences in performance between ethnic and gender groups. Every instance of such an outcome (usually termed 'adverse impact') is important and must be rigorously investigated and, if found valid, must be remediated. In the balance of this book, we will discuss such issues in various circumstances in the detail required.

Because of their importance we would like to end this chapter by highlighting two instances of such concerns that are too often not given the attention they deserve.

1. **Adverse impact is not the same as bias** – A ruler that shows females are, on average, shorter than males does not necessarily have a gender bias. It is merely reflecting a biological reality. So, if a particular test score shows adverse impact we must see if it is incorrectly predicting the validity criterion for which that test score is being used. There is a race difference on SAT scores – White scores are, on average, higher than Black scores. This adverse impact would be a bias if Black students' subsequent

---

[9] As the 2020 U.S. Presidential election illustrated, simply because someone lost doesn't mean the process was unfair. Sometimes the loser actually lost – and complaining doesn't change facts.

performance is better than what was predicted by the test score. In fact, tests like the SAT tend to slightly *over-predict* Black students' subsequent performance in college relative to Whites (see Chapter 12, particularly Section 12.3, for a more detailed explanation of this phenomenon). So, if there is a bias, it is in the direction of a bias against Whites (and Asian-Americans).

2. **Test scores are perhaps the most effective, practical way of finding outstanding minority candidates** – Since 1955 the Merit Scholarship program has used the inexpensive and easily available PSAT to screen 1.5 million students annually to find the 1,500 winners of a Merit Scholarship. There is no other way this could be accomplished without the search using up all the resources that were to have been given to the winners. And for many decades highly competitive colleges have used SAT scores to find hidden jewels to increase diversity within their student bodies while at the same time assuring that those students uncovered have a good chance to prosper within the rigorous programs that have made those schools so sought after.

2.6 And Finally, A Crucial Observation and A Segue

Hitchen's Razor
What can be asserted without evidence can also be dismissed without evidence. (Hitchens, 2009)
Christopher Hitchens (1949–2011)

All claims about test scores are, either implicitly or explicitly, causal. So, if we hear a claim akin to "With SAT scores like this we have no doubt Suzie will do well in college" it can be stated more explicitly as, "We believe that Suzie will do well in college *because* of the performance of prior students with SAT scores like Suzie's." Even more vague claims like "Tests are unfair" have hanging, just after them, unstated, the inevitable "because." All thoughtful audiences for such claims anticipate hearing supporting evidence for what must be a causal syllogism. If such supporting evidence is not provided, most audiences will (properly) use Hitchen's Razor and dismiss the claim as baseless. But when additional material is appended, the claims become causal, and once we move into the realm of causal inference, we enter a mine field of difficult and complex ideas. But there is hope. The justly famed eighteenth-century Scottish philosopher David Hume (1711–1776) set us on a path toward understanding causation, but his explicit focus on the crucial role played by the conditional counter-factual warned us of dangerous shoals ahead. In Chapter 11 we will take a deep dive into the modern views on causal inference, especially Rubin's Model (Holland, 1986; Rubin, 1974), and we will describe how we can use it to evaluate claims made about tests and test scores (as well as the causal relation between fracking and earthquakes in Oklahoma).

Chapter 3
The Origins and Consequences of Mental Testing in the U.S. Military

*The difference between basic and applied research
is that basic research has so many more applications.*
Harold Gulliksen (1965)

In Chapter 1 (Section 1.2) we briefly mentioned Robert Yerkes' remarkable, all-star committee that convened in 1917 in Vineland, New Jersey. The consequences of that committee's work so profoundly affected the future of testing that it would be a true disservice to leave its description to a mere mention. In this chapter we will expand our description of that committee and its work and lay out its consequences for testing in general and military testing in particular.

3.1 Testing Military Recruits

For the first 3,000 years or so of their existence, tests were constructed to focus on specific skills: horsemanship, writing, bookkeeping, reading, and so on – including military skills. Tests have been used to select only the best soldiers for centuries. Flavius Vegetius Renatus, in his *De Re Militari* (circa 380 AD) cautioned:

> *On the careful choice of soldiers depends the welfare of the Republic, and the very essence of the Roman Empire and its power is so inseparably connected with this charge, that it is of the highest importance not to be entrusted indiscriminately, but only to persons whose fidelity can be relied on.*

His description of the necessary physical standards would be appropriate for male recruits today:

> *The young soldier, therefore, ought to have a lively eye, should carry his head erect, his chest should be broad, his shoulders muscular and brawny, his fingers long, his arms strong, his waist small, his shape easy, his legs and feet rather nervous than fleshy.*

Not just anyone can join the armed forces. In addition to physical ability, mental acuity is crucial in military activities. Visions of a test taker struggling to successfully place a square peg into a round hole are not completely apocryphal. Current U.S. law prohibits the enlistment of persons who score below the 10th percentile on an entrance test. The motivation behind this law is likely twofold: the individual (a) would be put at an extreme disadvantage on the battleground and (b) might end up costing other lives besides their own due to incompetence.

3.2 The Birth of Modern Military Testing

World War I saw the development of the first mental test used for enlistment. Given that the U.S. entered the war late and needed to quickly convert large numbers of untrained soldiers into an efficient combat unit, the U.S. Armed Forces solicited and received help from the American Psychological Association (APA) as some of its leading scholars volunteered their services. A group of applied psychologists, led by APA president Robert Yerkes and including Lewis Terman and Henry Goddard, gathered at the Vineland Training School in Vineland, New Jersey to address the question of how they might help the war effort. An initial step was determining which soldiers should lead and which should follow in battle. "Democracy," Goddard argued (1919, p. 237), "means that the people rule by selecting the wisest, most intelligent and most human to tell them what to do to be happy. Thus, Democracy is a method for arriving at a truly benevolent aristocracy."

Yerkes' committee debated the relative merits of very brief individually administered tests versus longer group-administered tests. For reasons of objectivity, uniformity and reliability, they decided to develop a group test of intelligence in a modification of Lewis Terman's (1877–1956) expansion of Binet and Simon's original work. The committee felt that they were merely modifying a test built to be given one-on-one to a form that could be mass administered. In fact, they were changing the very notion of what a test tests. We will elaborate more fully in Section 3.4, but let us first lay out the structure of the tests they constructed.

The criteria they adopted (described in detail beginning on page 62 of Philip DuBois' 1970 *A History of Psychological Testing*) for the development of the new group test were:

1. adaptability for administration to several individuals at once;
2. correlation with measures of intelligence known to be valid;
3. measurement of a wide range of abilities;
4. objectivity of scoring, preferably by stencils;
5. rapidity of scoring;
6. possibility of many alternate forms to discourage coaching;
7. unfavorableness to malingering;
8. unfavorableness to cheating;
9. independence of school training (not tied to school curricula);
10. minimum writing required in making responses;
11. material intrinsically interesting;
12. economy of time.

In just seven working days they constructed ten subtests with enough items for ten different forms. They then prepared one form for printing and experimental administration. The pilot testing was done on fewer than 500 subjects. These subjects were broadly sampled coming from such diverse sources as: a school for the developmentally disabled, a psychopathic hospital, a reformatory, some aviation recruits, some men in an officers' training camp, 60 high school students and 114 marines at a Navy yard. They also administered either the Stanford–Binet intelligence test or an abbreviated form of it. They found that the scores of their test correlated 0.9 with those of the Stanford–Binet and 0.8 with the abbreviated Binet.

The items and instructions were then edited, time limits revised, and scoring formulas developed to maximize the correlation of the total score with the Binet. Items within each subtest were ordered by difficulty and four alternate forms were prepared for mass administration.

By August statistical workers under E.L. Thorndike's direction had analyzed the results of the revised test after it had been administered to 3,129 soldiers and 372 inmates of institutions for intellectually challenged. The results prompted Thorndike to call this the "best group test ever devised." It yielded good distributions of scores, correlated about 0.7 with years of school completed and 0.5 with ratings by superior officers. This test was dubbed *"Examination a"*.

In December of the same year, *Examination a* was revised once again. It became the famous *Army Alpha*. This version had only eight subtests; two of the original ones were dropped because of low correlation with other

Table 3.1 *The eight component tests and their lengths that comprised the original Army Alpha*

	Test	Number of items
1.	Oral Direction	12
2.	Arithmetical Reasoning	20
3.	Practical Judgment	16
4.	Synonym–Antonym	40
5.	Disarranged Sentences	24
6.	Number Series Completion	20
7.	Analogies	40
8.	Information	40

measures and because they were of inappropriate difficulty. The resulting test (whose components are shown in Table 3.1) bears a remarkable similarity to the structure of the modern ASVAB. This testing program, which remained under Yerkes' supervision, tested almost two million men. Two thirds of these received the *Army Alpha*; the remainder were tested with an alternative form, *Army Beta,* a nonverbal form devised for illiterate and non-English speaking recruits. At the time of WWI, the U.S. had many immigrants who could not read but were capable of serving the war effort in some capacity. Together, Army Alpha and Army Beta represented the first large-scale use of intelligence testing for personnel selection.

The success of the *Army Alpha* led to the development of a variety of special tests. In 1919 Henry Link discovered that a card-sorting test aided in the successful selection of shell inspectors and that a tapping test was valid for gaugers. He pointed out that a job analysis coupled with an experimental administration of tests thought to require the same abilities as the job and a validity study that correlated test performance with later job success yielded instruments that could distinguish between job applicants who were good risks and those who were not; L.L. Thurstone developed a "rhythm test" that accurately predicted future telegraphers' speed.

Testing programs within the military became even more extensive during World War II. In 1939, a Personnel Testing Service was established in the Office of the Adjutant General of the Army. This gave rise to the *Army General Classification Test* (AGCT) and Naval General Classification Test (NGCT), which were updated versions of the *Army Alpha*. The chairman of the committee which oversaw the development of the AGCT was Walter V. Bingham, who served on the 1917 committee that developed *Alpha*. This test eventually developed into a four-part exam consisting of tests of (1) reading and vocabulary, (2) arithmetic computation, (3) arithmetic reasoning, and (4) spatial relations. Supplemental tests for mechanical and clerical aptitude, code learning ability, and oral trade were also developed. By the end of the war, more than 9 million men had taken the AGCT or NGCT. The Navy and the Army Air Forces participated in the same program, but each with some additional tests that they required for their own purposes.

In 1960, the *Armed Services Vocational Aptitude Battery (the ASVAB)* was instituted to be used as a screening instrument for all services. It was designed to ensure appropriate allocation of talent to all branches. These will be described in more detail in Chapter 9.

3.2.1 The Armed Services Vocational Aptitude Battery and Scores Derived from it

The ASVAB consists of nine subtests, each of which is scored separately. These are:

1. Arithmetic reasoning
2. Mathematics knowledge
3. Word knowledge
4. Paragraph comprehension
5. General science
6. Electronics information
7. Auto & shop information
8. Mechanical comprehension
9. Assembling objects

The scores on the first four of these subtests are combined into a composite score and dubbed the AFQT score, which specifically determines whether a candidate is eligible for enlistment in the military. Each branch has a different minimum AFQT score requirement. The Air Force has the highest, the Army the lowest. The Air Force has more complex jobs, whereas there are more jobs in the Army and Navy of lower complexity. The Marine Corp was and is highly selective.

3.3 Why Were the Military Tests Different from all Other Tests that Preceded Them?

The 1917 Vineland committee successfully found a way to measure individual mental potential in a group-administered test that had previously only been done with individually administered tests. This satisfied the goal of Yerkes' committee to go beyond testing for specific skills and instead test for something latent that would then be much more broadly predictive. This underlying trait has come to be called 'g'. They had constructed a set of tests that leaned on wisdom gleaned from the long experience that also generated Harold Gulliksen's later observation (quoted at the beginning of this chapter). A test built to measure a specific bit of expertise measures only that expertise – but a test built to measure a trait that underlies broad ranges of expertise is suitable for many uses, even some inconceivable at the time.

The value of Army Alpha and its successors led the way to the development of the SAT and ACT exams that are broadly used to predict future college performance and hence to aid in selecting students for college admission. But this was just the beginning. As the pathway to improved prediction broadened, there emerged an alphabet soup of other exams for similar purposes: the Graduate Record Exam (GRE) for admission to graduate school, the Law School Admission Test (LSAT) for admission to law school, Medical College Admission Test (MCAT) for admission to medical school and on and on. All of these tests lean heavily on 'g' for their validity, and it is g that predicts later performance in education and vocations (Gottfredson, 2003).

Because the goal of Yerkes' committee was to build a test whose basis was the measurement of potential rather than some specific skill, they anticipated that it would be more broadly useful in the future for multiple purposes that they were considering as well as some that had yet to even have been thought of. Thus, first emerged the Army Alpha, and subsequently the ASVAB, the SAT, and many others. After this there was no turning back.

These initial military tests proved to be enormously successful and allowed a substantial improvement in the efficient utilization of both human resources and the physical resources needed to train them. Their success is testified to by their continued use more than a century later. Indeed, in the latter part of the twentieth century, the military invested in a major expansion of the ASVAB by supporting a substantial effort to transform the ASVAB into an adaptive test, which yielded the same accuracy and validity of the traditional test but did it in about half the time (Wainer, 1990/2000).

The wisdom of building a test based on measuring the underlying potential of the examinees rather than on their subject matter knowledge proved decisive (Ree & Earles, 1992) and allowed the efficacious expansion of the ASVAB's use for personnel selection well beyond the training programs for which it was originally intended. This confirmed Gulliksen's observation that a well-chosen theoretical structure yields far more applications than a testing program focused only on specific skills.

The lessons learned from the military's pioneering effort were not lost on the rest of those who were faced with selecting wisely for scarce resources. In subsequent chapters we will discuss how building tests focused on selecting examinees based on their ability led to the tests used for admission to training programs at all levels (secondary, collegiate, graduate, and professional), for licensing applicants to practice a profession (e.g., physicians, fire fighters, pilots), and for awarding scholarships and prizes to promising recipients.

3.4 What's 'g' and Why Does its Very Name Excite such Emotion?

As huge numbers of service members participated in the military testing programs, the military's various research programs designed to evaluate the tests gained increased experience. What they uncovered was not all sunshine and roses.

They learned that all the various, carefully defined, subscales were essentially identical, and, in words repeated in several formal research reports "Not much more than g" (see numerous reports by Malcolm Ree and his colleagues at the Air Force Human Resources Laboratory – now Air Force Research Laboratory). This was also the conclusion of statistician Frank Schmidt, who commented on the findings of the Army Selection and Classification Project in the 1980s (Campbell, 1990), "So, this is what you get for ten million dollars of research, 'not much more than g'?" These conclusions were well described by Sandip Sinharay's wise parents (quoted in Chapter 9), that "anything is possible except reporting subscores for unidimensional tests."

By g we are referring to Spearman's g, a variable he considered a measure of general intelligence, which Carroll (1993) called the general mental ability factor, and which we will refer to as mental potential. The early Army Alpha and Beta tests, followed by the AGCT, the AFCT, the AFQT, and the ASVAB all correlated very highly with g. The same is true for the ACT, SAT, GRE, and so on. This factor of g typically explains around 50 percent of the variance among individuals on any given cognitive test. It is by far the largest explainer among all other factors. Thus, most researchers acknowledge that g represents what might be commonly called intelligence – no matter the specific verbal definition one chooses.

The breadth of the predictive power of g extends so broadly it is often surprising. The assessment of g during childhood strongly predicts later adult socioeconomic position (Deary et al., 2005). Even after controlling for socioeconomic status (SES) in early life, g is negatively correlated with cardiovascular disease and hypertension (Deary et al., 2005), thus the lower the g, the greater the likelihood of dying from heart health issues. No one has ever developed a test of a mental ability that does not also mostly measure g (Gottfredson, 2005).

The percentage of individual differences in g that can be attributed to genetic differences increases from about 40 percent in early childhood to 80 percent by middle age (Plomin et al., 2001). Thus g is about as genetically determined as height. This parent–child relationship ($r = 0.7$) controls the rank order of children's g, but not its level – for example, Japanese children born after WWII were 10 cm taller on average than their parents, although shorter parents still had relatively shorter children (Cole & Mori, 2018).

3.5 How has the ASVAB been Used to Guide both Entrance and Placement Decisions in the Military Since WWII?

3.5.1 Making Informed Decisions

A continuous theme in this book is that tests as tools are often remarkably useful, but they can also be used to cause mischief. A hammer is fine for driving in a nail but ought not be used to bop people over the head. Thus, it is wise to focus on what are the uses to which test scores are put. The character and impact of the decisions that test scores are used to support can be controversial. Tests used for entrance and placement purposes in the military are no exception. The controversy is not as active in all circumstances; for example, it is diminished for a person who volunteers to join the military during peacetime and wants to be a pilot, but, due to a low test score, is instead assigned to an air force ground crew. Contrast this disappointment with someone who is drafted during a war whose low test score led him to be assigned to an infantry battalion and is thence sent to the front lines.

We will focus now on using exam scores to guide decisions about entrance into the armed forces. As mentioned earlier (Section 3.1), there is a federal law that prohibits the enlistment of persons who score below the 10th percentile on the test. The motivation behind this law was to prevent putting low-scoring individuals and others at a disadvantage on the battlefield.

Further, 10 U.S. Code, Section 20, limits the enlistment of persons who score between the 10th and 31st percentile to 20 percent of the total number of persons enlisted in a given year.[1] This law, designed to protect those who score low, also provides a way to avoid enlistment by those who are smart enough to

---

[1] That is their proportional representation should be no greater than it is in the general population.

deliberately score low and not be detected. These attempts have raised legitimate concerns during the time of the draft and numerous methods have been developed to detect deliberate test failure.[2]

But what happens when the number of eligible draftees is not sufficient to meet the demands of war (as was the case in 1965 when the U.S. was faced with escalation of the war in Vietnam)? The policy at the time was that no one who scored below the 31st percentile was eligible to serve. This effectively ensured that almost one third of all test takers would never wear a uniform.

3.5.2 The Case of Cassius Clay

January 17, 1960 was Cassius Marcellus Clay's eighteenth birthday. And so, as federal law then required, he registered for the military draft. Between 1960 and 1964 there were a torrent of events that filled his life: he easily won the Gold Medal as a light heavyweight in the Rome Olympics; upon his return home to Louisville, he turned professional, and in 1964 defeated Sonny Liston for the heavyweight championship of the world and changed his name to Muhammad Ali. In the years following he earned the reputation as the greatest boxer of all time. But at least some of his fame was accrued from events outside of the ring.

In 1962, his draft classification was 1-A – eligible to be drafted – and so in 1964, he was required to take pre-induction mental exams, including the AFQT. He performed poorly – 16th percentile or 84 percent of all test takers scored higher than he did.[3] This was far below the 30th percentile cutoff score required to be draft eligible. Thus, he was classified as 1-Y – fit for service only in times of national emergency. However, in 1965, this threshold was lowered to the 15th percentile. Thus, Ali, and many other young men who had been ineligible due to low AFQT scores, suddenly became eligible for the draft (Foley, 2003).

Ali refused to be drafted into the military, citing religious opposition to the Vietnam War. In 1967, Ali was found guilty of draft evasion and stripped of

---

[2] While cheating is a serious concern throughout testing, it usually focusses on getting a higher score than is deserved. Military testing may be unique in that it also must contend with some candidates who cheat to get a lower score than is appropriate. This double-sided concern is a difficult one to resolve. The military (and more specifically, the Air Force Research Laboratory) has been a leader in supporting research into this problem. At the moment, the most successful methodology for discovering and correcting for test-taking anomalies is described in Wainer and Sakworawich (2020). This sophisticated methodology relies on a procedure that combines methods of robust estimation with Jackknife technology and has been shown to correct anomalies in both directions automatically.

[3] We now strongly suspect that his poor performance was at least partially due to his then undiagnosed dyslexia.

his boxing titles. His conviction was appealed and, in 1971 the U.S. Supreme Court ruled 8–0 to overturn Ali's conviction.[4] Although he avoided serving time in prison, he did not fight for almost 4 years when he was in his athletic prime. His actions and his fame elevated him to a highly visible position among those in opposition to the war. Ali's legacy would be much different had it not been for one man's plan.

3.5.3 Project 100,000: Its Claims and Its (Lack of) Evidentiary Support

Secretary of Defense Robert McNamara came up with a plan that would be sold to the American public as providing an opportunity to thousands of young men who were stuck in poverty. The timing was ideal as President Lyndon Johnson had just declared his War on Poverty. By lowering the minimum required score on the AFQT from the 30th to the 15th percentile, Project 100,000 immediately made 354,000 previously ineligible young men now draft eligible. Forty-one percent of these were African American, compared to 12 percent of the armed forces overall.

But was Project 100,000 successful at helping the poor test takers in terms of improved opportunity and quality of life? A study sponsored by the Department of Defense (Laurence et al., 1989) over 20 years later concluded that when compared to non-veteran peers who were similar on many demographic and SES measures, the draftees had lower income, educational attainment, and employment status. Project 100,000 draftees were also more likely to be divorced. Not exactly the evidence McNamara had hoped for. But it emphasizes the importance of gathering suitable data to allow us to assess the efficacy of any policy.

Secretary McNamara could have chosen other options to increase the draft pool, such as eliminating student deferments for college or calling up more reserves. Instead, he placed thousands of young men from poor families in harm's way, resulting in numerous deaths (MacPherson, 2002). This decision, supported by Johnson, remains controversial. Muhammad Ali wasn't the only one affected by Project 100,000, although he was the most prominent. By lowering the test standards and selling it as an opportunity to improve lives, test scores were used in a way to affect, disproportionately and negatively, the lives of thousands of minorities.

---

[4] The Supreme Court found that Ali's resistance to the draft on religious grounds was sincere and he should not have been forced to serve.

3.5.4 Another Project 100,000 in Higher Education?

Almost 60 years later, we are experiencing something similar in college admissions. It is being sold to the American public as a way to increase diversity at selective colleges – especially given the recent Supreme Court ruling banning affirmative action. But rather than lower the standards by lowering the cutoffs for SAT and ACT scores to be admitted to colleges, there is a more radical movement to do away with the tests entirely. Of course, the proper question to ask in evaluating such a policy where tests are not used to make admission decisions is "compared to what?" What will colleges use instead? Applicants will now be evaluated "holistically"[5] by basing decisions on other metrics (e.g., application letters, letters of recommendation, high school GPA, etc.). The success of this recent policy will be measured similarly – will the lives of the minorities affected be improved or will they end up worse off? Will those who are admitted under the new policy graduate at the same rate as before? Will those who do not graduate be able to find suitable employment? That topic is explored further in Chapter 6, although this discussion is limited because too often outcome data (e.g., graduation rates, rates of bar exam passage, etc.) that would allow us to evaluate the efficacy of this policy are either not being gathered or not being made publicly available.

---

[5] What does the term "holistic" mean? It was used earlier by the famed Scottish polymath Sir D'Arcy Wentworth Thompson (1860–1948) in his iconic book *On Growth and Form*. He carefully defined the term, explaining that it was not derived from a root in the word "whole" (everything altogether) nor from "holy" (implying the input from some deity). Instead, he credited a Greek origin, from the word αρμονικός, implying a kind of special harmony. A definition we find more than suitable. Unfortunately, we do not believe that its current usage implies any sort of harmony, but rather is used to mean an idiosyncratic mixture of various objective and subjective measures with arbitrary, and usually unstated, weightings.

Chapter 4
Testing in Grades K-12

4.1 Introduction

Horace Mann (1796–1859), who successfully pushed for universal public education, is known as the Father of American Education (Carleton, 2009). He is also credited (or blamed) with initiating what is now known as "high stakes" testing in which student test performance is a determinant of the fate of teachers, principals, superintendents, school board members, and ultimately schools. In this chapter, we take a closer look at the history of testing in U.S. schools and conclude with one of the oldest and continuous misuses of testing in modern history – using student test scores for school accountability and to drive educational reform efforts.

Testing has been used to evaluate learning in primary and secondary (K-12) education for centuries. The types of tests that appear in K-12 education range from the subject-based ones created by teachers to the standardized IQ and achievement tests built by professional testing organizations.

In the United States, prior to 1845, tests were teacher-made and generally administered orally with no paper or pencil needed. Individual students would sit in a private room with a teacher and answer questions or recite what they had learned. The oral method of testing obviously saved many trees, but scoring such tests was also somewhat subjective as the teacher could be influenced by many things other than what the student said, including body language, nervousness, fluency, social skills, and personality. This process changed dramatically when Horace Mann, then secretary of the Massachusetts State Board of Education (1837–1848), returned from his 1843 visits to European schools, where he became convinced that written exams were better than oral exams. He gave the rationale:

> *When the oral method is adopted, none but those personally present at the examination can have any accurate or valuable idea of <u>appearance of the school</u>*

> *(emphasis ours) . . . Not so, however, when the examination is by printed questions and written answers. A transcript, a sort of Daguerreotype likeness, as it were, of the state and condition of the pupils' minds, is taken and carried away, for general inspection. Instead of being confined to committees and visitors, it is open to all; instead of perishing with the fleeting breath that gave it life, it remains a permanent record. All who are, or who may afterwards become interested in it, may see it.*
>
> (Caldwell & Courtis, 1923, pp. 43–44)

With written exams, every student would read the same questions and answer in a way that was less subjectively graded. However, Mann's goal in promoting written exams was not simply to demonstrate which students were superior and which were less so. Rather, as the phrase, "appearance of the school" indicates (highlighted in the Mann extract), his goal was to reveal how well the schools and teachers were doing. If nothing else, Mann fancied himself as an educational reformer.

Mann's plan for written exams was soon realized and over 30,000 students in the Boston area were tested. The average score on the exams was 30 percent correct, raising an alarm among parents. Unfortunately, as with most standardized tests, the teachers were neither the ones who wrote the questions nor were they privy to what content was being covered. Thus, they did not know if the content they were teaching matched that measured by the test. Tables were published that showed school performances and compared them to the then very affluent Roxbury schools. Teachers whose students performed poorly were called out publicly for emphasizing rote learning rather than understanding.

Test fraud soon showed its ugly head when the test examiners caught one teacher leaking the questions to his students. The head teacher at the Smith school, which was segregated, was censured for not realizing the potential of African American students whose scores were substantially lower than those of White students. High-stakes testing was thus born, along with conversations about school failures and accompanying calls for school reform. Thus began a tradition of firing teachers and even school administrators based on poor student test performance that remains to this day.

> *What transpired then still sounds eerily familiar: cheating scandals, poor performance by minority groups, the narrowing of curriculum, the public shaming of teachers, the appeal of more sophisticated measures of assessment, the superior scores in other nations, all amounting to a constant drumbeat about school failure.*
>
> (Reese, 2013)

4.2 From Intelligence to Achievement

Horace Mann's push for commonality among school curricula and tests initiated the start of school testing that was not limited to measuring only what one teacher taught in one subject at one school, but rather the development of tests that would measure more general knowledge and skills that every student ought to know and have. In the early twentieth century, Binet's first IQ test was designed to identify low-scoring children who would not benefit from schooling. In the U.S. in 1911, Goddard was the first to advocate for IQ tests in the public schools to similarly identify children who would struggle to be successful. A few years later, Terman (1916) developed the individually administered Stanford–Binet Test of Intelligence to help with placement and tracking of students. By 1919, Terman had taken what was learned from the Army Alpha test (Chapter 3) and developed the group-administered National Intelligence Tests for schoolchildren. Over 400,000 tests were sold during the first year (Hanson, 1993). With this began the academic tracking programs that grouped students of similar abilities into similar curricular paths, restricting choices for many (Zanderland, 1998).

These early IQ tests successfully measured the type of general knowledge and skills that most agreed students should acquire in school. The focus began to shift away from tests that were used to identify students and track them in school and more toward tests that successfully measured the learning of a common curriculum that students should master by the end of a particular grade. The Stanford Achievement Tests appeared in 1923 and combined a battery of smaller content-area tests into one exam. This was followed in 1929 by the first statewide achievement tests – the Iowa Test of Basic Skills (ITBS), which were used for over 50 years as the primary achievement tests for most states (Peterson, 1983).

4.3 Educational Reform

Results from statewide tests like the Iowa Test of Basic Skills(ITBS) continued to highlight the poor test performances of minority and high-poverty groups of students – and continued the calls for school reform that began with Horace Mann's initiatives in Massachusetts. The launch of Sputnik in 1957 brought these concerns into sharp focus as the quality of education in the United States was tied to the Cold War space and arms race with the Soviet Union. But modern educational reform accelerated sharply in the mid-1960s with Lyndon Johnson's Great Society. Johnson's first order of business was to commission reports on just how badly the nation's schools were failing underrepresented minority (URM) children.

In 1964, the Exploratory Committee for the Assessment of Progress in Education was established. The committee soon created what has become known as the National Assessment of Educational Progress or NAEP – a congressionally mandated project that assesses K-12 students in most subjects by administering specially developed tests. NAEP tests remain to this day and results are used to assess student progress, assist in developing ways to improve education, and, unfortunately, also drive educational reform.

In 1965, Assistant Secretary of Labor Daniel Patrick Moynihan and his staff wrote a commissioned report entitled, *The Negro Family: The Case for National Action*. Among the report's conclusions was that civil rights legislation would not be enough to repair the damage done to African Americans.

> *In this new period the expectations of the (African) Americans will go beyond civil rights. Being Americans, they will now expect that in the near future equal opportunities for them as a group will produce roughly equal results, as compared with other groups. This is not going to happen.*
>
> (emphasis added)

What would produce equal results? Some believed that education was the solution. Ensure all citizens receive the same, quality education and the tide would turn for URM.

4.4 Money for Schools with Impoverished Students

Later that year, President Johnson sat in the same rural Texas schoolhouse where he had sat as a student and signed into law the Elementary and Secondary Education Act (ESEA), which provided federal money to schools that served poor children – many of whom were URM, under what was called Title I. Prior to 1965, education had been primarily left to the local and state governments. The goal was noble indeed – to increase the academic performance of poor students who had struggled to keep up with their richer counterparts. Enter educational reform solution number one: spending more on poor students' education. But would spending more on education lead to better achievement performance for poor students? The congressionally mandated Coleman Report (aka The Equality of Educational Opportunity report) (1966) explored influences on student achievement. The massive study involved almost 600,000 students and 66,000 teachers from over 4,000 schools. It remains one of the largest educational research efforts ever undertaken.

The federal government expected that schools with mostly minority students, especially in the South, provided a poor education for URM students.

4.4 Money for Schools with Impoverished Students

On the contrary, the report concluded that school quality measures (e.g., per pupil expenditure) had minimal correlations with student achievement scores, whereas family background (e.g., income) had large correlations with test scores. Thus, it was concluded that increased spending on education would not lead to equality of student achievement.

> *Taking all these results together, one implication stands out above all: That schools bring little influence to bear on a child's achievement that is independent of his background and general social context; and that this very lack of an independent effect means that the inequalities imposed on children by their home, neighborhood, and peer environment are carried along to become the inequalities with which they confront adult life at the end of school.*

But does the Coleman Report's conclusion hold true today? A recent examination of data from 1992 to 2015 confirmed that increased spending had little to no effect on achievement (Hanushek, 2016). Incidentally, the one erroneous finding in the Coleman Report, that the backgrounds of other students at the school were related to a student's achievement, ultimately led to forced desegregation and busing. Enter educational reform solution number two – desegregation. The federal orders to desegregate cost millions, were very controversial, and still did not result in decreased gaps between African American and White student achievement scores.

Johnson had said when signing the ESEA, "By passing this bill, we bridge the gap between helplessness and hope for more than 5 million educationally deprived children." Yet, despite numerous attempts to dismiss the reports by Moynihan and Coleman, their conclusions concerning failure to improve the conditions of URM were, unfortunately, prophetic. In 1965, the Black–White achievement gap was roughly a standard deviation. Fifty years later, the achievement gap remained about a standard deviation (Hanushek, 2016). Similarly, Barshay (2024) reported that gaps between Black and White 9- and 13-year-olds on NAEP reading and math scores have remained consistent for the past 50 years. Despite this disappointing counter evidence, federally ordered school reform efforts to improve the achievement scores of impoverished children, many of whom are URM, have continued. How many dollars have been spent on these reform efforts? In 2021, $6.5 billion was spent on Title I programs alone.

> *One of the saddest lessons of history is this: If we've been bamboozled long enough, we tend to reject any evidence of the bamboozle. We're no longer interested in finding out the truth. The bamboozle has captured us. It's simply too painful to acknowledge, even to ourselves, that we've been taken. Once you give a charlatan power over you, you almost never get it back.*
>
> (Sagan, 1997)

4.5 A Nation at Risk – 1983

In 1983, the Reagan administration commissioned *A Nation at Risk: The Imperative for Educational Reform*, which continued the apparently baseless pursuit of educational reform. The report concluded, based on disappointing test scores, that our educational system was broken. Rather than simply recommending more spending, the conclusion was similar to Mann's over a century earlier: the quality of teaching in American public education was subpar. The report recommended performance-based salaries to improve teaching. The rationale was that low student test scores could be raised simply by motivating some lazy teachers or replacing them with motivated ones. Certainly, something or someone needed to be blamed for low student achievement. Enter educational reform solution number three – the teacher. If increased spending and desegregation could not fix education, then getting rid of bad teachers would.

4.6 An Inconvenient Truth

An erroneous assumption has been used to support the continuation of educational reform efforts. That assumption, despite the conclusions of the Coleman Report, is that student academic success as measured by achievement test scores is mostly "caused" by factors that exist inside the walls of the classroom and school building (e.g., per pupil spending, teaching quality, administrator quality, classmates, etc.). Thus, students who have the good fortune of getting "good" teachers, for example, tend strongly to succeed academically, whereas students who have the misfortune of getting "bad" teachers tend strongly to fail academically. The truth is closer to the conclusions of the Coleman Report – education has much less to do with a child's success compared with other influences outside of school. Thus, not surprisingly, educational reform efforts that attempt to increase student achievement by improving teaching have failed.

Consider the head-scratching teacher value-added system (see Chapter 8) employed by the Houston, Texas independent school district recently. Teachers, principals, and even the superintendent were fired or awarded merit raises based on how much students' scores improved on state tests. Superintendent Terry Grier was awarded an almost $100,000 merit raise based on calculations that are so lacking in reliability and validity that they are not worth taking the time to describe (Amrein-Beardsley et al., 2016).

The repeated failure to reduce achievement gaps has been consistently ignored by politicians, government regulators, faculty of university teacher training programs, school administrators, and teachers. All are guilty of failing to acknowledge that the emperor is indeed marching naked. The strong correlation between poverty and student achievement is well known and consistent (Lacour & Tissington, 2011). The average academic test performance of randomly grouped K-12 students is inversely proportional to the level of financial poverty of those students. Bad teachers are not disproportionally assigned to teach financially impoverished students nor are good teachers disproportionally assigned to teach non-impoverished students.

4.7 Miracles

Famed Scottish Philosopher David Hume (1748) defined a miracle as a violation of a law of nature (understood as a regularity of past experience projected by the mind to future cases) and argued that the evidence for a miracle is never sufficient for rational belief because it is more likely that a report of a miracle is false as a result of misperception, mistransmission, or deception ("that this person should either deceive or be deceived"), than that a violation of a regularity of experience has actually occurred.

4.7.1 No Child Left Behind and the Texas Miracle

As previously mentioned, iterations of ESEA have continued with lofty goals and equally disappointing results. The efforts to improve teaching ability by getting rid of 'bad' teachers spurred by the *Nation at Risk* report did not result in reduction of achievement gaps. Undaunted, in 2001, President George W. Bush signed the *No Child Left Behind Act* (NCLB) as a reauthorization of ESEA. This law required statewide testing in public schools (if they were to continue to receive federal funds for education) and demanded that student test performance improve, or teachers *and principals* would be removed from the school. Bush was influenced by the "success" of Houston, Texas schools under Superintendent Rod Paige. By holding principals accountable, the schools had improved dramatically. Enter educational reform solution number four: fire bad principals. Principals joined teachers in terms of being accountable for poor student performance, despite evidence that principals account for much less than the paltry 1 to 7 percent of variance in student achievement outcomes attributed to teachers (Detterman, 2016; Hanushek, 1997). Unfortunately, it was later revealed that the improved student test scores and decreased dropout rates reported by Houston schools were due to falsifying records. But not before Bush chose Paige to be Secretary of Education and lead the charge for NCLB.

How have the "fire or replace principals" educational reform efforts fared? Heissel and Ladd (2018) evaluated the federally funded North Carolina school reform effort called "Turning Around the Lowest Achieving Schools". To be eligible to receive the School Improvement Grant, states had to employ one of four models – two of which involved replacing the principal. There was no evidence that replacement of principals led to an increase in leadership quality or student test scores at the low-performing schools. Robinson and Bligh (2019) reported three other "miracles," in addition to Houston where large urban school districts in high poverty areas reported incredible "turnarounds" due to the improved test performance of poor students during the NCLB era. Unfortunately, for each turnaround, they also found where principal accountability led to test and/or reporting fraud by the school leaders similar to the Houston story. We will summarize these next.

4.7.2 The New Orleans Miracle

In 2005, Hurricane Katrina devastated large areas in New Orleans, displacing much of its population – especially those in the poorest areas of the city. The city decided to replace the traditionally "bad" public schools with charter schools. According to Chait (2015), the new charter schools "produced spectacular results." The proportion of New Orleans students who performed at grade level had been only half of that which was found in the rest of the state. By 2015, it trailed by only 6 percent.

Were the charter schools the cause of this great success? Prior to Katrina, there were 65,000 students enrolled in the New Orleans public school system. Five years after Katrina, that number was 45,000. Most of the 20,000 students who left lived in the poorest areas of the city and never returned as their homes were destroyed. Many relocated to Houston, TX and a year later, they were failing the Texas competency tests (Tucker, 2006). Those same students scored low on tests and were more likely to drop out, and so on. Obviously, if you take any large urban school district and simply remove its 31 percent poorest students, average test scores will shoot up and dropout rates will decline. The results will appear to support any kind of reform someone might claim.

4.7.3 The District of Columbia Miracle

The District of Columbia public school system had been singled out as a national model for educational reform. Former Secretary of Education Arne

Duncan used DC schools as an example of what happens when you embrace innovative reforms. Former chancellor Michelle Rhee implemented accountability policies that linked principal and teacher salaries and job security to student test scores and graduation rates. In early 2018, the FBI, U.S. Education Department, and D.C. Office of the Inspector General began investigating the school system about graduation fraud. At one particular school, Ballou High School, it was revealed that over 900 students should not have graduated. Although the district had a record graduation rate of 73 percent in 2017, a city investigation concluded that roughly one-third of those students should not have graduated (Jamison & Nirappil, 2018).

4.7.4 The Atlanta Miracle

In February 2009, Beverly Hall was named Superintendent of the Year by the American Association of School Administrators which Ms. Hall was applauded for raising test scores and graduation rates and called Atlanta a model of school reform. In August of that same year, Hall referred to the Atlanta public schools as a model urban school district with double-digit test score gains. In February 2010, the state Board of Education ordered districts to investigate fifty-eight schools in Atlanta for cheating. In November 2010, a study confirming the cheating was made public and Hall announced her intent to retire. The *Atlanta Journal-Constitution* reported that Hall and other officials had overseen a campaign to suppress allegations of widespread cheating. Eighty educators later confessed to cheating.

4.8 Every Student Succeeds

The most recent reauthorization of ESEA, *Every Student Succeeds Act* (ESSA), was signed in 2015 by President Barack Obama and moved much of the enforcement of the demand for improved academic performance in public schools back to the states, with federal oversight. ESSA also moved away from firing teachers and principals to simply shaming schools whose students did not perform well on state tests by requiring the grading of schools (A, B, C, D, or F or some other form of categorization) based upon academic achievement test performance. Enter educational reform solution number five: shame the schools themselves. If spending more money, desegregation, and firing teachers and principals does not work, then shame the schools. Peterson et al. (2022) examined the results of a decade of reform efforts in the state of Nebraska. Despite spending billions of dollars and costing hundreds of teachers and principals their jobs, there were absolutely zero gains in student test scores. Today, we are witnessing a reduction in the numbers of college students who enroll in teacher education programs. Public confidence in education is at an all-time low.

4.9. Is Educational Reform Failure Unique to the U.S.?

Horace Mann, who first made his appearance at the beginning of this chapter, was responsible for many things in American education, both good and bad. Among the good things were his efforts to make public education free and universally available to all children beginning in the 1830s. Over a century later, the United Kingdom followed suit with the passing of the Education Act in 1944. Prior to that, few students from poor families were admitted to the state-aided grammar schools. Admission decisions were based mostly on the ability of the parents to pay rather than on student performance (see Saunders, 2022, for a more extensive coverage of what follows).

To complete the conversion from class-based to merit-based admissions, a new national examination was created, the "11-Plus," to allow high-scoring children from poor families to be admitted to grammar schools, regardless of their parents' financial means. Did this move to meritocracy ensure equal success among poor and rich kids? Unfortunately, no. Performance on the new exam and representation in grammar schools was still much higher among middle-class kids compared to their working-class counterparts. What was the source of this gap?

Some claimed that teachers were discriminating against poor students by using a language that they were not used to. The curriculum was also blamed as it was foreign to most poor kids. Finally, the new 11-Plus exam was blamed as being culturally biased and favored middle-class kids. After 20 years of failure to reduce consistent, stubborn achievement gaps, most grammar schools were replaced with "comprehensives" that were forbidden to admit students based solely on ability. Selection at age 11 ceased to occur and instead all children were taught together in the same schools.

Did this reform effort result in the elimination or reduction in gaps? Again, no. Middle-class children continued to outperform working-class children on the post-16 and university entrance exams. What could be blamed next? Testing in the classroom was scaled back and progressive methods of teaching were implemented. Teachers were required to have graduate training and understanding social class disadvantages was part of the curriculum. School district boundaries were redrawn in an effort to have more heterogenous

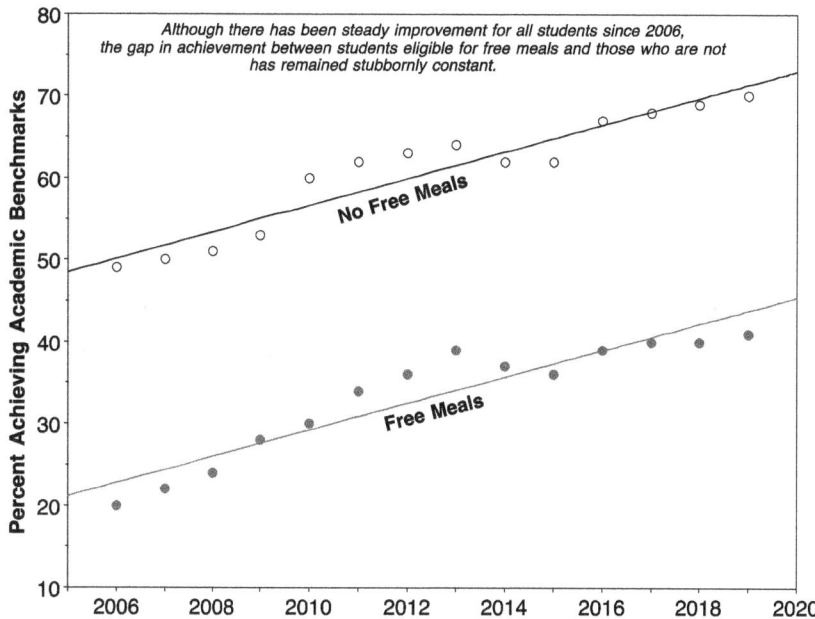

Figure 4.1 Percent of students achieving benchmarks on the General Certificate of Education shown separately by their eligibility for free school meals.

classrooms with regard to social class. School choice was removed to promote desegregation – similar to the forced busing occurring in the U.S. at the same time. Compulsory education was extended to age 16 as a way to help underperforming poor kids by keeping them in school longer. In 2008, this was extended to age 18. Despite all these school reform efforts, the poorest children saw little benefit. A 2022 report (Tahir, 2022) showed that the achievement gap had remained remarkably consistent over a 20-year period. Figure 4.1 shows the percentage of UK students who reached General Certificate of Secondary Education (GCSE) benchmarks. The GCSE is a set of exams given to students after two years of secondary education. The top line represents students not eligible for free lunches whereas the bottom line represents students who were eligible. Both groups showed the same pattern of improvement since 2016 yet the difference in performance has remained constant.

The story of educational reform in the UK over the past 70 years is very similar to that which has occurred in the U.S. over the same period. Numerous reform efforts have resulted in wasted spending, wasted hours of implementation, and worst of all, cost countless educators their jobs. Testing continues to reveal race and class differences that are resistant to any reform efforts. Rather than chasing windmills by aiming to eliminate the achievement gaps, perhaps a more sensible goal is to view testing as information that can be used to guide both instruction and social policy so that every student may reach maximum potential.

4.10 Coda

The truth is rarely pure and never simple

Oscar Wilde

Is there a coherent message to be drawn from this decades-long tale of well-meaning, but ultimately unsuccessful, attempts to make public education the pathway to a better life for all citizens that was envisioned by education's pioneers? We believe that there is, although Oscar Wilde's Algernon's[1] comment was certainly prophetic in this instance.

We must start by returning once again to the false conflict between the romantic idea of the good and the classic goal of truth. We may be able to have both, but the path is not going to be easy, nor short, nor inexpensive. In the area of testing, the good is represented by having no differences among groups – not among ethnic groups nor among gender groups. And truth is represented by the empirical evidence generated by those tests and other sources of relevant information. Further, the path toward progress is not by denying evidence. We cannot get rid of group differences by getting rid of tests any more than we can rid ourselves of obesity by getting rid of bathroom scales.

Indeed, we must go in quite the opposite direction and take the test results and the various studies of them very seriously indeed. The beginning of a solution is to find the cause of the differences observed. As we will learn in Chapter 11, finding the causes of effects is often an insuperably difficult task – even with extensive data and careful detective work and is evocatively illustrated by John Snow's historic attempt to find the cause of the 1854 London Cholera epidemic. We have seen in this chapter how attempts to eliminate group differences caused by teachers, or principals, or schools have had minimal success. Obviously, all these potential causes have some effect on student learning and performance. But the size of their combined causal effects is clearly not enough to explain group differences and make a serious dent in the problem. What are we to do?

As we discussed in Section 4.4, the most likely candidate to resolve the discouraging resistance to reduction of group differences in the effectiveness

---

[1] A character in Wilde's play *The Importance of Being Earnest*.

4.10 Coda

of education, are the differences in home environments of the students. And these differences are the result of societal inequities that are centuries old. Why has this not been addressed in a vigorous manner? In a very real way this is reminiscent of the old story of the good Samaritan, who on a particularly dark night was walking along a lonely street when he happened upon a friend who was crawling around on his hands and knees in the area around a streetlamp. The Samaritan stopped and asked what was wrong, and could he help. The friend replied that he had lost his car keys and was trying to find them so he could drive home. So, the Samaritan got down on his knees and helped in the search. After some time passed, they had covered the area thoroughly and had not found the missing keys. The Samaritan then asked his friend if he was sure this is where he had misplaced them. The friend replied that he believed that he lost them in a very dark alley further up the block but chose not to look there because finding anything there was surely to be difficult, if not impossible. So it is with trying to reverse centuries-long social inequities. It is bound to be difficult, expensive, and time consuming. But that is where the missing keys lie, and our repeated attempts, over decades, to find them elsewhere have not led to a happy solution in the past, nor is it likely to in the future.

Chapter 5
Licensing Examinations
Physicians, Pilots, and Teachers as Examples

5.1 Introduction

The theme expressed repeatedly in this accounting is that there has always been a conflict, grown more acute recently, between the romantic idea of "The Good" and the classical notion of "The Truth." In testing, "The Good" is most often the event of having no differences in scores among societal groups (e.g., racial, ethnic, gender) on the variables being measured; "The Truth" is the recognition that there are differences. As we discussed in Chapter 4, sometimes the costs of down weighting (or ignoring altogether) existing real differences so as to get closer to the ideal of The Good is small enough to justify such policies. But sometimes those costs are too large to ignore. It is hard to imagine anyone urging the abandonment of high-performance liquid chromatography (HPLC)[1] testing because it showed substantial race differences, or mammograms because of their huge sex differences.

One specific area of application in which the truth revealed by test scores is often too impactful to be ignored is when tests are used for licensing. The costs may be to individuals, to institutions, and/or to society; but, if they are large enough, they cannot be ignored in service to The Good. In Chapter 10 we will learn of a Canadian lifeguard chosen for his bilingualism rather than his swimming ability. It seems a flawed policy, but its supporters argued that the need to actually make an in-water rescue was very rare, whereas the need to be understood by all at the pool was common; thus, they argued it would be a mistake to overweight that one particular skill in hiring when it was needed so rarely. Similarly, a test for firefighters included "items" like "carrying a heavy hose up a ladder'" and "carrying a person down a ladder"

---

[1] HPLC is the most reliable blood test methodology to detect sickle cell disease.

that were objected to because they showed a substantial adverse impact on female candidates. The logic of the objection parallels the Canadian argument for lifeguards: of the many tasks firefighters have to perform, carrying heavy things up and down a ladder occurs relatively rarely, too rarely they (successfully) argued, to allow such requirements to have a large influence on the hiring of an entire class of plausible candidates. The counterargument in both cases was that while such tasks were relatively rare, when they were needed, they were crucial.

The comparative cost functions represented by The Good and The Truth sometimes lean toward the former and sometimes toward the latter. As we suggested in the examples cited above, one area of testing, in which moving too far away from The Truth is likely to be too expensive to the public welfare, is licensing. And licensing spans a very broad range well beyond lifeguards and firefighters; it includes pilots and truck drivers, teachers and lawyers, accountants, barbers and electricians.

We cannot go into details of the licensing of all of the activities and professions for which society requires a license, but will instead focus on just three: physicians in part A of this chapter, airline workers in part B, and teachers in part C. We believe that these serve as three important illustrative examples.

Part A. Licensing of Physicians in the U.S.

5.A.1 History of Medical Licensing

Using a test of some sort to license individuals before they are allowed to engage in selected activities is centuries old. Among the oldest of such activities is found in the practice of medicine. We find a *History of Licensure* in the Parsis collection of sacred books known as the *Avesta*, which contain regulations for physicians (specifically surgeons). In 931 A.D. the ruler of Arabia required that all potential physicians undergo examination by the most respected physician of the land, Sinan ibn Thabit of Harran (Sigerist, 1935).

Licensure of physicians was both a means of protecting the vulnerable public and protecting the current practitioners of that profession from too much competition. Typically, when the state did the licensing, it was because of concern for the public's welfare; however, in the Middle Ages, crafts and professions of all kinds were organized into guilds. From these guilds came strict standards and regulations regarding the quality of professional services, which almost surely were to protect the incomes of current practitioners by limiting entry. This was as true for the practice of physicians as it was for any other skilled trade.

The testing procedures initially adopted for medical licensure followed in the long and storied history exemplified by the university exams that began at the University of Bologna in 1219 and continued in 1257 by Robert de Sorbon, chaplain of Louis IX, in the community of scholars at what would evolve into the Sorbonne. These exams were entirely oral – written exams came centuries later and did not even begin to show up until the sixteenth century with the work of the Jesuits, which is described in greater detail in McGucken (1932).

Thus, it should not be surprising that nineteenth-century medical training in the United States followed the same sort of apprenticeship model that was used by carpenters, plumbers, and other skilled professions. The Shibboleth that allowed them to practice was a combination of the endorsement of their master and some sort of licensure procedure established by the areas in which they intended to practice. In the early 1880s, West Virginia became the first state to enact and implement a genuinely restrictive medical license law. The challenges to this law eventually ended up in the U.S. Supreme Court, whose 1889 decision (*Dent v. West Virginia*) upheld the licensing law and confirmed a state's right to regulate the practice of medicine. Thus, began state licensing of physicians in the United States (Mohr, 2013).

At that time, when a formal exam was administered, it was typically oral and neither its content nor its scoring was objective and standardized. Marmaduke Dent, the attorney representing his cousin Frank before the U.S. Supreme Court, challenged the West Virginia statute on these very grounds. Dent asserted (and the court agreed) that there were "no objective criteria against which to measure the board's completely subjective assessment of what distinguished a passing performance from a failing performance." And even if the board members agreed upon appropriate standards, "the standards could not be consistently applied when every candidate was examined separately, and every examination was different."

Originally, the Medical Society of West Virginia provided three paths to licensure. The first was having been in practice for at least 10 years – the grandfather pathway. The second was graduation from a "reputable medical program". And the third, of relevance here, was passing an oral exam given by one or more examiners based on "anatomy, physiology, chemistry, *materia medica*, pathology, pathological anatomy, surgery, and obstetrics" at "a sufficiently strict" level to justify public practice. So far so good. But the examiners were free to set the exam in any form they wished and free to determine for themselves whether any given candidate's answers merited passing. Clearly the lack of standardization and objectivity was a disaster waiting to happen. And, on Saturday morning, March 7, 1891, it did.[2]

On that morning, at a busy intersection in downtown Wheeling, West Virginia, Dr. George Garrison met Dr. George Baird. The 62-year-old Baird was a popular physician, Civil War veteran, and former mayor of Wheeling. The 39-year-old Garrison was a generation younger, had been Baird's apprentice and his protégé. By 1891 Garrison had been a practicing physician for 7 years and was enjoying a flourishing medical practice. But the terms of the newly adopted licensing law precluded his being grandfathered in and so he had to present himself for an examination. He did not pass and blamed Baird, who was one of the two examiners who failed him. And so, when they met on that fateful Saturday morning, Garrison pulled out a pistol and shot Baird twice – the first went through his skull emerging from his left eye, and the second in his chest where it severed a major artery before lodging beneath his shoulder blade. Baird managed to stumble into a local store and told the shopkeeper that Garrison had shot him. He was pronounced dead 20 minutes later. In the meantime, Garrison calmly walked to a local police station and surrendered himself, explaining to the shocked duty officer exactly what had happened.

Garrison was tried and finally, after three trials, convicted of involuntary manslaughter. He was sentenced to seven more months of jail time (in addition to the fifteen that he had already served) and a $250 fine.

Although the Wheeling shooting took place more than 130 years ago, it should still give pause to any who would seek to deprive a person of their profession in ways that can be seen as subjective, unstandardized, or capricious.[3]

The shift to a more rigorous standardized approach in our national licensing program was motivated both by the 1889 Supreme Court decision and the 1891 Wheeling murder; but it had its formal beginnings on May 5, 1914 in the Willard Hotel in Washington, DC (Johnson & Chaudhry, 2012).

5.A.2 Multiple Choice Exams, John Hubbard, and Modern Medical Licensing

Medical licensing exams in the first half of the twentieth century were surely influenced by the Garrison tragedy, but nevertheless they initially followed the

---

[2] Mohr (2013) pp. 3, 66, and 184.
[3] In the November 14, 2023 issue of the *New York Times* (p. A11) is an article by Troy Closson describing a change in New York State's Regents exams, passage which had, for generations, been required for a Regents High School Diploma. Instead, they will be substituting "capstone projects, presentations, or performance-based assessments." One cannot help but wonder how this policy change will meld with policies that allow "concealed carrying of firearms."

centuries-old tradition of constructed response items, some written and some oral, rigorously administered over several days and scored by multiple expert raters. As discussed in Chapter 1, this changed mid-century with the happy confluence of three major events.

1. The success and growing popularity of the College Entrance Exam produced by the College Board which led, in 1947, to the founding of the Educational Testing Service. Here, in one place, was concentrated the psychometric experience and expertise developed over the previous four decades.
2. The publication, in 1950, of Harold Gulliksen's *Theory of Mental Tests*, which finally provided a rigorous consilience of the statistical and theoretical methodologies required to both support the scoring of modern tests and to measure their efficacy.
3. The ascension of the renowned pediatric cardiologist John P. Hubbard (1903–1990) to be the head of the National Board of Medical Examiners (NBME), a post he held from 1950 until 1975.

Let us reiterate and elaborate on the effect of these three events in order.

The need for economically practical mass administration of tests that faced the U.S. military during the First World War gave rise to a huge increase in the development of multiple-choice items. Then, as now, there was concern that such a format was incapable of testing certain proficiencies that were crucial. Sometimes these concerns were well founded, but surprisingly often it turned out that the multiple-choice option worked better than even its most ardent supporters could have hoped. Why?

The answer draws on the psychometric/statistical developments described in Gulliksen's foundational book and stems from the basic fact that scores derived from any test format are imperfect. They contain errors. These errors fall principally into two broad categories.

(i) The estimates fluctuate symmetrically around their true values, due to variations in the examinee and the scorer. On some days we perform better than on others. As mentioned earlier (Chapter 1, Section 1.2), variation among raters of essays has always been substantial and seems relatively insensitive to improved rater training. In addition, scores also fluctuate due to the specific realization of the test item; if we want to study writing and so ask for an essay on Kant's epistemology, we are likely to get less fluid responses than if we asked for one on "My Summer Vacation."
(ii) The estimate can also contain some bias if the item used is measuring a proficiency that is similar to, but not exactly what we are specifically concerned about. Suppose, for example, we are interested in measuring

writing ability and instead of testing it in the obvious way, by asking the examinee to write an essay, we use multiple-choice items designed to measure general verbal ability (e.g., items involving verbal analogies, antonym/synonym interpretation, sentence completion). We are measuring something related to writing ability, but not writing ability specifically.

The test that is most predictive of future behavior is one that minimizes the sum of both kinds of errors. What the experience gained in the first half of the twentieth century (and reconfirmed many times since) was that in a remarkably wide range of proficiencies, multiple-choice items were superior to their much older cousin, the essay. This surprising result is because the bias that multiple-choice items might introduce was much smaller than the errors introduced by subjective scoring and the limitations in breadth of subject matter coverage that are the unavoidable concomitants of essay style exams. In one study, examinees were given a test made up of three half-hour sections (Wainer et al., 1994). Two of the sections required the writing of an essay; the third comprised 40 multiple-choice verbal ability items. The essays were each scored with two raters (and sometimes a third to adjudicate any large disagreements), and the multiple-choice section was scored automatically. It was found that the score on the multiple-choice section was more highly correlated with either essay score than the two essay scores were with one another. What this means practically is that if we want to predict performance on a future essay test, we could do so more accurately with a multiple-choice test than we could with a parallel essay test. Some argued that 30 minutes is too short for a valid essay test – perhaps, but if the essays were allocated an hour, the one-hour multiple-choice test would also improve, probably more than the essays.

It is worth emphasizing the advantage that asking many small questions has over asking very few large ones. In the latter case an unfortunate choice of question can yield an equally unfortunate outcome ("I knew just about everything in that subject except that one small topic.") In the former case, there is still the possibility of such unfortunate choices, but through the larger sampling of topics, the effect of such bad luck is ameliorated considerably.

This brings us to the third and final crucial component in the development of the modern medical licensing exam: the 1950 ascension of John P. Hubbard to lead the National Board of Medical Examiners. Even prior to Hubbard's arrival, NBME's reach was extensive. Most states accepted the NBME Certifying Exam as meeting their examination requirement and many drew on NBME's item pool for their own, state-developed tests (Johnson & Chaudhry, 2012). Recognizing the NBME's growing influence, Hubbard began to investigate how medical licensing exams could be improved soon after he took office; how NBME's continuing goal of measuring more precisely the knowledge and competence of medical students and physicians, and thus better assessing their qualifications for medical practice, could be achieved. He recognized the limitations of the traditional oral and essay formats of exams[4] and so in 1951 instigated collaboration with the then newly hatched ETS to explore shifting to a more accurate, objectively scorable, format.[5] After careful consideration, and extensive study, action was taken in 1954 to discontinue essay testing and to substitute multiple-choice testing for the NBME Part I and II examinations. While not without controversy,[6] the adoption of more objective testing formats paved the way for the NBME to test larger numbers of examinees and eventually expand its services to other markets.

With this running start, let us next discuss some of the technical work of the last century that has made the United States Medical License Examination (USMLE) the Shibboleth for modern medical practice.

There have been two fundamental changes in testing over the past century. The first grew from the realization that the subjectivity involved in scoring answers that were constructed by examinees yielded enormous error. And so gradually there has been a shift toward constructing items that could be scored objectively. A little of the evidence supporting this shift was discussed previously.

The second shift was in test construction paradigms that went from considering the test as a single entity (where the examinee's score was usually represented as the proportion of items answered correctly), to a much more flexible form in which the test is drawn from a large pool of components – some of which are selected as needed to estimate the examinee's ability in

---

[4] As documented in minutes of the NBME's Examination Committee as early as 1949, the NBME was having difficulty "handling the large number of papers, the variance in grading, and the difficulty in obtaining grades in time to meet the needs of medical schools."

[5] At an Annual Meeting in May 1950, Hubbard reported that the Examination Committee had reviewed the advantages and disadvantages of such a change and that both the Examination Committee and the Executive Committee had decided that this subject merited further study and investigation.

[6] At this time, sixteen states withdrew from having NBME do their licensure testing. Among these were some big states: for example, Florida, Texas, Pennsylvania, which reverted to their own tests, primarily oral/interview formats (we will learn in Chapter 10 how a nonstandardized selection method for medical school resulted in an unacceptable sex-bias). They ignored the 350-year-old lessons cited by the Jesuits and the 60-year-old precedent laid out in *Dent v. West Virginia*. Hubbard's courage and determination cannot be overstated. The loss of income caused by the departure of 1/3 of NBME's participating boards threatened its very existence. But he was right, and most of the secessionist states must have recognized this because they returned to the fold within 6 years. The one holdout (Texas) returned with the start of the USMLE in 1992.

some optimal fashion. Thus, the individual test item, or sometimes a fixed combination of items – a testlet – became the fungible unit of the test.

This shift in test structure was captured by three signal events in the four decades between 1950 and 1990. The first was the 1950 publication of Harold Gulliksen's *Theory of Mental Tests*, which provided the machinery necessary for rigorous scoring of tests using what has become known as True Score Theory. The unit of measure was the test itself, and so the proportion of the test that was answered correctly characterized performance. Different forms of the test were equated so that the scores on different forms could be compared (Thissen & Wainer, 2001).

The second breakthrough was the 1968 publication of Fred Lord and Mel Novick's *Statistical Theories of Mental Test Scores*. It signaled a new era in which tests could be built that were customized for each examinee and yet still be standardized. It put a capstone on True Score Theory while simultaneously providing a rigorous statement of a new approach in which the test item becomes the fungible unit of measurement – IRT (item response theory).[7] IRT was crucial if the dream of efficiently creating standardized tests that were individualized for each examinee was to be realized. Such a dream was instigated by the growing power and availability of high-speed computing. A combination of individually calibrated test items, a statistical theory that allowed us to calculate comparable scores for tests that might be made up of wildly different mixtures of items, and a computer that could construct such tests on-the-fly. IRT also made it possible to use a large pool of items from which one could sample to make up any particular individual's test. This portended a major improvement in test security.

The shift from an essay to a multiple-choice format in 1954 yielded enormous benefits; the material covered by the test was expanded, the test forms were scored much more accurately, and thus the inferences made from tests' scores became more valid, the scores themselves were more reliable, and simultaneously the exams were much cheaper to administer. Hubbard's revolutionary and courageous change in the tests' format in one swoop expanded the capability of the National Board while improving the services it provided.

Military testing (detailed in Chapter 3), which had played such an important role in shifting the testing paradigm to the multiple-choice format in 1917, made possible the third breakthrough 50 years later, which developed from the possibility of computerizing the test administration.

---

[7] There were earlier statements of IRT, the most relevant here was the 1960 monograph by the Dane Georg Rasch, which, though much more limited in application than the general models in Lord and Novick, was the test-scoring model adopted by NBME.

As we outlined in Chapter 1, the military took the lead in increasing the efficiency of large-scale testing still further with their support of the development of computerized adaptive tests (CAT) in which a computer chooses among a large array of possible questions to ask only those that will add significant information about the examinee's ability. This work was first used in the CAT-ASVAB and the general theory was laid out in the widely used text *Computerized Adaptive Testing* (Wainer, 1990/2000).

Computerized Adaptive Testing explained how to make the administration of a large test more efficient, but it could not explain unambiguously when such an approach would be a good idea. In the more than three decades since its publication wisdom enough to know when it can be efficaciously used is still being gathered. When adaptive tests will be the rule rather than the exception is hard to predict.[8] But the spectacular growth in cheap high-speed computing coupled with the astounding success of various Artificial Intelligence (AI) models, suggests that the near universal use of CATs is close at hand – but not just yet. The inertia of the status quo can be substantial.

In 1998, for example, NBME, after perhaps a decade of consideration, decided to computerize the administration of major parts of the USMLE, but chose not to make the test adaptive. The decade of experience accumulated since that time has confirmed the wisdom of proceeding slowly. The computerized administration has provided a big gain in control and security, although at significant cost. But it has yielded a test bed in which new item-types can be tried. And, while the move to a fully-fledged adaptive administration is not yet justified, CAT remains an attractive option if the use of the test includes instructional diagnosis. For this purpose, the ability to efficiently isolate precisely those areas that need remediation is likely invaluable.

The evolution of medical licensing exams has moved a great distance over the past century, with the modifications instituted by John Hubbard having yielded the most profound improvements. But this evolution is not done yet. As technology continues to provide us with new tools as well as new challenges to security, the character of the USMLE – as well as the platform on which it is presented – is likely to undergo startling changes in the coming decades. One vexing problem associated with computerized administration is the practical requirement that tests be administered continuously. It was just too expensive to utilize the old tactic of gathering hundreds of examinees in a gymnasium three or four times a year and passing out #2 pencils; while #2 pencils are cheap, laptop computers are not. So instead, testing centers are set

---

[8] The difficulty of this prediction was explained by Yogi Berra, who pointed out that "predictions are hard, especially of the future."

up and examinees are scheduled to come to them a few at a time. Such an approach has some economic challenges: maintaining testing centers is expensive, and the continuous testing required by computerized testing yields security challenges. Giving a test continuously means that the items used on the tests must be changed very often; consequently, there must be a lot of them.

But there is no going back: the modern USMLE has many item types that cannot be administered in a paper and pencil format (e.g., ones where the examinee listens to a recorded heartbeat and must make a diagnosis). But technology may again provide a solution. Tablet computers have become both capable and relatively inexpensive. We may soon be able to return to the old style of a few mass administrations in which the twenty-first century #2 pencil is instead a specially made tablet. This is but one of the likely future possibilities of exams for medical licensure.

But it is the orienting attitude of questioning the status quo that John Hubbard instilled in the DNA of the National Board that continues the drive toward improvement through change. This attitude melds perfectly with the tenets of modern quality control. Whenever we have a complex system, whether it is a manufacturing process or the licensing of physicians, it is well established that the worst way to improve matters is to convene a blue-ribbon panel to lay out the character of the future of licensure exams. This doesn't work because the task is too difficult. What does work is the institutionalization of a constant process of experimentation in which small changes are made and evaluated. If the change improves matters, make a bigger change in the same direction. If it makes matters worse, reverse field and try something else. In this way the process gradually moves toward optimization and so when the future arrives the licensing process of the future is waiting for it.

5.A.3 How Far Have We Come?

We began this chapter with a brief discussion of the modern conflict between a societal desire to not enshrine methods and procedures that differentially affect subgroups of society while at the same time making efficient use of both human and material resources. Testing has come under increased scrutiny because it can yield results that, if utilized directly, can have an adverse impact on one or more subgroups of concern. The seriousness of the conflict is because there are mountains of evidence, reaching back millennia, indicating that making decisions about the use of human resources based on test scores, improves those decisions – usually profoundly. So, what is to be done?

Some decisions can tolerate errors more easily than others – errors in admission to nursery school have smaller impact than improperly licensing an airline pilot or neurosurgeon. The relative costs of decision errors – both false positives and false negatives – vary with the situation. But, in general, most would agree that, *ceteris paribus*, we would like to minimize errors of both sorts. Certainly, that is true for tests for COVID or cancer. And when we are utilizing tests for decisions we care about, we should get the most out of them that technology allows. Licensing in general, and medical licensing in particular, represents a set of decisions that serves us all best if we can get them right. The remarkable history of medical licensing in the U.S. told here illuminates two important points that underlie testing everywhere and were emphasized in the 1889 U.S. Supreme Court Decision of *Dent v. West Virginia*.

1. The test must eschew subjectivity as much as possible: subjectivity in the content of the test, its scoring, and what distinguishes passing performance from failing performance.
2. The standards that are decided upon (in 1) must be consistently applied.

The development of professionally built tests in general, and for medical licensing in particular, has shown remarkable advances since the initial licensing methods used in nineteenth-century West Virginia. The contents are decided upon through armies of subject matter experts and endless committee meetings abetted by pretesting that provides accurate estimates of how well the items work in practice. The tests are long enough to satisfy even the most stringent psychometric concerns. And what level of performance constitutes a passing score is validated through both expert judgment and psychometric procedures. In addition, errors of false negatives (failing a candidate who should have passed) are remediated through easy retaking of those parts of the exam the candidate might have failed originally. The lessons learned from George Garrison 130 years ago have not been forgotten.

Medical licensing (the USMLE) provides an exemplary example of how to simultaneously protect the public from incompetent physicians, while at the same time providing the opportunity for all competent candidates to practice the career they trained for.

Perfect? No. We don't yet know all that makes for a good doctor, only what makes for a knowledgeable doctor. The licensing procedure assures us that anyone who succeeds will be knowledgeable, but the evidence that they will be a good doctor requires more circuitous reasoning. Physicians who have lost their licenses due to malpractice tended to have somewhat lower scores than average. This could be ameliorated by raising the passing cut-score, but in doing so we would fail many candidates who have turned out to be competent physicians – it is a balancing act in which we must weigh the costs of false positives with false negatives.

Finally, although someone being a knowledgeable doctor does not guarantee they will be a good doctor, we can rest assured that an ignorant doctor is likely to be a bad doctor. Most prospective patients would certainly agree to such reasoning.

We believe that the reasoning behind building an exemplary system for licensing physicians (although perhaps not as rigorous) has been widely applied to building systems for licensing pilots and teachers and electricians and ... We only regret that there is not a similar system available to license prospective elected officials.

5.A.4 But Even Medical Licensing is not Immune from "Good vs Truth" Issues

Unfortunately, despite the impressive improvements in testing for medical licensing over the past 70+ years, like any test that measures human mental abilities, such tests still show race and sex differences. Although Hispanics make up about 18 percent of the U.S. population, and African Americans make up about 13 percent, combined they make up less than 4 percent of orthopedic surgeons (AAOS, 2017). The Institute of Medicine has called for more diversity among healthcare workers to reduce racial health disparities (Smedley et al., 2003).

To get into a medical school, after an undergraduate Bachelors degree, students must take the Medical College Admission Test (MCAT). The MCAT is a 7.5-hour exam that also shows race differences: that is, scores of underrepresented minorities are lower, on average, than those of White students (Davis et al., 2013). Similarly, these differences are also observed with undergraduate grades of medical school applicants.

The dean of the City University of New York School of Medicine, Carmen Green, recently said that they have successfully diversified the health profession by removing barriers to entry. Thus, they do not require the MCAT for admission to their programs. Other medical schools, including George Washington University, Montclair State University, and the University of Missouri Kansas City, do not require the MCAT by having a BS to MD degree plan. However, those aspiring to be doctors must still take a licensing exam.

The USMLE includes three steps. Step 1 is an 8-hour exam with 280 multiple choice items that measure student knowledge of science, including physiology, pharmacology, pathology, microbiology, biochemistry, and anatomy. It is taken at the second year of medical school. Steps 2 and 3 are additional exams taken after clinical rotations and the first year of residency, respectively.

As with the MCAT, Black and Hispanic students have scored lower on average than White students on the Step 1 exam (Williams et al., 2020). Underrepresented minority students also receive lower clinical grades in medical school (Low et al., 2019). Finally, a smaller proportion of underrepresented minority students have residency interviews (Edmond, 2001). Men tend to score higher than women on the Step 1 exam (Case et al., 1993).

On February 12, 2020, the USMLE announced that the Step 1 test would be scored only as pass/fail starting in 2022. Gary LeRoy, President of the American Academy of Family Physicians, responded on February 20, 2020:

Pass/fail scoring is also vitally important for creating a more equitable student evaluation and residency selection process, as it will reduce the impact of racial and other biases on residency selection. Factors that impact student experience with standardized testing (such as access to test preparation) perpetuate inequities and disparities that impact test performance, but do not predict or capture competency or skills for future physicians.

As Nolen (2020) has noted, Step 1 was the only objective metric that residency programs could use to evaluate candidates. By de-emphasizing Step 1, more emphasis is placed on research experience, publications, and more subjective evaluations (students of color receive lower evaluations during clinical years), which are more a reflection of access to resources, which are limited for students from lower socioeconomic backgrounds. De-emphasizing objective measures in favor of more subjective ones effectively means that the chances of lower ability examinees getting into more competitive residency programs are increased.

After the move to pass/fail scoring, the USMLE passing rate for Step 1 fell from 88 percent in 2021 to 82 percent in 2022. Thus, medical licensing tests, with all the improvements, still suffer from the same "Good vs. Truth" problems that plague other tests.

Part B. Airline Licensing

As with medical licensing, the consequences of licensing untrained individuals who are responsible for flying, taking off, and landing commercial airlines are staggering. In this section, we focus on two types of individuals, pilots and air traffic controllers.

5.B.1 Pilot Licensing

Most U.S. pilots in WWI were not licensed. The U.S. started requiring airplane pilots to be licensed in 1926, as part of the Air Commerce Act. On April 6, 1927, the new Assistant Secretary of Commerce for Aeronautics, William MacCracken, received the very first pilot license. He had offered the honor to Orville Wright, but Wright declined because he no longer flew. Secretary of Commerce, Herbert Hoover, had established the Aeronautics Branch to oversee aviation regulations. Shortly after, Phoebe Omlie became the first female to receive a pilot license on June 30, 1927. Six months later, James Banning became the first African American to receive a pilot license.

The end of WWII saw an influx of 200,000 military pilots returning to civilian life. The airlines feasted on this glut of trained pilots and has continued to employ many military pilots who have retired after 20 years of service. These individuals continue to be eligible to fly until age 65 – the mandatory retirement age for commercial pilots. Of the 200,000 eligible pilots in 1945, 1,000 were Black men and 1,000 were women. However, it wasn't until 1964 when the first Black pilot was hired at a major airline. White women were not hired until 1973 and the first Black woman pilot was hired in 1978 (Bjorkman, 2023).

In 2022, there were about 750,000 licensed pilots in the U.S., with about 10 percent of them women (FAA, 2023b). White men continue to dominate the airline pilot industry. About 3 percent of pilots are Black, about 2 percent are Asian, and less than 1 percent are Hispanic. Fewer than 5 percent are women (WIIAB, 2022).

To become licensed, candidates must take flight training. For most certificates, a written knowledge test is also required. As an undergraduate, those seeking to become pilots in the Air Force can do so through Reserve Officer Training Corp programs or Officer Training School. Candidates must take two tests: the Air Force Officer Qualifying Test that measures general aptitude and knowledge and the Test of Basic Aviation Skills, a computer-assisted test that measures psychomotor skills, multitasking, and spatial orientation.

A 2016 study commissioned by the Air Force (Schulker et al., 2018) found that attrition rates were higher for non-Whites for both initial flight training (White – 7%, Black – 19%, Hispanic – 17%, and Asian – 17%) and primary pilot training (White – 7%, Black – 11%, Hispanic – 16%, and Asian – 16%). They were also higher for females for both (Male – 8%, Female – 15%). Fifty-three percent of female candidates and 48 percent of Black candidates ranked only in the 25th percentile in Pilot Candidate Selection Method scores, which is the largest predictor of attrition rate.

The crash of Colgan Air Flight 3407 in Clarence, N.Y. on February 12, 2009 was a turning point in U.S. aviation history. All 49 people on board were killed. The Airline Safety and Federal Aviation Administration (FAA) Extension Act of 2010 was a response to the National Traffic Safety Board's investigation of the crash blaming inadequately trained pilots. One result was the "1,500-hour rule," that required first officers to have a minimum of 1,500 hours of flight training time. Prior to the new rule, first officers were required to have only 250 hours of flight training (the same as what is currently required for licensing in Europe). According to the Air Line Pilots Association, in the 20 years prior to the Act of 2010, there were over a thousand passenger deaths due to airline accidents. Since the Act, fatalities have decreased by 99.8 percent (Higgins et al., 2023), with no more than ten per year.

Despite these encouraging numbers, in 2023, the FAA reauthorization bill was debated, with some regional airlines calling to roll back the 1,500-hour rule due to a severe pilot shortage. During the pandemic, many airlines offered early retirement buyout packages to avoid furloughs. Now airlines are forced to increase pay to attract and retain pilots.

United Airlines went so far as to create its own flight school – Aviate – in 2021. Its goal is to train 5,000 new pilots, half of whom will be women or people of color. The truth remains that getting a pilot's license is an expensive venture. Accumulating 1,500 hours of flight time costs a great deal of money.

5.B.2 Air Traffic Controller Licensing

Air traffic controllers must be at least 31 years old and must retire by age 56. They do not need a college degree and instead are certified simply by passing the Air Traffic Selection and Training (AT-SAT) exam (2002–2016). The AT-SAT measures memory, attention, visuospatial skills, and so on. Soon after its introduction, studies found, again like any other standardized test measuring cognitive skills, the AT-SAT revealed race and gender differences (King et al., 2007).

An FAA report concluded that

> [w]hile results of statistical analyses indicated that AT-SAT could be considered a valid tool for use in placement, based on technical considerations only, it was concluded that it should not be used in that way due to lack of utility and potential for adverse impact ... Furthermore, using AT-SAT ... might have adverse impact on blacks, Hispanics, and females. (Byrne & Broach, 2014)

Thus, in 2014, the FAA changed the AT-SAT and added a Biographical Questionnaire (BQ). The inclusion of the BQ eliminated some qualified candidates and there were lawsuits. The FAA then got rid of the BQ and created a new exam in 2016, the Air Traffic Skills Assessment (ATSA) that retained some of the kinds of questions in the BQ.

How the move to the ATSA will affect air traffic fatalities remains to be seen. The most recent FAA report acknowledges that there is no plan to evaluate the effectiveness of the ATSA (FAA, 2023a). A common strategy with many tests that are likely to reveal race differences is to either collect no data or suppress available data to avoid controversy.

Part C. K-12 Teacher Licensing

5.C.1 Introduction

Similar to the licensing of physicians and flight professionals described in the previous sections, teacher licensure has traditionally been a means of protecting the vulnerable public. Though not as life threatening as having simply anyone from off the street suddenly hang a shingle and proclaim themselves to be a physician, or step into an airplane and claim to be a pilot, we also don't want just anyone teaching our children. Despite licensure requirements, threats to all three professions remain. In medicine, the issue concerns what is legitimate practice. For example, although most states do not consider homeopathy to be a legitimate medical practice, the states of Arizona, Connecticut, and Nevada nonetheless provide homeopathic medical licenses. Similarly, most states license chiropractors despite the lack of any evidence that supports the benefits of subluxation (spinal adjustments). The public is left wondering what is legitimate and what is not.

Education suffers from a different problem. Some states have recently relaxed K-12 teaching certification requirements. Arizona, for example, now allows persons to teach if they are simply *enrolled* in a teacher preparation program. They are not required to take a certification test, nor have passed required college courses. The public is again left wondering whether teaching is a legitimate profession or not. In this section, we trace the history of requiring teacher licensing exams in an effort to legitimize the profession and end with the role they play in debates about educational reform.

According to the *Standards for Educational and Psychological Testing* (AERA, APA, and NCME, 2014)

Tests used in credentialing are intended to provide the public ... with a dependable mechanism for identifying practitioners who have met particular standards. The standards may be strict, but not so stringent as to unduly restrain the right of qualified individuals to offer their services to the public. Credentialing also serves to protect the public by excluding persons who are deemed to be not qualified to do the work of the profession or occupation. (pp. 174–175)

Most states require prospective teachers to take a standardized test to obtain certification. The strongest argument for requiring teachers to be licensed via exams is that content knowledge is a necessary condition for pedagogical ability. Sure, it's not a sufficient condition, but it is difficult to argue that someone can be excellent at teaching high school chemistry and not know anything about chemistry. The sufficient validity evidence for licensing exams would consist of correlating test performance with later teaching performance. Unfortunately, measuring teaching performance has proven to be an elusive, latent variable.

> *Criterion-related evidence is of limited applicability because credentialing examinations are not intended to predict individual performance in a specific job but rather to provide evidence that candidates have acquired the knowledge, skills, and judgment required for effective performance ... In addition, measures of performance in practice are generally not available for those who are not granted a credential* (AERA, APA, and NCME, 2014, pp. 175–176).

Yet see John Flannagan's validity study described in Chapter 9 (Section 9.3), which accomplished exactly this.

About half of the states require teacher candidates to take a national exam, whereas other states have their own version of a teacher licensure test. For example, if you want to teach in the state of New York, you need to pass the New York State Certification Examinations. In California, you must pass the California Basic Education Skills Test. The national exam that is most common is the Praxis. ETS published the Praxis I test (also known as the Pre-Professional Skills Test or PPST) in 1989. In 2014, the test changed to the Praxis II (or CASE – Core Academic Skills for Educators). Another national exam used by some states is the National Evaluation Series administered by Pearson. States decide minimum test scores required to pass. For example, as of 2023, most states that used the Praxis required a score of 150 to pass the Core mathematics test, but the state of Mississippi required a score of only 130.

The first teacher licensing tests originated in medieval Europe for universities that were sponsored by churches (Wilson, 1985). Similar tests first appeared in the United States in colonial New England and largely focused on demonstrations of faith and morality, in addition to knowledge of the common school subjects. With the rapid increase in Normal Schools (colleges created for teacher training), testing was replaced by transcripts showing completion of required courses. However, teacher testing did persist into the early twentieth century. For example, in some rural schools where qualified teachers were scarce, tests were used to grant "emergency" licensure to persons who had not completed teacher training. Today, this practice is becoming more common due to teacher shortages. We mentioned earlier how the state of Arizona allows persons to teach as long as they are enrolled in a teacher training program.

Despite the early use of requiring teacher licensing tests and transcripts of required courses, concerns about the academic preparation of teachers increased by the end of the nineteenth century (National Education Association, 1895). These concerns eventually led to a massive study to investigate the health of K-12 education. In 1928, all high school seniors in Pennsylvania were given a battery of intelligence and IQ tests as part of what came to be known as the Pennsylvania Study. Over 4,000 college seniors were given similar exams that same year. The study was led by Ben Wood, director of Collegiate Educational Research at Columbia University. Wood was no educational research lightweight. His doctoral advisor had been Edward Thorndike and his dissertation was published with an introduction by Lewis Terman. One of the findings of the study was that teacher candidates scored considerably lower than students in other fields (Learned & Wood, 1938). It also concluded that "high-school teaching attracts college students who ... fall below a knowledge minimum in a large proportion of cases" (pp. 38–39). Teaching candidates were deemed to be "narrower people" with "uninformed and incompetent minds". Terman (1939), upon viewing the results, called some teachers "congenital ninth graders" (p. 112).

In his critical review of the Pennsylvania study, Goodwin Watson (1938), a professor at Teachers College, Columbia University, acknowledged that teachers needed better academic training in some areas but also suggested increasing teacher pay and changing the public perception of teachers to attract higher quality persons to teaching – a proposal still often heard today. Learned and Wood recommended the required use of better, standardized tests for teacher candidates.

Thus, the development of standardized testing for teacher candidates coincided with the development of other standardized tests such as military placement and student achievement tests. In the 1920s and 1930s, the Bureau of Public Personnel Association, the Carnegie Foundation for the Advancement for Teaching, and the Teachers College Personnel Association all initiated large-scale teacher testing projects (Wilson, 1985). In 1939, the National Committee on Teacher Examinations held its first meeting. Later that year, the committee released an announcement of a teacher examination service, authored by Ben Wood, that mentioned challenges due to varying standards at universities with teacher preparation programs. Wood (1940a) was concerned that too many teacher candidates were part of "the horde of semi-literates who flaunt their diplomas before the credulous eyes of employer superintendents" (p. 381) and that "educational classes are as much if not more amply populated with morons than other departments" (p. 498).

Not surprisingly, such comments angered many teachers and teacher training faculty. Wood (1940b) realized this and pleaded with the American Association of Teachers Colleges,

> ... the only possible hope for our children lies in having them educated, so far as possible, by persons who are themselves educated. I believe that the wise and judicious use of examinations such as those provided by the National Committee on Teacher Examinations will help assure this boon for our school children. (p. 19)

In March 1940, the first National Teacher Examinations were administered and, similar to the significant change in the medical licensing exams, all items were multiple choice. The first tests were based on three areas that Ben Wood thought could be measured: a) communication skills, b) general knowledge, and c) professional knowledge. For the next 40 years, those three areas continued to comprise the tests.

The initial results of those first National Teacher Examinations were reported in 1940 by none other than John Flanagan – the same person who would later carry out the first true test of validity for testing pilots. The first thing Flanagan noticed was that despite the teacher candidates having met the legal requirements for certification and passed the required courses, "some of them know so little in various fields that they are able to answer correctly practically none of the questions in the examinations" (p. 239). He continued:

> there are quite a number of applicants for teaching positions in the city school systems included this year who know the answers to hardly any of these questions. These individuals, all of whom have fulfilled the necessary requirements for teaching certificates and many of whom have actually obtained teaching positions, get a few items correct, partly by chance, but when their scores are corrected for guessing, they are very close to zero (p. 247).

This finding, similar to the conclusions of Wood a few years earlier, that those training to be teachers were below average in terms of intelligence has continued for the past century, along with the concerns associated with it. For example, the Coleman Report (Coleman et al., 1966) discussed in Chapter 8 also mentioned that the nation's teachers were poorly equipped to teach. Based on data from the College Board, in 2014, education majors received an average score below 500 on all three (reading, writing, and math) SAT sections. Similarly, Gunn et al. (2020) found that education majors scored lower than all other majors on the SAT except "parks recreation fitness" and "security law enforcement". Wai et al. (2009) examined composite test scores for about 400,000 participants in a longitudinal study. The only group scoring below the mean on all three composite measures (verbal, mathematical, and spatial ability) received Bachelors, Masters, and Doctorates in education, and for those whose occupation was classified as education (see their Figure 5 reproduced below as our Figure 5.1). For the GRE, education was the only group that scored below the mean on both the math and verbal tests. Thus, the relatively low performances noted by Wood a century ago remain true today.

In addition to revealing the unsatisfying state of affairs with regard to teacher preparation, the NTE, like most tests that measure academic knowledge, also revealed race differences. Black teacher candidates scored considerably lower than did their White counterparts. Makers of a test cannot control how some people will use the scores. Just as student achievement tests are misused to evaluate teachers and administrators, similarly, teacher licensure tests like the NTE were soon misused. Wood was later criticized by the NAACP because NTE scores were used to determine pay scales for teachers in southern states (Baker, 1995). The NTE program director for ETS, Richard Majestic, revealed that the NTE was being used to get rid of Black teachers in southern states in the wake of the *Brown v. Board of Education* decision in the mid-1950s. He said, "(y)ou can build the best test available, but if there's malice in somebody's heart, it can be used to eliminate Blacks" (Fenwick, 2022, p. 42).

This issue of using the NTE to prevent Blacks from being hired as teachers in the south came to a head with the 1971 Supreme Court case, *Bettye Jo Baker et al. v. Columbus Municipal Separate School District of Lowndes County, Mississippi*. In 1970, the school district required all applicants to have a minimum combined score of 1000 on the Common and Teaching Area Examination of the NTE. The court ruled that the district had "purposely discriminated against Black teachers and Black applicants on account of their race" (*Baker v. Columbus*, 1971).

> *The 1000 NTE cutoff score established by defendants creates a racial classification. Under this standard, 90% of the white graduates from Mississippi institutions of higher education are eligible to teach in Columbus school district and 89% of the Black graduates from Mississippi institutions are disqualified. This amounts to racial classification.*

The court ruled that the NTE test score could not be required for employment in the school district. Yet, states continue to use the tests and the cutoff scores for employment continue to negatively affect minority candidates. Nettles et al.

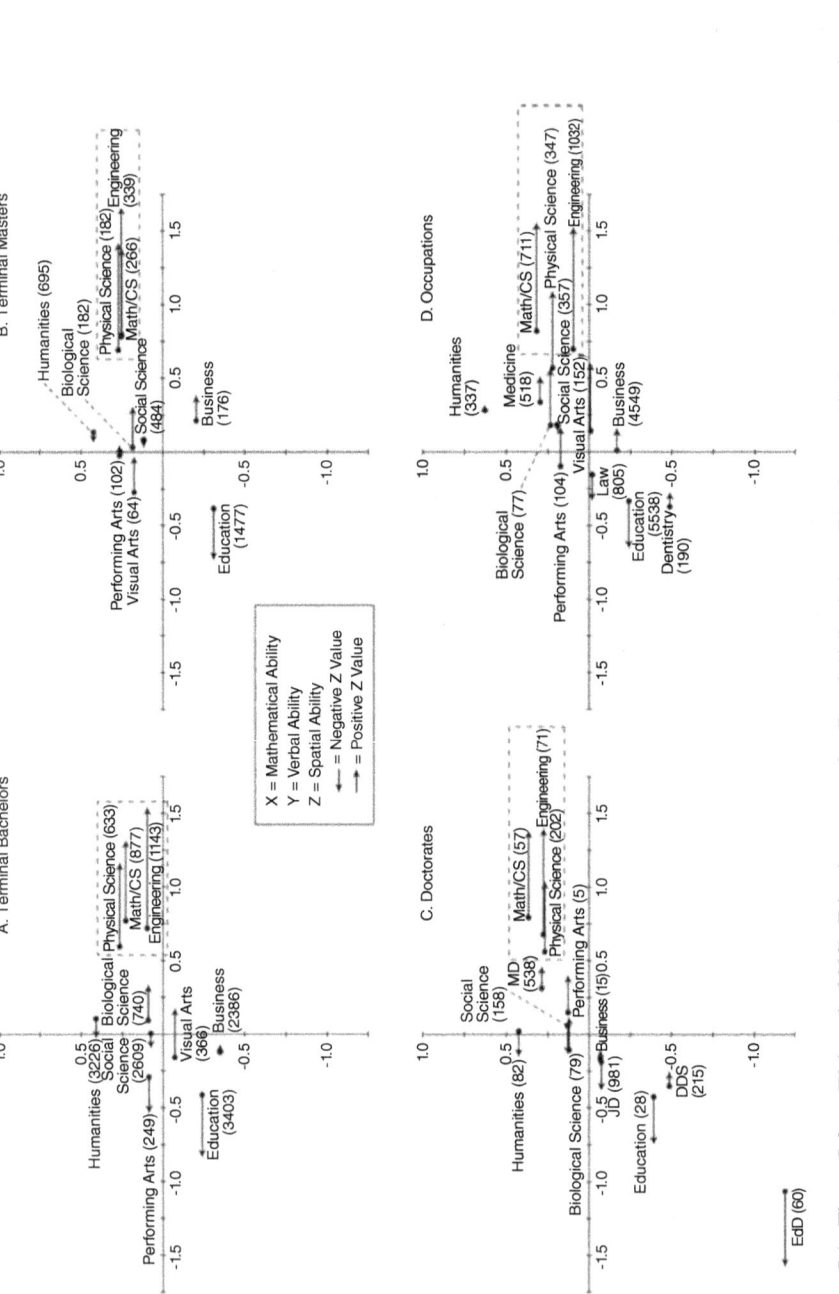

Figure 5.1 (Figure 5 from Wai et al., 2009). Trivariate means for (Panel A) Bachelors, (B) Masters, (C) Doctorates, and (D) occupations of those individuals whose data were included in Panels A, B, and C. Panels A through D are standardized across sexes. Mathematical ability is on the x-axis, and verbal ability is on the y-axis; an arrow from each group mean indicates either positive (to the right) or negative (to the left) spatial ability. Breakdowns by sex for $n = 500$ was 0.04 and for $n = 1,000$ was 0.03. Data are from Project TALENT. CS = Computer Science. The standard error of the mean for $n = 500$ was 0.04 and for $n = 1,000$ was 0.03. Data are from Project TALENT. CS = Computer Science.

(2011) found that first time passing rates for Blacks on the Praxis reading, writing, and math tests ranged from 37 to 44 percent, whereas it was 78 to 82 percent for Whites.

5.C.2 Problems with Using Teacher Licensure Tests

Thus, three major problems emerge when using tests to license teachers. First, and most importantly, there is poor validity evidence that doing well on such tests is related to being an effective teacher. At best, such tests measure content knowledge, but not pedagogical content knowledge – how to teach the content. This is principally due to the difficulty in measuring teaching ability. As will be shown in Chapter 8, attempts to measure teaching quality in terms of how much students improve their test scores in a year is wrought with statistical and logical problems. Until evidence for criterion-related validity is found, controversy surrounding teacher licensure tests will remain.

Validity is indeed important. Whereas tests for military placement and college admissions have had consistently high validity (e.g., higher military test scores correlate with higher ratings from commanding officers and higher SAT scores correlate with higher graduation rates), there has never been evidence that higher teacher license exam scores correlate with higher teaching ability. But that is not what the tests purport to measure. Instead, passing scores ensure minimal competence of subject matter knowledge. This parallels what we found with medical licensing. High scores on teacher licensure tests don't guarantee a good teacher, but low scores portend a bad teacher. Excluding candidates with low subject matter knowledge, regardless of race, is not a bias. Rather, it protects their potential students against incompetence.

Second, having teacher candidates take any type of test reveals that they score among the lowest of all college majors. This fact does nothing to help the cause of paying teachers more to eventually attract higher scoring persons to the profession.[9] And third, similar to other tests that measure general knowledge, teacher licensure tests reveal race differences. Almost 40 years ago, differences in pass rates for Black and White teacher candidates on the Praxis I were substantial. For example, in Alabama, 78 percent of Whites passed compared to only 15 percent of Blacks (AACTE, 1988). The last problem is what fuels the calls for getting rid of all tests that reveal race differences because they are thought to be biased.

---

[9] Inevitably, visions of the difficulty of establishing priority between chickens and eggs spring to mind.

5.C.3 The Latest Ill-Fated Attempt

In an attempt to move away from standardized multiple-choice tests that introduce the problems noted above, the latest effort to measure the readiness of teaching candidates is the Educator Teacher Performance Assessment (edTPA). Developed in 2013 by faculty at Stanford University, edTPA is performance based and subject specific. Candidates prepare a portfolio of materials during student teaching including unedited videos of them teaching. The portfolios are then scored. The cost, $300, is substantially higher than the Praxis, as is the time investment. The edTPA system was quickly adopted in eighteen states and approved in twenty-one others. But if portfolios, including videos, are scored based on individual judgment, rather than objectively, is the reliability and validity of edTPA acceptable? In a review of the edTPA documentation, Gitomer et al. (2019) raised serious concerns regarding the scoring and reliability of the assessments. Such concerns were reminiscent of the Vermont Portfolio Assessment in the early 1990s. Rather than using tests, the state of Vermont decided to evaluate student work through portfolios. The project had wide appeal as it claimed to promote formative, rather than just summative, evaluation. Unfortunately, similar to the edTPA, the reliability coefficients were around 0.3 to 0.4, causing serious concern about the usefulness of such measures (Koretz et al., 1992). The Vermont project, like edTPA, was also much more expensive than standardized tests. Finally, the project failed as a formative assessment because it took too long to score, and students had already moved on to the next subject and grade before receiving feedback.

Besides the relative subjectiveness in scoring compared to standardized tests, portfolios are also constructed out of the sight of examiners. Thus, there is always an uncertainty concerning whose work is being evaluated. This tends to benefit the rich over the poor as the former have the means to pay someone to write or construct portfolio materials that are not reflective of the examinee's work. Similar to the failed Vermont experiment, several states scrapped use of the edTPA, including Texas, New Jersey, New York, and Washington. Among the reasons for discontinuing the edTPA, besides the psychometric shortcomings noted by Gitomer et al., was that minority teacher candidates scored lower than Whites.

5.5 Coda – Learning to Keep the Beat

We have seen in the licensing of physicians, pilots, and teachers that tests can do a good job in measuring the extent to which a candidate knows the factual material required for the job, but less well in the more subjective skills required

5.2 Coda – Learning to Keep the Beat

to be a master. Thus, our conclusion (in Section 5.A.3) that medical licensing test scores can assure us that those who pass are knowledgeable doctors, but not necessarily that they are good doctors. Yet, we are reasonably well assured that less knowledgeable doctors are less likely to be good doctors. The same is true for teachers; teachers who know the subject matter they are to teach may not be good teachers, but those who don't know their subject are likely to be ineffectual.

This conclusion is reminiscent of a 1958 conversation[10] between the renowned conductor Pierre Monteux, then rich in years and reputation, and a young conductor in one of his master classes at Tanglewood. The student told him that he was desperately seeking "the ineffable essence of Mozart". Monteux congratulated him on his high aim, and then said that it would do him no harm, meanwhile, to "learn how to keep the beat."

The "ineffable essence" of what it takes to excel in various professions varies with the profession. Perhaps sobriety for air traffic controllers, probity for bankers and lawyers, empathy for clergy, and so on; we will leave it to others to try to figure out how to measure the extent to which candidates in these various fields possess these traits/abilities. But all of them will still need to be able to keep the beat in order to perform their duties successfully – and testing has been measuring the extent to which that is true for centuries.

---

[10] Reported by Marvin Bressler (1992).

Chapter 6
Admission Testing for Higher Education[1]

6.1 Introduction

In Chapter 4, we discussed the uses of standardized testing in grades K-12 to assess not only student performance but also, and more controversially, that of using students' test scores to evaluate teachers and administrators. This is a big business. The state of Texas alone spent $388 million over 4 years to administer the State of Texas Assessments of Academic Readiness to third through twelfth graders that determines whether students can move up to the next grade or graduate. Despite coherent scientific and epistemological objections (Chapter 8) to the notion that standardized tests can be used to evaluate teachers, such testing appears to remain alive and well.

Rather than using a test specific to the state, like Texas does, twenty-five states use college admission tests, such as the ACT or SAT, as a statewide assessment for high school students. Fourteen states currently require students to take the ACT, eight require the SAT, and three require either the ACT or SAT. These tests serve a double function – one as an assessment of how well students (and unfortunately, teachers, administrators, schools, etc.) are doing, and the other helps students in applying for admission to colleges and universities by removing a financial barrier and getting more students to take a college admission test. For example, Michigan implemented this policy in 2007 and the percentage of students who took an admission test went from 54 to 99 percent. More impressively, the new policy resulted in more poor students enrolling in

---

[1] SAT – Current name for a test produced by the College Board originally termed the Scholastic Aptitude Test, but because of concerns that the word Aptitude implied some sort of innate ability it was given its current name SAT with no deeper meaning implied. The ACT is a parallel college admissions test developed and administered by the American College Testing service in Iowa City, Iowa. The two exams have surface differences but fundamentally measure the same thing. Most colleges that require an admissions test score will accept either one.

and graduating from 4-year colleges (Hyman, 2017). Making the requirement of college admission tests universal would increase college enrollment of minorities. Yet, the sentiment at the time of this writing concerning college admission testing is overwhelmingly against using them.

Helping poor students gain entrance to college has been a goal since the Land-Grant College (or Morrill) Act of 1862, which allowed public colleges to be funded by sales of federal land grants and opened opportunities for working citizens who had previously been excluded from higher education. A century later, the Higher Education Act of 1965 provided financial assistance for students to further create opportunities for those who had previously been excluded from the college experience. President Lyndon Johnson, in addition to everything he did to aid K-12 students, also sought to level the playing field for college students.

Standardized college admission tests, like the SAT and ACT, were also originally designed to help to level the playing field for college admissions. Prior to their creation, mainly rich, White, Protestant students who had attended elite high schools were admitted to the elite universities. Today, a century after their creation, and somewhat ironically, the current trend is to not require scores from such tests as part of the admission process to better level the playing field. The University System of Georgia, for example, in 2023 announced that most of its public universities and colleges will not require applicants to submit ACT or SAT scores. Officials informed the regents that requiring the tests "would likely drive students to other colleges" (Amy, 2023). The State University of New York System's (SUNY) 64 campuses also stopped requiring the tests. "Each SUNY campus will continue with its longstanding commitment to a holistic review of student applications that includes grades, program of study, academic achievements, non-academic achievements, and other activities that allow for the evaluation of the potential success of a candidate for admission" (Cordero, 2023). Vassar College President Elizabeth Bradley defended her institution's decision to stop requiring the tests, saying, "(s)tudies have shown that test scores do not always accurately measure the qualities we are looking for in students. Standardized testing simply shows who is a good test taker" (Spitalniak, 2023).

The GRE is a similar exam and is to graduate school what the SAT and ACT are to undergraduate programs. Recently, the GRE has been under attack. According to the 2022–2023 *Graduate Study in Psychology* survey, most graduate psychology programs reported not using GRE scores as criteria in the admissions process. Rather, letters of recommendation and personal statements were rated as the most important criteria (Assefa et al., 2024).

6.2 A Short History of Admission Test Use

The number of high school students in the U.S. who take the ACT or SAT dropped considerably from pre pandemic 2019 to 2022. For example, in California, about 273,000 students took the SAT in 2019, compared to 102,000 in 2022. According to the fairtest.org website, in 2019, just over 1,000 colleges were test optional. In 2023, there were over 1,800. Currently, there are over eighty colleges that do not consider ACT/SAT scores in the admissions process even if an applicant submits them. These colleges are using a test-free or test-blind admissions policy. In 2022–2023, only 43 percent of applicants included entrance exam scores, compared to 75 percent in 2019–2020 (Bauer-Wolf, 2023).

A common reason for no longer requiring admission test scores is the argument that standardized admission tests are biased against poor minority students and serve as a barrier to getting a degree. To examine the validity of this argument, we must first trace the history of college admission tests.

Up until the late nineteenth century, each college typically had its own admission test. Prospective students had to visit the college and take the test in person. As one can imagine, this required considerable cost for the applicants (favoring families of means). In 1900, presidents from twelve leading universities in the northeast formed the College Entrance Examination Board, better known as the College Board. The purpose was to administer a standardized admission test (the College Boards) for all applicants. The test was all essay questions, covered Greek, Latin, English, German, French, physics, chemistry, and math, and lasted five days. Almost all students came from private high schools. Much like Horace Mann's K-12 tests 50 years earlier, the validity of the test was questionable as students could, for a fee, access much of the content prior to taking the test. The admission testing system also naturally ensured that certain racial and ethnic groups' access to an elite higher education was limited.

This soon changed in the early 1920s when there was a major concern about the increasing number of Jewish students who attended the elite colleges. Harvard's president at the time was A. Lawrence Lowell. Lowell decided that he would set a quota of 15 percent Jewish students. Franklin Roosevelt, who was a member of the Harvard Board of Overseers, supported the quota (Beran, 2021). The quota system employed by most Ivy League schools at the time was about to be challenged by a new admission testing system that was created to promote meritocracy rather than aristocracy.

Remember Robert Yerkes who had assembled a team of psychologists during WWI to create the Army Alpha test? A member of that team was

Carl Brigham, a professor at Princeton. After the war, in 1926, Brigham transformed the Army Alpha into a more difficult test to create the first college admission test. He called it the SAT (Scholastic Aptitude Test). Lowell's early objections to the SAT was that it would result in too many Jewish students being admitted. In 1933, the new Harvard president, James Conant, was interested in extending the reach of Harvard recruiting from small, elite schools in the northeast to the entire country and including young men from different backgrounds. Conant tasked Henry Chauncey, then an assistant dean, with this mission.

6.3 Using Admission Tests to Combat Bias

Chauncey quickly discovered a challenge. The small set of elite schools from which Harvard normally recruited students had grading systems that were well known. When a student received an "A" from one of those schools, the admissions officer knew what it meant. When evaluating students from rural high schools in other parts of the country, it was difficult to know what an "A" meant. Thus, Chauncey wanted a way to evaluate candidates regardless of where they went to school. Chauncey's search eventually led him to Brigham and the SAT. Conant liked the SAT because he thought it measured intelligence regardless of the quality of one's high school education (aka aptitude for learning). By 1935, all applicants to Harvard were required to submit SAT scores.

In an interview, Chauncey recalled an example of the SAT helping to recruit a young man who normally would have been missed.

> ...there was a fellow from Kentucky, not far from Nashville, Tennessee. He happened to see a poster on the bulletin board of the school about the Harvard national scholarships, and somebody suggested to him he ought to apply. And so, he did apply. He did well. The principal didn't have much excitement about this, but I sent a letter to the boy asking if he could meet me in Nashville for an interview. Well, the principal then took him down, got him a haircut, and got him properly dressed and drove him down. And I interviewed him, and he won a scholarship. He came from a family where he was the seventh of fifteen children, virtually none of whom had had any significant time in school. He himself had been in school for only about a year's worth at the time he had an accident, which is what caused it all. His brother was chopping down a bushy tree, and by mistake, hit him on his top of his foot and severed some tendons, so he couldn't work on the farm. So, he was allowed to go to school. And then because of the test score, he was found out.

Chauncey was able to convince the other members of the College Board to use the SAT for all incoming students to help identify such diamonds in the rough.

During WWII, Chauncey was placed in charge of the Army Qualification Test and became further interested in identifying candidates based on merit. In 1948, the newly formed ETS, with Chauncey as its president, was assigned the responsibility for administering, scoring, and reporting the SAT. In 1959, the ACT organization was born and became the leading rival of ETS.

Either SAT or ACT scores were commonly required as part of applications for admission to college and universities until the COVID-19 pandemic of 2020. Given the difficulties in administering the tests in large, in-person settings, and the impossibilities of preventing cheating that could occur in remote (unsupervised) testing environments, most colleges and universities stopped requiring applicants to submit SAT or ACT scores. The percentage of applicants who submitted test scores dropped from 75 percent in 2019–2020 to 43 percent in 2022–2023 (Bauer-Wolf, 2023). As of 2023, long after the last pandemic restrictions had been lifted, still over 80 percent of colleges and universities continued to either not require test scores or made them optional. The reason? Many claimed that standardized admission tests present a significant barrier to minority students who hope to attain a college degree. Some also claimed the tests were born out of the eugenics movement in the early twentieth century and were intended to keep minorities out of prestigious schools. Partly to address this perception, in 1993, the SAT was renamed the Scholastic Assessment Test to avoid the impression that the test measured aptitude that was innate and resistant to change. The fact that Black, Hispanic, and Native American students consistently score lower than do White, Asian, and Jewish students have continued to fuel perceptions that the tests are biased and should not be used.

But are the SAT and ACT really biased against minority students? The answer depends on how one defines bias. If bias is defined as one group, on average, scoring consistently lower than another group, then such tests are indeed "biased," but it is usually more accurately described as having 'adverse impact.' The Black–White difference on the SAT and ACT remains about one standard deviation – as it has for over 50 years. This racial gap also exists for most other tests of cognitive ability, including IQ tests and standardized state assessments, for *every* grade level beginning with kindergarten. Thus, race differences do not suddenly emerge when high school students take college admission tests in their junior or senior year. Instead, racial gaps are present before students enter formal education.

But test bias does not simply mean group differences in scores. Instead, bias is revealed if the test predicts performance differently for groups. The purpose of the SAT and ACT is to predict academic performance in college, typically measured by GPA. For example, the correlation between college GPA and

Table 6.1 *Percentage of SAT test takers who reported a high school GPA of "A" by SAT score level and racial/ethnic group*

Racial/ethnic group	SAT score level		
	High	Middle	Low
White	59	10	2
Asian	57	14	4
Hispanic	55	15	3
African American	46	14	3

Data reported by Bridgeman and Wendler (2005, p. 9)

SAT score is about 0.5 (Westrick et al., 2022), which is about the same as the correlation between high school GPA and college GPA. More importantly, admission test scores predict performance for various groups equally well (Marini et al., 2019). Thus, there is no evidence of test bias for either the SAT or the ACT.

The focus on average gaps between racial groups diverts attention away from the fact that many minority students defy stereotypes and succeed in rigorous high school courses, receive high SAT scores, and do well in college. In their 2005 report Brent Bridgeman and Cathy Wendler (see Table 6.1) found that after controlling for academic background, the percentage of students scoring over 500 on the SAT was identical across racial groups. Further, among students who scored high on the SAT, a smaller percentage of African American students (46%) reported having a high school GPA of "A" than both White (59%) and Asian (57%) students. Thus, the SAT score allows high-performing minority students to be found more readily and reliably than using such unstandardized measures like high school GPA or letters of recommendation.

Although admission tests are not biased against minority students, there still remains the problem of group differences in test scores. Critics will argue that admission tests, because they are used to make decisions regarding who gets in and who does not, present an unfair barrier to minority students. Get rid of the tests, they say, and things will be fairer. Whether things will actually be fairer depends, again, on how one defines fairness. If fairness means that minority students will have a better chance of being accepted without using admission test scores, then it depends on what is used instead. Is the SAT the only barrier among the many metrics admission officers use to decide who gets in? Suppose admission officers decide to use high school GPA exclusively. Remember, high school GPA predicts college performance about as well as admission test scores. The problem is that race differences also exist for high school GPA. For example, Black students consistently receive lower high school GPAs than do White students (Sanchez & Moore, 2022). Thus, getting rid of admission test scores and relying solely on high school GPA still leaves us with the problem of race differences and admission barriers.

6.4 Using Admission Tests to Find those Applicants More Likely to Succeed

In 2018, two years before the pandemic, the University of California system tackled this problem when it considered whether to continue its policy of requiring admission test scores. The system commissioned a task force to study the efficacy of including test scores in admission decisions. Perhaps somewhat surprisingly, they found that the SAT and ACT scores predicted college first year GPA *better* than high school GPA for all underrepresented groups. The decline in the predictive utility of high school grades was likely due to grade inflation and greater variability in standards across high schools – the same problem Chauncey dealt with a century ago (Geisinger, 2022).

The task force did not recommend getting rid of test requirements or making test scores optional. Nonetheless, a year after the report was released in 2020, the UC system announced that it will be "test-blind" for in-state students, meaning that test scores will not be used in making admission decisions. Using test scores simply appeared to interfere with the goal of achieving diversity.

When a college decides to do away with test scores, what does that mean for admission decisions? What other materials are applicants typically required to submit? Admission officers also consider letters of application, letters of recommendation, lists of extracurricular activities, and so on. The problem with these metrics, in addition to being much more subjective than test scores, is that they also reflect race differences. For example, affluent families can more easily afford to pay someone to write a brilliant letter of application for their children. They also typically have more connections with people who can write excellent letters of recommendation. White students consistently get letters of recommendation that are more positive than do minority students (Brown et al., 2021). Finally, they usually are better able to afford to participate in more extracurricular activities that impress admission officers. Thus, getting rid of admission tests and replacing them with other metrics will not improve things for minority applicants. Barriers still remain.

The only way to completely remove any advantage for rich, White applicants is to stop considering metrics altogether and go with decisions based on

6.4 Admission Tests to Find Applicants

randomization instead. If fairness is defined as simply giving everyone an equal opportunity, then the solution is straightforward: ensure all groups are accepted equally. For most universities that are less selective, this is not a problem as they do not enroll as many students as they can serve. For highly selective schools, like Harvard, unfortunately, they cannot accept everyone because there is limited space – they simply do not have room for everyone who wants to enroll. Such highly selective institutions would need a lottery system where students are accepted randomly up to the point where the capacity is filled.

The random selection solution still presents one major, completely different kind of problem. We know, based on consistent findings over the years, that some students will succeed, and others will fail based on widely available academic predictors that are known well before students begin college. Admitting students randomly ensures equal representation of students at all institutions. There can be no better solution to "fair" admissions. But not all groups will succeed (i.e., graduate) equally. In fact, some students will drop out after a year or two, owe money if they received need-based loans, and have nothing to show for their efforts. It is this latter cost – poor graduation rates for some students – that forces schools to consider student metrics that are good predictors of graduation success.

One of those predictors is admission test scores. In fact, if one looks at the correlation between the 6-year graduation rates and average admission test scores (ACT and SAT) of colleges and universities, it hovers around 0.90 (Wainer & Robinson, 2023). This means that universities with higher graduation rates typically admit students with higher admission test scores. The inverse also holds true. This relationship is conveyed clearly in Table 6.2, which displays the 25th percentile ACT composite score, percent admitted, and 6-year graduation rate for various groups of colleges and universities.

For an egalitarian lottery admission system, this presents a huge problem. Many students who are admitted to a selective university with high academic standards and rigorous curriculum, will unfortunately never graduate. They will spend (or owe) thousands of dollars and walk away from the experience poorer and without a degree. In Chapter 10, we will elaborate on other situations akin to the cost function that comes into play here. Is it better to admit everyone and have many that never graduate, or is it better to not admit everyone, and have a higher percentage of admitted students succeed? If the latter is better, then admission test scores serve a useful purpose in predicting which students will succeed. Finally, please remember that being denied admission to a selective school does not mean one cannot go to college. It simply means one cannot go to that particular college.

Table 6.2 *Graduation rates by type of college, admission selectivity and admission test score*

	25th percentile of ACT composite	Percent admitted	Six-year graduation rate (%)
Private schools			
Princeton	33	6	98
Harvard	33	5	97
Yale	33	6	97
Brown	33	7	96
Penn	33	8	96
LeMoyne-Owen College	14	80	18
Andrew College	14	41	17
Brewton-Parker College	16	96	16
Paine College	14	65	8
Bacone College	13	72	7
State schools			
Virginia	30	24	95
California-Berkeley	31	16	93
Michigan	31	23	93
UCLA	29	12	92
North Carolina	28	23	91
South Dakota	19	86	59
Montana State	21	82	57
Maine	21	90	57
South Dakota State	19	90	56
New Mexico State	18	55	48

Is the battle over whether to use admission tests unique to the U.S.? We refer to the excellent paper by Saunders (2022) to draw parallels between the U.S. and the UK.

Over the past 50 years, enrollment in UK universities experienced an explosion similar to that in the U.S. In the 1960s, there were only 200,000 university students in the UK, compared with 2.6 million in 2023. For the U.S., in 2023 there were almost 19 million university students compared with just under 6 million in 1965. The recent surges were influenced by the pronouncements by Tony Blair and Barack Obama that more young people should have a college education, along with the loosened requirements for need-based student loans. Admitting a larger percentage of the population into higher education presents some difficulties.

The majority of the students being admitted who previously had no chance of being admitted represented poor students whose academic preparation was not up to par for college work. The solution in the UK was to lower standards and grade inflation rose. More graduates were being released into the workforce with inadequate skills. Employers responded by turning to the top universities for recruits, knowing that an A grade at Cambridge or Oxford actually meant something. Similar to what happened in the U.S., government officials then pressured the best universities to admit more poor students. Some even suggested that the top universities prioritize diversity over ability and use a lottery system for admissions.

Despite these efforts to get more poor kids into college and graduate with a useful degree, rich kids remain much more likely to graduate and obtain a high-level job than are poor kids. This holds true in both the U.S. and UK. Admissions tests provide useful information. Ignoring this information risks wasting the time and money of those who are intended to benefit from such extreme policies.

Fortunately, as of this writing, the tide appears to be turning slightly back in favor of using test scores for admission decisions. In the Spring of 2024, a few highly selective schools (e.g., Brown, Yale, Dartmouth, Johns Hopkins and MIT) announced that they will return to requiring applicants to submit SAT and/or ACT scores when applying for admission. Among the reasons given for the decision is that they found that getting rid of the test requirement actually harmed low SES students.

Insisting on random acceptance rules represents one extreme end of the tension between admission based on diversity vs. ability. The costs of such a policy should be calculated so that we may weigh less extreme policy implementations. Of course, the other extreme – only using ability – has its own costs. These costs too should be made explicit. It is only by having the costs of proposed policies being made explicit that the balance between diversity and ability can be made wisely. We explore this issue of costs more deeply in Chapter 10.

Chapter 7
Tests Used for Merit-Based Scholarships

7.1 Introduction

In Chapter 6, we discussed using tests to aid decisions about who should be admitted to colleges and universities. Such decisions are not just important for the prospective student but also for the institution. Some institutions have limited space and lots of applicants (e.g., Princeton), and thus wish to admit only those students who will make the most of this incredible opportunity. Others have higher acceptance rates, with many accepting all applicants (e.g., The University of Texas at El Paso) (https://www.usnews.com/best-colleges/rankings/highest-acceptance-rate). For these latter institutions, admission tests still serve a role in that they can be helpful when advising students to select majors and take coursework that maximizes their chance of success.

Even before an applicant is accepted and enrolls, a challenge to all but the wealthiest families is finding the money to pay for college. In 2024, the cost of tuition and fees at a public college in the U.S. for one year averaged about $10,000 for in-state students and $42,000 for a private college (Kerr & Wood, 2023). Adding in books, supplies, and daily living expenses, the average cost per year for public colleges is over $38,000, and when figuring lost income and student loan interest, the total price of a 4-year bachelor's degree can be over half a million dollars for some private schools (Hanson, 2024). Making college more affordable has been a consistent goal since the first land-grant schools emerged after the Civil War, intended to open higher education to not just the rich but also to less affluent citizens who could demonstrate that they had potential to succeed. For a person who does not have the money to go to college, there are four types of financial support options that have emerged in the last 90 years: work–study, loans, grants, and scholarships. The National Youth Administration (1935–1943), part of FDR's New Deal designed to put Americans back to work, included over a half million dollars for college work–study jobs (e.g., janitorial, cafeteria, etc.). Today's Federal Work–Study program pays 75 percent of the students' wages; the remaining 25 percent is paid by the institution. In 2019–2020, over 450,000 college students received work-study awards totaling over $830 million, for an average award of just over $1,800 (NASFAA, 2022), which doesn't put much of a dent in college expenses.

A common theme of many 1940s films involved young students "working their way through college." This is no longer a practical option and has instead given way to the modern variant of "borrowing their way through college." Federal student loans emerged in 1958 as a response to the Soviet Union's launch of Sputnik. The National Defense Education Act made the loans available to students majoring in STEM and education fields. Federal loans were made much more widely available with the Higher Education Act of 1965. Although such loans might enable a person to attend college, eventually, the borrower must repay the loan (although as of this writing in Spring 2024, the U.S. government is forgiving billions of dollars in student loan debt). In the U.S., about half of all students who attend college each year borrow money to cover the costs (Hess, 2017). In 2021, about 45 million Americans had student loan debt averaging about $30,000 (Nova, 2021).

Grants, unlike loans, do not need to be repaid. An example of a need-based grant is the federal Pell Grant program that also began in the 1960s as part of President Johnson's agenda to provide financial assistance to students who demonstrated exceptional financial need. In 2022–2023, a student could receive up to $6,895 per year for educational expenses.

Scholarships, like grants, do not need to be repaid. However, unlike the other three types of financial aid, scholarships usually require demonstration of potential (i.e., merit). In 1944, the G.I. Bill and the United Negro College Fund (UNCF) provided college scholarships for soldiers returning from overseas and struggling Black students, respectively. The question addressed in this chapter is what role tests should play, if any, in deciding who gets a merit-based scholarship. As with admission decisions, scholarship decisions should be determined both by applicants' merits (giving awards to students who have a high likelihood of succeeding at college) and needs (using scarce resources to enable qualified students to attend who might not be able to otherwise) and not by biases that have little to do with either.

7.2 Merit-Based Athletic Scholarships

Perhaps the best-known merit-based college scholarships exist in college athletics. Merit-based athletic scholarships were first allowed by the National

Collegiate Athletic Association (NCAA) in 1952. One percent of student-athletes are awarded a true "full-ride" in the sense that tuition, room and board, fees, books, and so on are paid as part of the full "cost of attendance." In contrast, only one-tenth of one percent of academic scholarships constitute a full-ride (Wignall, 2021). Notwithstanding the recent college admission scandal that saw falsified ACT and SAT scores and the recruiting of student athletes regardless of athletic ability, most athletic scholarships are awarded based on athletic ability. Additionally, the issue of fairness was addressed by Title IX of the Education Amendments Act of 1972, which requires that athletic scholarship dollars must be proportional to male and female participation. There is no such requirement, however, for proportional distribution of scholarships by race. According to the U.S. Census Bureau, in 2019, African Americans made up about 14 percent of all college students, whereas Asian students made up about 7 percent. Black students received 23 percent of athletic scholarships in 2007–2008, compared to 0.1 percent for Asian students (Westfall, 2011). About 75 percent of scholarship football and basketball student athletes in the Power Five conferences are Black (Grantham, 2015).

Quite simply, the disparity among races in which athletic scholarships are awarded is astounding. Across the 131 schools in Division I of the NCAA, one out of every sixty-seven White male students has an athletic scholarship, compared to one in nine for Black male students (Jackson, 2022). Does the NCAA at least ensure that minority student athletes are well prepared for college academic success? In 2023, the NCAA voted to remove the admission test score requirement for incoming freshmen student-athletes. Sadly, only 47 percent of Black athletes graduate compared to 80 percent for Whites. Students who did not receive an athletic scholarship in 2007–2008 scored about a half standard deviation higher than those who did on both the SAT and ACT (Westfall, 2011). To our knowledge, no one has publicly complained about these race discrepancies. On the other hand, when it comes to scholarships based on academic merit, underrepresentation of groups that have been historically marginalized has been a major issue.

7.3 Merit-based Academic Scholarships

In 1955, the largest scholarship awarding organization in the United States, the National Merit Scholarship (NMS) Corporation, was created to support academically talented students. The NMS is one of the most prestigious scholarships awarded to high school graduates in support of their college education. Beginning in 1958, to be considered, students had to take the NMS Qualifying

Test and in 1971 the NMS Corporation partnered with College Board to cosponsor the Preliminary SAT (PSAT/NMSQT). About 1.5 million students take the PSAT/NMSQT each fall which consists of two verbal sections, one writing section, and two math sections. The top 4 percent or ~50,000 students qualify for letters of commendation. One third of those (~16,000) qualify as semifinalists as the highest scorers in their state and are then further considered for scholarships after they take the SAT. In the end, about 8,000 students, or roughly half of one percent, receive one-time NMS monetary awards, which in 2024 totaled $2,500 each. But this amount, like a work–study award, is hardly enough to be a game-changer in terms of making college affordable for most families. It certainly pales in comparison to the full-ride athletic scholarships. Then why even bother going through such an arduous process for such a small return on your effort?

Regardless of whether a student is commended, a semi-finalist, finalist, or NMS Awardee, such recognition can afford the student other advantages. Such students are heavily recruited by elite institutions with some receiving full scholarships – tuition paid for 4 years (Nankervis, 2013). As mentioned earlier, full academic scholarships funded by the institution are even more rare than receiving an NMS scholarship. Even if a full-ride is not offered, several universities still provide substantial merit-based funding for NMS-recognized students. For example, in 2019, the University of Florida had only thirty-nine students who received the NMS; yet another 231 received funding due to their semi-finalist or finalist standing (NMSC, 2019). Thus, while the NMS program provides only a small amount of funding, more importantly, it is an honor/distinction that helps recognized students gain admission to prestigious institutions and receive funding from other sources.

7.4 Group Differences on the PSAT/NMSQT

If the story of the NMS ended here, it would be considered a success. However, as happens with most tests of cognitive ability, when group differences are noticed the issue of adverse impact rears its ugly head. Soon after the NMS was established, it was observed that girls, despite earning higher grades in high school, scored lower on the PSAT/NMSQT, on average, than boys. A writing section was added to reduce the gender gap in scores, but the gap remains. Also, not surprising given consistent differences on other tests of cognitive ability (e.g., IQ, ACT, SAT, etc.), African American/Black and Hispanic students score substantially lower than White and Asian students and thus, very few qualify for the scholarship (College Board, 2017).

In response to the 1964 Civil Rights Act, the NMS Corporation acted to address race differences in performance by creating the National Achievement Scholarship Program specifically for academically talented Black students. This program partnered with the United Negro College Fund (UNCF) and transitioned to the Achievement Capstone Program (ACP), which provides financial assistance only to underrepresented college graduates who are academically talented. Underrepresented high school students are still eligible to be considered for the NMS, but they no longer have access to separate scholarship monies for only minority students.

Despite the creation of the ACP to distribute scholarships more equitably, the inequity among Black and Hispanic vs. White and Asian students receiving the NMS remains obvious and a target for criticism. At Amherst College, a highly selective school, out of 286 graduates who were National Merit Scholars from 1983 to 1997, not one was African American (Editor, 2001). For these reasons, both the National Association for College Admission Counseling and the National Center for Fair and Open Testing publicly criticized the NMS Corporation for using the PSAT/NMSQT as the sole measure for screening the top candidates (NACAC, 2009; NCFOT, 2010). The University of California System and the University of Texas at Austin do not support the NMS program and instead award scholarships based on students' educational backgrounds (BOARS, 2005; Nankervis, 2013; The Chronicle of Higher Education, 2009).

Race differences have also presented problems for other merit-based scholarships. In 2004, Massachusetts' governor Mitt Romney introduced the John and Abigail Adams Scholarship Program. Students who scored in the top 25 percent on the Massachusetts Comprehensive Assessment System (MCAS) would be guaranteed 4 years' tuition free at any state or community college (Romney, 2004). The MCAS English and math is given to all students in the tenth grade. Romney's scholarship program was immediately criticized as primarily favoring suburban White students (Vaishnav & Dedman, 2004). By ranking all students in the state, 28 percent of White students and 34 percent of Asian students would qualify for the scholarship, compared to only 5 percent of African American students and 4 percent of Hispanic students (Heller, 2004).

Other states have addressed this problem by reconsidering how students are ranked. The Florida Bright Futures Scholarship and the Michigan Merit Award are similar merit-based scholarships awarded to high school students based on SAT or ACT scores. By ranking students by district or school instead of simply statewide, these two states have higher percentages of African American and Hispanic students qualify for the scholarships. Compared to white students in Florida (32 percent) and Michigan (34 percent) who qualified for the scholarships, 9 percent and 8 percent of African Americans and 18 percent and 25 percent of Hispanic students qualified, respectively. Yes, gaps remain, but considering school variability in terms of SES helps to narrow those gaps (Heller, 2004).

Rather than rank students by district or school, the NMS program ranks students only by state. Semifinalists are determined by the number of students in the state who take the test. If a state has 5 percent of the nation's graduating seniors, it can expect that same percentage of its seniors to qualify as semifinalists. Because states differ in racial and SES composition, they also differ in minimum scores required to be a semi-finalist. Thus, it is easier to qualify for an NMS in some states than in others. As Rebecca Zwick and Neil Dorans (2016) noted, if a student moves from Virginia to West Virginia, the required qualifying score on the PSAT/NMSQT drops from 222 to 203. Is this fair to a student who lives just across the border in Virginia who scores a 205 on the test?

7.5 Issues of Fairness

What is a reasonable method for reducing adverse impact in the determination of NMS semifinalists? The reader is referred to Zwick and Dorans' (2016) thoughtful perspectives on these questions for a deeper discussion. Should the cutoff scores be different for girls, for example, so that the proportion of semifinalists who are female matches the general population or that of the test takers? Should there be different cutoff scores by race to also match proportions? Is it fair to allow more students from one state who score lower to advance than those from another simply due to a geographic disadvantage? Perhaps racial gaps would be narrowed if the NMS program would simply follow the lead of Florida and Michigan and rank students by school.

Ranking students within high schools is similar to an approach currently used by the University of Texas System for admission decisions. But rather than rank students by admission test score, they are ranked by high school GPA. By guaranteeing acceptance for students who rank near the top of their public high school graduating class (originally the top 10 percent but currently the top 6 percent), the UT System hopes to achieve greater diversity than if they based admission decisions solely on SAT or ACT scores. For example, the percentage of UT Austin freshmen who were Hispanic increased from 23 percent in 2009 to 31 percent in 2020 (McGee, 2023).

Is this a workable solution? An important question that is rarely asked is does admitting students or awarding merit-based scholarships by considering performance within subgroups to ensure a more representative distribution also ensure that college academic success (i.e., GPA) is equally representative among races? Unfortunately, the College Board does not release such data for NMS awardees.

We do, however, have Fall 2016 student data from UT Austin. The state requires that 75 percent of admitted students are automatic admits (based on their placement in the top 7 percent of their graduating public high school class), whereas 25 percent are admitted based on other considerations (e.g., test scores). Also, if a student attended a private high school, the automatic admission rule did not apply. To declare such a program a success, we would need to see data that show that students from lower income families, who are automatically admitted, achieve about the same academic success as those who are not automatically admitted. Otherwise, it could be argued that UT Austin is admitting less academically able students to achieve diversity but not ensuring their success.

Let's take a closer look at only those students whose GPA was low enough to place them on academic probation. Table 7.1 shows UT Austin students who received a Fall 2015 GPA of 2.0 or less and compares students who were automatically admitted based on their high school rank-in-class with those students admitted on the basis of their grades and other variables, presumably including admission test scores.

We see that rank-in-class predicts success in college more poorly than other variables for students whose family incomes was less than $80,000/year – we infer that they attended less competitive high schools than students from wealthier families. However, there is a shift for students from families with incomes over $80,000/year, for they are *more* successful than students admitted on the basis of more information than just rank-in-class. This suggests that

Table 7.1 *Percentage of students with GPAs below 2.0*

Annual family income (in thousands $)	Automatic admission	Non-automatic admission
Less than 20	14	9
20–40	21	11
40–60	16	12
60–80	12	11
80–100	10	14
100–150	14	19
150–200	6	9
Greater than 200	7	15

the high schools these students attended were more competitive and hence their high rank portended greater likelihood of college success.

7.6 Conclusion

Financial aid for students not only helps the students but also helps colleges recruit the types of students they want. When it comes to athletics, colleges offer free-ride scholarships to students who will help them win games and secure money through TV contracts. In early 2024, the National Labor Relations Board ruled that college student athletes are considered employees and are allowed to unionize. This comes on the heels of the NIL (Name, Image, and Likeness) ruling that allows athletes to profit off the college's use of their NIL which can lead to substantial additional income in the hundreds of thousands of dollars. But what about the academic "superstar" students?

For many colleges, when it comes to recruiting students based on academic prowess, they also want the very best students as higher graduation rates improve their national rankings (e.g., *US News and World Report*). The NMS program helps identify such students. However, another goal for most colleges in academic recruitment is diversity. As we have shown, awarding scholarships or admitting students based on their class rank in high school may help to increase diversity but these practices do not fix the problem of poor academic performance as predicted by low family income. Improving diversity numbers is simply window dressing for colleges, universities, and yes, even scholarship programs. Until there is evidence showing that increased diversity also leads to increased academic success for poor and minority students, such programs should not be touted as models for others to consider following. The Florida Bright Futures Scholarship, the Michigan Merit Award, and the NMS should make such data public and transparent. For those who complain that the use of the PSAT/NMSQT in awarding NMS is unfair for minority students, we suggest withholding judgment until the data are made available. UT Austin prides itself on having a diverse student body. But at whose expense? Admitting and awarding merit-based scholarships to more underrepresented students who are at risk for academic failure is not a solution. It's a big problem. Ignoring the information that tests provide is hurting, rather than helping, these students.

Chapter 8
Using Student Test Scores to Evaluate Teachers: An Assessment of Value-Added Models

8.1 Introduction

As we learned in Chapter 4 the 1960s saw several major developments in education in the U.S. Most were influenced heavily by President Lyndon Johnson's War on Poverty. Francis Keppel, U.S. Commissioner of Education from 1962 to 1965, wanted a means to assess the knowledge, skills, and abilities of our school children. In 1964, NAEP was created, known popularly as the Nation's Report Card. The first assessments in citizenship, writing, and science were administered in 1969 to 9-, 13-, and 17-year-olds.

The 1980s witnessed more changes in education, but these were different than the ones driven by democratic presidents in the 1960s. The Reagan years began with the *A Nation at Risk* report in 1983 that suggested poor teachers were the main source of failure in schools. Over time, testing was ramped up and, in addition to teachers, principals and superintendents were also held accountable for student achievement test scores. In the past 40 years, we have witnessed "high stakes" testing in most subjects for most grades as a way to evaluate schools and separate them into "failing" and "exemplary" categories. Not surprisingly, most of the former were in poor districts, whereas most of the latter were in wealthy districts. Thus, the relationship between poverty and student achievement that was obvious in the 1960s remains today. The "achievement gap" between attendees of poor schools and rich schools has stubbornly remained about the same, despite the landmark 1971 *Serrano v. Priest* decision (and several subsequent ones) mandating equal per pupil expenditure and numerous efforts at educational reform.

Using K-12 achievement test scores to either incentivize or punish teachers and administrators has never worked. Continuing with *No Child Left Behind* (2001) and the *Every Student Succeeds* act (2015), educational reforms have attempted to hold teachers and administrators accountable for student performance. The Coleman Report in 1966 concluded that education has relatively little influence on student achievement compared to factors outside of school. Nonetheless, educators have been subjected to various reform efforts over the past half century that cost billions of dollars, cost countless educators their jobs, and alas have little to show for it. The Black–White achievement gap was about a standard deviation in 1965, where it remained 50 years later (Hanushek, 2016).

The latest efforts to reform education have included requirements to fire or replace school principals when student test scores are not sufficient or improving. This has led to numerous examples of test or reporting fraud in large school districts (Robinson & Bligh, 2019). A recent study by Peterson et al. (2022) traces these failed attempts and examines the state of Nebraska's failed school reform efforts over a decade.

Let us now focus narrowly on one much ballyhooed program, *Race to the Top,* the Obama administration's program to help reform American education, has much to recommend it – not the least of which is the infusion of much needed money. So, it came as no surprise to anyone that resource-starved states rushed headlong to submit modified education programs that would qualify them for some of the windfall. A required aspect of all such reforms is the use of student performance data to judge the quality of districts and teachers. This sounds like a fine idea, not original to Race to the Top, but is it one of those ideas that only makes sense if you say it fast? We explore this issue in more detail in the rest of this chapter.

In a 1991 interview, late Marvin Bressler (1923–2010), Princeton University's renowned educational sociologist, said:

> *Some professors are justly renowned for their bravura performances as Grand Expositor on the podium, Agent Provocateur in the preceptorial, or Kindly Old Mentor in the corridors. These familiar roles in the standard faculty repertoire, however, should not be mistaken for teaching, except as they are validated by the transformation of the minds and persons of the intended audience.*

But how are we to measure the extent to which "the minds and persons" of students are transformed? And how much of any transformation observed do we assign to the teacher as the causal agent? These are thorny issues indeed. The beginning of a solution has been proposed in the guise of what are generally called "value-added models," or VAMs for short. These models try to partition the change in student test scores among the student, the school, and the teacher. Although these models are still very much in the experimental stage, they have been seized upon as "the solution" by many states and thence included as a key element in their reform proposals. Their use in the evaluation of teachers is especially problematic.

Let us describe what we see as three especially difficult problems in the hope that we might instigate some progress toward their solution.

8.2 Problem 1 – Causal Inference

One principal goal of VAMs is to estimate each teacher's effect on their students. This probably would not be too difficult to do if our goal was just descriptive (e.g., Freddy's math score went up 10 points while Ms. Jones was his teacher.). But description is only a very small step if this is to be used to evaluate teachers. We must have a causal connection. Surely no one would credit Ms. Jones if the claim was "Freddy grew 4 inches while Ms. Jones was his teacher," although it too, might be descriptively correct. How are we to go from description to causation? As we will elaborate in Chapter 11, a good beginning would be to know how much of a gain Freddy would have made with some other teacher. But alas, Freddy didn't have any other teacher. He had Ms. Jones. The problem of the counterfactual plagues all of causal inference. We would have a stronger claim for causation if we could randomly assign students to teachers and thence compare the average gain of one teacher with that of another. But students are not assigned randomly. And even if they were, it would be difficult to contain post-assignment shifting. Also, randomization doesn't cure all ills in very finite samples. The VAM parameter that is called "teacher effect" is actually misnamed; it should more properly be called "classroom effect." This change in nomenclature makes explicit that certain aspects of what goes on in the classroom affects student learning but is not completely under the teacher's control. For example, suppose there is one fourth-grader whose lack of bladder control regularly disrupts the class. Even if his class assignment had been done at random, it still does not allow fair causal comparisons.

And so, if VAMs are to be usable, we must utilize all the tools of observational studies to make the assumptions required for causal inference less than heroic.

8.3 Problem 2 – The Load VAM Places on Tests

VAMs have been mandated for use in teacher evaluation from kindergarten through twelfth grade. This leads through dangerous waters. It may be possible for test scores on the same subject, within the same grade, to be scaled so that a 10-point gain from a score of, say, 40 to 50 has the same meaning as a similar

8.3 Problem 2 – The Load VAM Places on Tests

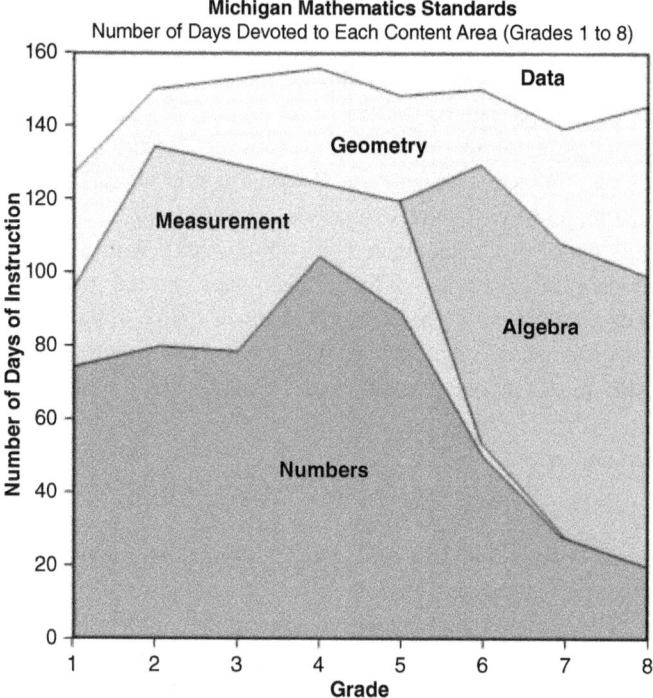

Figure 8.1 The amount of time that the Michigan math curriculum standards suggest be spent on different components of math from first to eighth grade (Braun & Wainer, 2007 after Schmidt et al., 2005).

gain from 80 to 90. It will take some doing, but we believe that current psychometric technology may be able to handle it. We are less sanguine about being able to do this across years. Thus, while we may be able to make comparisons between two fourth-grade teachers with respect to the gains their students have made in math, we are not sure how well we could do if we were comparing a second-grade teacher and a sixth-grade one. Figure 8.1 gives a depiction of the math curriculum (Braun & Wainer, 2007 after Schmidt et al., 2005) in Michigan from first grade through eighth. While we may be able to make credible comparisons between students in adjacent grades, the contents of what is being called "mathematics" changes profoundly even before high school specializations make the differences even more obvious.

Trying to compare a third-grade math teacher with a seventh-grade teacher on the test performance of their students would require heroic assumptions. Tests that were properly aimed for these two distinct student populations would have little in common because the topics covered on the two math tests are certain to be wildly different. Thus, a 10-point gain on one test would bear no relation to a similar gain on the other

If these difficulties emerge on the same subject in elementary school, the problems of comparing teachers in high school seem insurmountable. Is a 10-point gain on a French test equal to a 10-point gain in physics?

Even cutting-edge psychometrics has no answers for this.

Are you better at French than I am in physics? Was Mozart a better composer than Babe Ruth was a hitter? Such questions are not impossible to think about – Mozart was a better composer than I am a hitter – but only for very great differences. What can we do to make some gains on this topic? Judging differences among teachers is usually much more subtle.

8.4 Problem 3 – Missing Data

Missing data is always a huge problem in all practical situations, it is made even more critical because of problems with the stability of VAM parameter estimates. The sample size available for the estimation of a teacher effect is typically about thirty (the size of a typical class). This has not yielded stable estimates. One VAM study showed that only about 20 percent of teachers in the top quintile one year were in the top quintile the next. This result can be interpreted in one of two ways.

1. The teacher effect estimates aren't much better than random numbers.
2. Teacher quality is ephemeral and so a very good teacher one year can be awful the next.

If we opt for (1), we must discard VAM as too inaccurate for serious use. If we opt for (2), the underlying idea behind VAM (that being a good teacher is a relatively stable characteristic we wish to reward) is not true. In either case, VAM is in trouble.

Current belief is that the problem is (1) and we must try to stabilize the estimates by increasing the sample size. This can be done in lots of ways. Four that come to mind immediately are:

(a) increasing class size to 300 or so,
(b) collapsing across years,
(c) collapsing across teachers,
(d) using some sort of intermediate strategy akin to an empirical Bayes trick and gain stability by borrowing strength from other teachers and other time periods.

Option (a), despite its appeal to lunatic cost-cutters, violates all we know about the importance of small class sizes, especially in elementary education. Option (c) seems at odds with the notion of trying to estimate a teacher effect, and it would be tough to explain to a teacher that her ranking was lowered this year because some of the other teachers in her school had not performed up to par. Option (d) is a technical solution that has much appeal to us, but we don't know how much work has been done to measure its efficacy. Option (b) is the one that has been chosen in Tennessee, the state that has pioneered VAM, and has thence been adopted more-or-less pro forma by the other states in which VAMs have been mandated. But requiring longitudinal data increases data-gathering costs and the amount of missing data.

What data are missing? Typically, test scores, but also sometimes things like the connection between student and teacher. But, let's just focus on missing test scores. The essence of VAM is the adjusted difference between the pretest and the posttest scores. (These are often given at the end of the school year, but sometimes there is just one test given in a year and the pretest score is the previous year's post score.) The pre-score can be missing, the post-score can be missing, or both can be missing. High student mobility increases the likelihood of missing data. Inner-city schools have higher mobility than suburban schools. Because it is unlikely that missingness is unrelated to student performance, it is unrealistic to assume that we can ignore missing data and just average around them. Yet, often this is just what is done.

If a student's pre-test score is missing, we cannot obtain what the change is unless we do something. What is often done is the mean pre-score for the students that have them (in that school and that grade) is imputed for the missing score. This has the advantage of allowing us to compute a change score, and the mean scores for the actual data and the augmented data (augmented with the imputed scores) will be the same. This sounds like a plausible strategy, but only if you say it fast. It assumes that the people who are missing scores are just like the ones that have complete data. This is unlikely to be true.

It isn't hard to imagine how a principal under pressure to show big gains could easily game the system. For example, the principal could arrange a field trip for the best students on the day that the pre-test is to be given. Those students would have the average of all those left behind imputed as their pre-score. Then, at the end of the year when the posttest is to be given, there is a parallel field trip for the worst students. Their missing data will be imputed from the average of those who remain. The gain scores could thus be manipulated, and the size of the manipulation is directly related to the academic diversity of the student population – the more diverse, the greater the possible gain. Obviously, a better method for dealing with missing data must be found.

8.5 Concluding Remarks

There is substantial evidence that the quality of teachers is of importance in children's education. We must remember, however, the lessons brought home to us in the Coleman report (and replicated many times in the almost half century since) that the effects of home life dwarf teacher effects, whatever they are. If a classroom is filled with students whose home life is imbued with the richness of learning, even an ordinary teacher can have remarkable results. But, conversely, if the children's homes reflect chronic lack, and the life of the mind is largely absent, the teacher's task is made insuperably more difficult.

VAMs represent the beginning of an attempt to help us find, and thence reward, the most gifted teachers. But, despite substantial efforts, these models are still not ready for full-scale implementation. We have tried to describe what we believe are the biggest challenges facing the development of this methodology. We do this in the hope that once the problems are made explicit, others will add the beauty of their minds to the labor of ours and we may make some progress. But we must be quick, because the pressures of contemporary politics allow little time for extended reflection.

Marcel Proust likened aging to being "perched upon living stilts that keep on growing." We can see farther, but passage is increasingly wobbly. The amount of time that has passed during which these problems have been visible has given our eyes time to adjust to the relative dimness of scientific illumination. We can see further, but what we see does not provide solid answers. In that sense this chapter exemplifies Proust's metaphor.

Chapter 9
Dividing Test Scores into Subcomponents

Standardized tests, whether to evaluate student performance in coursework or to choose among applicants for college admission or to license candidates for various professions, are often marathons. Tests designed to evaluate knowledge of coursework typically use the canonical hour: admissions tests are usually 2–3 hours, and licensing exams can take days. Why are they as long as they are? To answer this question, we must consider the purposes of the test. Most serious tests have serious purposes – admission to a college or not, getting a job or not, being allowed to practice your profession or not. As we discussed in Chapter 2, the extent to which a test score can serve these purposes is its validity, which is usually defined as "the degree to which evidence and theory support the intended interpretations of those test scores." But the validity of a test's scores is bound by the test's reliability.[1] Reliability is merely a standardized measure of the score's stability, ranging from a low of 0 (essentially a random number) and a high of 1 (the score does not fluctuate at all). A test score that has low reliability must perforce have an even lower validity and its usefulness diminishes apace.

Thus, the first answer to the question "why are tests so long?" that jumps immediately to mind is derived from the inexorable relationship between a test's length and its reliability. However, even though a test score always gets more reliable as the test generating it gets longer, *ceteris paribus*, the law of diminishing returns sets in very quickly. In Figure 9.1 we show the reliability of a typical professionally prepared test as a function of its length. It shows that the marginal gain of moving from a thirty-item test to a sixty- or even ninety-item one is not worth the trouble unless such small additional increments in reliability are of practical importance. We must also note that reliability does

---

[1] More accurately, the validity is bounded by the square root of its reliability.

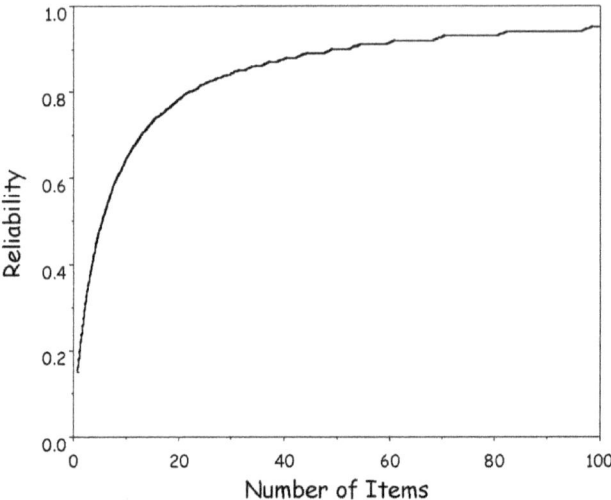

Figure 9.1 Spearman–Brown function showing the reliability of a test as a function of its length, if a one-item test has a reliability of 0.15.

drop precipitously as test length shrinks from thirty toward zero. But the puzzle still remains; why are typical tests so long if, after a test's length surpasses thirty it is about as reliable as we are likely to need. So, if such extra precision is rarely necessary, why are tests as long as they are?

9.1 A Clarifying Example – The U.S. Census

Our intuitions can be clarified with an example, the Decennial U.S. Census. On midnight of January 1, 2020, the year of the most recent Census, it was estimated that there were 331,449,281 souls living within the borders of the United States. The error bounds were $\pm 31,000$. The budget of the 2020 Census was \$14.2 billion, or approximately \$42.84 per person counted. Is it worth this amount of money to just get this single number? Before answering this question consider the function shown in Figure 9.2, which shows the results of all decennial censuses for the past 150 years. The curve shown is a fitted quadratic function to the data from 1870 through 2010. The large dot associated with 2020 is the actual population estimate from the 2020 census, the value of the curve, which passes slightly above it, is the estimate obtained from this fitted function – 331,943,913. The difference between the two is 494,632 people or 0.1 percent. Obtaining this estimate cost only about an hour of a statistician's time – totaling perhaps a couple of hundred dollars.

9.1 A Clarifying Example – The U.S. Census

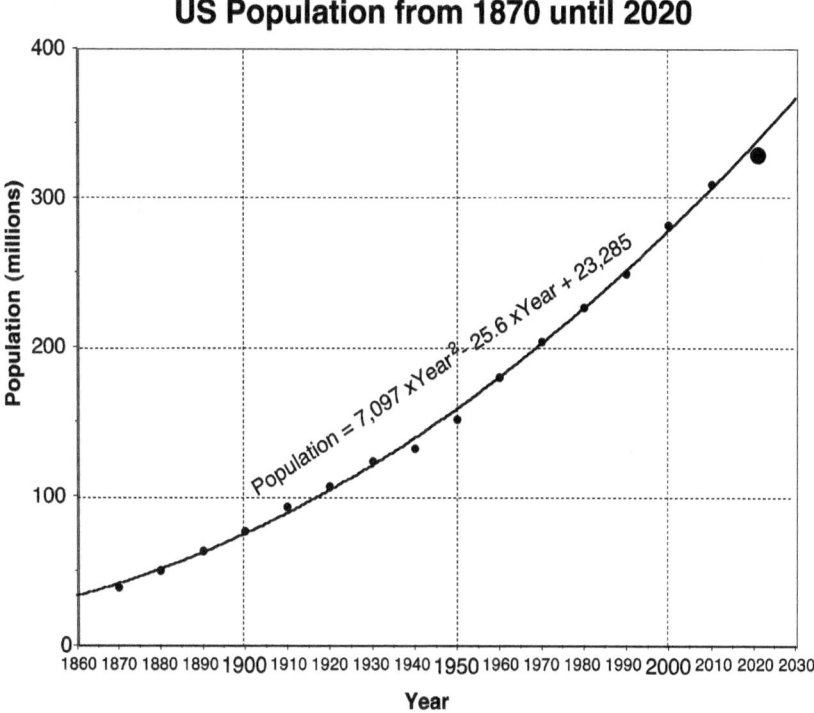

Figure 9.2 The population of the United States from 1870 until 2010. These counts were obtained by the U.S. Census. The data were well fit by a quadratic function. The large dot corresponding to 2020 is the result of the 2020 decennial Census.

Fitting a connecting function, like the quadratic shown in Figure 9.2, can have many uses. By far the most important purpose is to provide, at a glance, an accurate representation of more than a century's growth of a nation's population – Henry D. Hubbard (in the preface to Brinton, 1939) memorably characterized this use when he pointed out that, "There is a magic in graphs. The profile of a curve reveals in a flash a whole situation—the life history of an epidemic, a panic, or an era of prosperity. The curve informs the mind, awakens the imagination, convinces."

Although the fitted curve provides only an approximation of the population between censuses, we can, by adopting very credible regularity assumptions, confidently use the curve to interpolate between censuses and obtain accurate estimates for any time in the 150-year range of the data.

A third use, and the one that we have illustrated here, is extrapolation ten years beyond the 2010 census. Extrapolation, like interpolation, relies on regularity assumptions, but those assumptions become more heroic the further the estimate is from the data. As we have seen predicting the 2020 U.S. population from prior census results ending in 2010 yielded an estimate that is likely accurate enough for most applications. Were we to use the same function to predict further into the future we would be less sure, and our uncertainty would, naturally, expand with the size of the extrapolation. Of course, there are more data-rich methods that could improve the accuracy of such extrapolations by making their inevitable, underlying assumptions more credible.[2]

And so, returning to the original question, is it worth $14.2 billion dollars to just estimate this single number when it could have been determined almost as accurately in just a few minutes and be paid for out of petty cash? It doesn't take a congressional study group or the Office of Management and the Budget to tell us "No." If all the Census gave us was just that single number, it would be a colossal waste of census workers' time and taxpayers' money. However, the constitutionally mandated purpose of the Census is far broader than just providing a single number. It must also provide small area estimates. Broadly such estimates are used by states to allocate congressional representation, but also much, much narrower estimates, like "how many households with two parents and three or more children live in the Bushwick section of Brooklyn (NY)?" Such small area estimates are crucial for the allocation of social services and for all sorts of other purposes. The Census provides such small area estimates admirably well, but to be able to do so requires massive data collection and so incurs a huge expense. Yet the importance of providing accurate answers to many crucially important small area questions makes it worth its impressive cost.

There are two key lessons we should take from this census example.

1. Obtaining an accurate estimate of the grand total is relatively easy and cheap.
2. Obtaining accurate small area estimates is hard and expensive, and hence should not be attempted unless such small area estimates are important enough to justify the vast increases in the resources of time and treasure that are required.

---

[2] For example, the change in the population of the U.S. at any given time after a full census is the sum of four factors: (i) the number of births since the census, (ii) the number of deaths since then, (iii) the number of immigrants since then, and (iv) the number of emigrants. When all of these are added together we find that the net increase in the U.S. population since 2010 is one person every 13 seconds, and so to get an accurate estimate of the total population at any moment one merely needs to ascertain how much time has elapsed since the last estimate, in seconds, divide by 13 and add in that increment. Note that a single clerk, with access to a pocket calculator in a minute or two, could use this method to estimate the change from the previous census (to an accuracy of ± 0.1 percent).

9.2 Back to Tests

Now let us return to tests. Instead of characterizing cost in terms of dollars (a worthwhile metric, for sure, but grist for another mill) let us instead use examinee time. Is it worth using an hour (or two or even more) of examinee time to estimate just a single number – a single score? Is the small marginal increase in accuracy obtained from a sixty- or ninety-item test over, say a thirty-item test, worth doubling or tripling examinee time?

A glance at the gradual slope of the Spearman–Brown curve shown in Figure 9.1 as it nears its asymptote tells us that we aren't getting much of a return on our investment. And multiplying the extra hour spent by each examinee by the millions of examinees that often take such tests makes this conclusion stronger still. What would be the circumstances in which a test score with a reliability of 0.89 will not suffice, but one of 0.91 would? Off hand, it is hard to think of any.

But, returning to the lessons taught us by Census, perhaps there are other uses for the information gathered by the test, that require additional length; the equivalent of the small area estimates of Census. In testing such estimates are usually called subscores: small area estimates on aspects of the subject matter of the test. On a high school math test these might be subscores on algebra, arithmetic, geometry, and trigonometry. For a licensing exam in veterinary medicine there might be subscores on the pulmonary system, the skeletal system, the renal system, and so on. There is even the possibility of cross-classified subscores – perhaps one on dogs, another on cats, and others on cows, horses, and pigs. Such cross-classified subscores are akin to Census having estimates by ethnic group and also by geographic location.

Thus, the production of meaningful subscores needed for important purposes would be a justification for tests that contain more items than would be required merely for an accurate enough estimate of total score. What is a meaningful subscore? *It is one that is reliable enough for its prospective use and one that contains information that is not adequately focused (or is overly diluted) in the total test score.*

There are at least two prospective uses of such subscores:

(i) to aid examinees in assessing their strengths and weaknesses, often with an eye toward remediating the latter, and
(ii) to aid individuals and institutions (e.g., teachers and schools) in assessing the effectiveness of their instruction, again with an eye toward remediating weaknesses.

In the first case, helping examinees, the subscores need to be reliable enough so that attempts to remediate weaknesses do not become just the futile pursuit of noise. And, obviously, the subscore must contain information that is focused on performance on the specific topic of interest and is not diluted over the broad range of topics contained in the total test score. Let us call these two characteristics of a worthwhile subscore *reliability* and *specificity*. But for a subscore to have a specific focus apart from the total score, its information must be somewhat orthogonal to the total score, hence we shall designate this characteristic of a useful subscore *orthogonality*. Shortly, we will provide an introductory discussion of each of these two important characteristics but for the full story see chapter 3 in Haberman et al., 2024. But first, let us drop back in time and see where the concept and use of subscores came from.

9.2.1 A Brief Account of the Long History of Tests and Subtests, Scores, and Subscores

The use of mental tests appears to be almost as ancient as western civilization. As we described in Chapter 1, the Hebrew Bible (in Judges 12:4–6) provides an early reference to testing in western culture. But the test that the Gileadites used to uncover the fleeing Ephraimites hiding in their midst was only one item long and so could not have any subscores. But the much older Chinese civil service tests were longer and had subscores.

Tests have been around for at least 4,000 years, and so long as they have consisted of more than a single item, it appears that the appeal of computing subscores has been irresistible. For example, in 1115 B.C.E. at the beginning of the Chan dynasty, formal testing procedures were instituted for candidates for office. Job sample subtests were used, each with its own associated subscore. The candidate needed to demonstrate proficiency in archery, arithmetic, horsemanship, music, writing, and skill in the rites and ceremonies of public and social life.

The U.S. military has arguably one of the most widely used and consequential testing programs in the United States, both in terms of number of examinees and the length of time it has been in use. It also has been carefully thought through and researched over the better part of a century. Few testing programs can match the careful seriousness of its construction and use. We feel this makes it a worthy and informative illustration of the use of tests and subscores in support of evidence-based personnel decision making. In Chapter 3 we provided a brief history of military testing in the U.S., and so for our purposes here it will suffice to show the evolution in the use of subscores in modern military testing. The first test for military use in the U.S. was the Army Alpha, developed in 1917, which was developed to be a mass administered off-shoot of intelligence testing. It had eight parts, each with its own associated subscore.

Table 9.1 *The eight component tests and their lengths that comprised the original Army Alpha*

	Test	Number of items
1.	Oral Direction	12
2.	Arithmetical Reasoning	20
3.	Practical Judgment	16
4.	Synonym–Antonym	40
5.	Disarranged Sentences	24
3.	Number Series Completion	20
7.	Analogies	40
8.	Information	40

Note: This is a copy of Table 3.1, reproduced here so readers do not need to go back and forth to an earlier chapter.

Army Alpha evolved during the ensuing century: first, in 1950, to the *Armed Forces Classification Test* – the precursor of the *Armed Forces Qualification Test* (AFQT), which led in turn to the *Armed Services Vocational Aptitude Battery (the ASVAB)*.

The ASVAB consists of nine subtests, each of which is scored separately, and each of those scores range from one to 100 scaled so that the mean is 50. The nine subtests are:

1. Arithmetic reasoning
2. Mathematics knowledge
3. Word knowledge
4. Paragraph comprehension
5. General science
6. Electronics information
7. Auto & shop information
8. Mechanical comprehension
9. Assembling objects

The ASVAB works well, and one of the reasons for its success is because it is composed of test items that span a range of topics that panels of experts agree tap into abilities important for success in military performance. Crucial to this is the reliability of the total test (AFQT) scores, which range between 0.94 and 0.97, depending on the grouping of examinees being considered. Such reliability is generally agreed to match or exceed the standard for useful scores.

But what about the ASVAB's subscores and the various composites that are made from them? The reliability of ASVAB subscores vary depending on the subtest, the subpopulation of examinees, and the mode of administration, but are generally in the 0.8 range.[3] Why is the reliability of ASVAB subscores so much lower than the aggregate score (the AFQT)?

9.2.2 Subscore Reliability

Subscores' reliability is governed by the same inexorable rules of reliability as overall scores – as their length decreases, so too does their reliability. Thus, if we need reliable subscores we must have enough items for that purpose. A glance at the low end of the curve in Figure 9.1 shows clearly that the marginal value of each additional item to a score's reliability is much greater when there are few items than when there are many (the right side of the curve in Figure 9.1). But this means that to have reliable subscores the overall length of a test would have to be greater than would be necessary for merely a single reliable total score.

For the second use, helping institutions, the test's length might not have to increase: the reliability would be calculated over the number of individuals from that institution who took the items of interest. If that number was large enough, the estimate could achieve high reliability.

And so, it would seem that one key justification for what appears at first to be the excessive lengths of most common tests, is to provide feedback to examinees in subscores calculated from subsets of the tests. Certainly, that is what was conveyed by the military's guidance to examinees "so you can focus on specific areas you want to do well in" (Military.com, 2020). How successful were the ASVAB's test developers in providing such subscores? Actually, they ran into a problem that has continued to plague test developers and the users of test scores because they combine the nine test subscores into ten composite scores that are, alas, a long way from ten independent pieces of information. Users can easily be confused, thinking that the array of ten scores they see represent ten different facets of the examinee's ability. In fact, as we will soon see, it is more or less telling the score user the same thing ten times over. This will be clearer if we enumerate what are the components of some of these subscores.

The scores on the first four of these subtests (arithmetic reasoning, mathematics knowledge, word knowledge, and paragraph comprehension) are combined into a composite score and dubbed the AFQT score, which specifically determines whether a candidate is eligible for enlistment in the military. Each branch has a different minimum AFQT score requirement.

---

[3] See https://www.officialasvab.com/researchers/test-score-precision/ for technical details of ASVAB reliability

The five subtests that make up the balance of the ASVAB are not used for enlistment decisions but rather for placement in jobs within the military. Selected groups of the scores from these nine subtests are used for ten different composite scores. For example, five of these are:

- *Clerical Score* – same four subtests as the AFQT,
- *Combat Score* – uses word knowledge and paragraph comprehension but then also includes the scores from Auto & Shop Information and mechanical comprehension,
- *Operators and Food Score* – has, oddly, exactly the same components as the *Combat Score,*
- *General technical* – Same as *Clerical Score* except that it excludes mathematical knowledge
- *Field artillery* – Uses arithmetic reasoning and mathematics knowledge and then adds in mechanical comprehension.

It is striking to note that the various subscores are not used individually, but instead are combined into various scores based on longer tests that are to be used for impactful decisions by the military. So how is it anticipated that the actual individual subscores are to be used? The military answers this question in their advice to potential enlistees (quoted previously):

> *Understanding how your ASVAB scores are calculated will help you be strategic when studying, <u>so you can focus on specific areas you want to do well in</u> (emphasis ours).*
>
> (Military.com, 2020)

9.3 How Well Does the ASVAB Work?

The ASVAB, like any well-constructed mental test of sizable length, provides a reliable ordering of its examinees, and so interpreting the differences between candidates well separated by score is not likely to be interpreting noise. A dramatic illustration of its efficacy was described by John Flanagan in his 1948 monograph. He told of how military leaders were not fully convinced of the efficacy of using test scores to select candidates for aviation training. Accurate selection was of crucial importance because the training was expensive and failure in training could have catastrophic consequences. Flanagan convinced military leaders to test all of the candidates but then to ignore the results and select trainees on whatever basis they had been using. Then after training was complete, some candidates made it through, and some didn't.

He showed that their test scores were a very accurate predictor of success in aviation training. After this demonstration all subsequent candidate decisions were made on the basis of their test scores. Of course, once the population of trainees was highly selected, the strength of the relation between test score and training outcome was, predictably, diminished. Harold Gulliksen referred to Flanagan's work as "the only true validity study that has ever been done." Apparently military leaders eventually came to see the value of such a testing program, and they initiated work that 20 years later resulted in the inauguration of the ASVAB and the general practice of basing the lion's share of military personnel decisions on it.

One of the reasons that the ASVAB works well is because it is composed of test items that span a range of topics that panels of experts agree tap into abilities important for success in military performance. But remember the military's guidance to examinees "so you can focus on specific areas you want to do well in." How successful are test developers in providing such subscores? Not particularly, for such scores are typically based on too few items to provide the minimal levels of reliability to allow effective decisions about remediation.

9.3.1 Subscore Specificity

Earlier we proposed that a "subscore is meaningful when it is reliable enough for its prospective use and contains information that is not adequately focused (or is overly diluted) in the total test score." Having just discussed reliability let us turn our attention to specificity.

If a subscore is merely reproducing the same information that is in the total score we gain nothing from its use – indeed we are fooling ourselves into thinking that we have new, potentially valuable, information when we do not.[4] Continuing with our examination of the ASVAB, as an example of a professionally polished test whose subscores potentially have impact on the lives and careers of its examinees, let us ask the extent to which its various composite scores provide information that is at least somewhat orthogonal to the information obtained from total score.

The short answer is that they do not. In a sequence of reports in the early 1990s, Malcolm Ree, who for a decade was chairman of the ASVAB Technical Committee, and his colleagues, repeatedly showed that the ASVAB and all of its composite scores were essentially unidimensional and

---

[4] More technically, if the covariance matrix of all the subscores is of rank one, all of the subscores are saying the same thing as the total score, albeit less reliably.

so any index formed by combining the ASVAB subtests yielded the same result (within the bounds of stochastic variation).

So, while the ASVAB does an admiral job of rank ordering examines and so improve the efficacy of selection for military training, the use of the myriad of indices based on their score on subtests is a chimera.

9.3.2 Is the ASVAB Like the Census?

The ASVAB is a serious test taken annually by more than a million people. When it was a linearly structured, paper-and-pencil test it took more than three hours to complete. In the 1980s the military undertook an ambitious project to transform the ASVAB to a computerized administration and then to make it adaptive (W.A. Sands and his colleagues at the Navy Personnel Research and Development Center provide a full description in their 1997 technical report). This transformation allowed the test to be administered in only a little more than half the time with the same overall accuracy. The annual budget for the ASVAB is somewhere north of $20 million.[5] The ASVAB is not the same size project as the Census, but it is a serious test with serious goals. And although its developers desired efficacious subscores, only partial success has been achieved in supplying them – they are reliable enough for many purposes, but are not independent enough of one another to give guidance that is not more reliably given by the total score (AFQT).

Next, we shall compare the success of other testing programs with parallel goals.

9.4 Other Testing Programs That Want to Use Subscores

Over the last 20 years, due primarily to the passage of No Child Left Behind (and its sequel Every Student Succeeds), there has been a marked acceleration in K-12 testing in the United States. The Act requires assessment in Grades 3 through 8 with separate scores in mathematics, reading or language arts, and science. In a very real sense, the scores on each of these topics are a subscore. They are calculated on various subpopulations of examinees, designated by race, geographic location, and so on but are not reported back as individual scores to examinees and their families. Because what are calculated are mean scores over the subpopulations of interest, we probably need not be concerned

---

[5] $20 million budget for one million examinees yields about $20/examinee in cost.

about the reliability of the reported mean score. But concerns remain about the orthogonality of those subscores. The stated goal of these subscores is to guide remediation of schools and districts. The aim is for each school to make at least adequate yearly progress (AYP) as defined by the Act. Such goals are very serious indeed. Schools have at their disposal several, possibly draconian, actions to remediate less than AYP. These include "restructuring the school by: (1) reopening as a public charter school or (2) replacing all or most of the staff (which may include the principal) relevant to the AYP failure" (DiBase, 2005).

There is no doubt of the desirability of having subscores that are accurate enough to make judgments about both the overall level of students' performance in each of several subject matter areas and are also stable enough to estimate changes in them from one year to the next. This, however, simply cannot be done effectively without reliable and orthogonal scores.

The annual budget for this work is $250M to cover roughly 50M students, or $5/student. Compare this with the $40/person cost of census or even the $20/examinee cost of the ASVAB. We see that despite the seriousness of the consequences of poorly estimated subscores, the government has not seen fit to provide resources on the same level for them as they have for Census or for military testing.

9.5 Summing Up

The principal point of this chapter is that providing useful subscores may be important, but accomplishing this is neither easy nor cheap. Each subscore presented must be reliable enough (that means long enough) so that using it is not just interpreting noise. In addition, the subscore must be independent enough of the rest of the test so that its score is telling you something directly that is not being conveyed by the total test score. Noted statistician Shelby Haberman and his colleagues derived an empirical measure (the Proportional Reduction in Mean Square Error or PRMSE – Haberman et al., 2024) of the value of any proposed subscore. If a subscore's PRMSE value is large enough, it adds value and can be reported. If it is not, it does not add value and should not be reported.

Sandip Sinharay, Haberman's indefatigable colleague, gathered data on subscores from thirty-three major testing programs and examined them to see how many of those tests' subscores added enough value to be worthy of reporting. The short answer was that the vast proportion of reported subscores do not provide any information beyond what is available in the total test score. His results (from chapter 4 in Haberman et al., 2024) are shown in Figure 9.3.

9.5 Summing Up

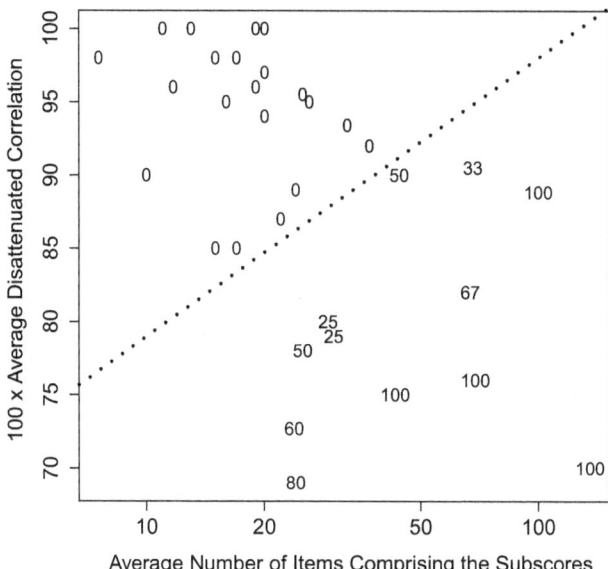

Figure 9.3 A graphic depiction of the percentage of subscores of each test that add value over that conveyed by the total score. The plotting symbol is that proportion. The diagonal line divides the twenty-one tests that had no subscores worth reporting from the twelve tests that had at least some of its reported subscores that add value (from 25 percent to all of them).

The tests are shown on two axes. The horizontal axis shows the average number of items in each subscore and the vertical axis is a measure of how independent the items in the average subscore are from the rest of the test – 100 means they all mean the same thing (the test is unidimensional); a 0 would mean that every item is independent of every other one. Values lower than 70 only rarely occur in practice.

What we see in Figure 9.3 is that to be of value a necessary (but not sufficient) condition is that there must have been at least twenty-two items and that there must be some (it need not be a great deal) of independent information contained in a subscore for it to add value.

We note that there are only four testing programs, out of the thirty-three examined, in which all of the subscores they report are of value.[6] The majority reported subscores that were not suitable for their proposed purpose.

---

[6] These four were: NBME's physicians' licensing exam, a dentists' licensing exam, the SAT, and a language mastery exam. The twenty-one that had no subscores of any added value span a great range of topics including all of the various state mandated exams that were included in the sample.

Or, paraphrasing Thomas Hobbes, who foresaw these results in his *Leviathan*, "No reliability; no original contribution; and which is worst of all, continual misleading worthlessness; and so we may characterize such subscores, as dependent, poor, nasty, brutish, and short."

9.6 Coda

In the dedication to their book on subscores, co-author Sandip Sinharay thanked his parents "who taught me that anything is possible except reporting subscores for unidimensional tests." This issue is always present whenever subscores are reported.

Chapter 10
On Cost Functions in Testing
Why Testing? Why Should it Cost You?

10.1 Introduction

During the first half of the twentieth century New York City was the scene of three much loved and celebrated Fall traditions: the changing of the colors of the leaves in Central Park, the Labor Day Parade in Crown Heights Brooklyn, and a Sunday trip to Orchard Street on the lower east side of Manhattan. Orchard Street was (and is) the location of many wholesale clothing purveyors. At that time these stores were principally owned by Jews, so they were closed on the Sabbath and open only "to the trade" during the week. But on Sundays they were open for retail.

And so, on the appointed autumn Sunday, tradition led many New York fathers to take their quickly growing children to Orchard Street to get outfitted for the coming year. There were many stops – Beckenstein's for underwear and socks, and Gus's for pickles. But the star of this story revolves around Max Schoenbaum's "Designer Discounts" whose motto, printed boldly on the store's front window, as well on his business cards, was "Quality clothing, why should it cost you?"

As Mr. Schoenbaum made abundantly clear, customers are concerned both with the quality of what they eventually decide to buy *as well as* what it costs. In this chapter we adopt the same attitude and make the costs of the inevitable errors that occur in any kind of decision making central to that decision.

In any binary decision there are always two kinds of errors that can be made – saying "yes" when you should have said "no" (a false positive) or saying "no" when you should have said "yes" (a false negative). Choosing a decision-making strategy by simply adding up the number of each of two kinds of errors is only sensible if the costs of each of the two errors are equal. This is only rarely the case.

We will discuss two different kinds of decisions – for college admission and for licensing – and consider the place of testing within each of them in terms of the costs of using tests and how those costs are likely to change if the use of tests is eschewed.

10.2 Admissions Testing

When an admissions decision is made, the two kinds of errors that can be made are (1) rejecting a student who could have graduated and (2) accepting a student who will not graduate. What are the costs of these two errors? What are the costs to the institution? To the individual? To society?

10.2.1 On the Costs of an Incorrect Rejection

It is of critical importance to remember that the cost of being turned down for admission to a college does not mean that that individual can't go to college – only that they can't go to *that* college. That decision is an error if that student could have been successful and graduated, but when we try to calculate the costs of that error, we must not weigh the costs of college vs. no college but rather that college vs. some other college. So, the cost of that error to that applicant must be what that student would have achieved had they gone there vs. what they achieved having gone someplace else. To answer this, we must assess what is the value added by the college compared with how much of a person's accomplishments are due to who they are and what they bring with them.

Charles Dillon Stengel, after considerable experience, came down strongly on the side of the person being the principal source of the final outcome. Professor Stengel (Casey, to all who knew him) was the manager of the enormously successful NY Yankees from 1948 through 1960, during which time they won ten American League pennants and seven world series; yet before he came to the Yankees Stengel managed the Dodgers (1934–1936) and the Braves (1938–1943) and never finished higher than fifth in an eight-team league. What happened? Casey explained, "I only became a genius after Mickey Mantle joined the team." The parallel in education is that the greatness of a university is determined to a large extent by the greatness of the students that it can attract. There is little doubt that had Mickey Mantle joined the Red Sox instead of the Yankees we would now be celebrating the genius of the long-forgotten Pinky Higgins.

Table 10.1 *The last eleven U.S. presidents and the college in which they initially enrolled*

Number	President	College
36	Lyndon Johnson	Texas State University
37	Richard Nixon	Whittier College
38	Gerald Ford	University of Michigan
39	Jimmy Carter	Georgia Southwestern College
40	Ronald Reagan	Eureka College
41	George Bush	Yale University
42	William Clinton	Georgetown University
43	George Bush	Yale University
44	Barak Obama	Occidental College
45	Donald Trump	Fordham University
46	Joseph Biden	University of Delaware

If Professor Stengel's observation broadly holds, it means that the cost to the individual student of being incorrectly rejected is perhaps more modest than we might assume based on the extraordinary efforts exerted to get into the "right school" (consider, for example, the recent admissions scandal involving Hollywood celebrities). But the cost to the school (team) could be substantial

If we were to define as one measure of success becoming President of the United States, we note that attendance at a *US News and World Report* "elite" school may help but is surely not required. For example, note that only two of the last eleven U.S. presidents initially enrolled at an Ivy League college (Table 10.1).

Or if the definition of the epitome of success is winning a Nobel Prize, note the absence of Ivy League or Seven Sister schools among laureates in all fields both in this century and the last one (Table 10.2).

Or suppose the goal is to make money. Does the choice of school help? In a list of the twelve richest people in America we see that fewer first enrolled in an Ivy League institution than those who didn't (see Table 10.3).

These admittedly exceptional examples demonstrate that a student with the requisite talent can reach the highest levels of success in their chosen field without attending one of the most sought-after schools. This is fortunate, because the number of extraordinary students, if they could be identified, would far exceed the capacity of the "elite schools."

10.2.3 On the Costs of an Incorrect Acceptance

But let us consider the costs associated with a false positive decision – admitting someone who cannot do the work. The costs to the student will depend on how quickly they fail. The longer they hang on, the more of the

Table 10.2 *Undergraduate Institutions for some twentieth-century Nobel Laureates*

Laureate	College	Field	Year
Milton Friedman	Rutgers	Economics	1976
George Stigler	Washington	Economics	1982
John Nash	Carnegie Mellon	Economics	1994
Jim Heckman	Colorado College	Economics	2000
Saul Bellow	Northwestern	Literature	1976
Toni Morrison	Howard	Literature	1993
John Bardeen	Wisconsin	Physics	1956 & 1972
Leon Lederman	CUNY	Physics	1988
Jack Kilby	Illinois	Physics	2000
And for some from the 21st century			
Richard Heck	UCLA	Chemistry	2010
Jennifer Doudna	Pomona	Chemistry	2020
Josh Angrist	Oberlin	Economics	2021
Paul Milgrom	Michigan	Economics	2020
Philip Dybvig	Indiana	Economics	2022
Bob Dylan	Minnesota	Literature	2016
Louise Gluck	Sarah Lawrence	Literature	2020
Harvey Alter	Rochester	Medicine	2020
Charles M Rice	Davis	Medicine	2020
David Julius	Berkeley	Medicine	2021
Ardem Papoutian	UCLA	Medicine	2021
Drew Weissman	Brandeis	Medicine	2023

Table 10.3 *The twelve richest people in America and the colleges in which they initially enrolled*

Billionaire	Wealth (Billions $)	Initial college
Elon Musk	195	Pretoria
Jeff Bezos	194	Princeton
Mark Zuckerberg	177	Harvard
Larry Ellison	141	Illinois
Warren Buffet	133	Penn
Bill Gates	128	Harvard
Steve Ballmer	121	Harvard
Larry Page	114	Michigan
Sergey Brin	110	Maryland
Michael Bloomberg	106	Johns Hopkins
Michael Dell	91	Texas
Jim Walton	78	Arkansas

student's time and money is spent that might have been used more fruitfully elsewhere.

Without putting too fine a point on it, it seems clear that both the long- and short-term consequences *for the student* of a false positive decision are worse than for a false negative.

10.2.4 What Role Does Testing Play in this Calculus?

There is little disagreement, even among the anti-testers, that the use of test scores has, at least for the past century, reduced the total number of errors of both types. The issue that is of most contemporary concern is the extent to which the use of admission tests disadvantages equally able applicants because they come from different backgrounds (e.g., SES, race, etc.). This is certainly a worthwhile concern, but extensive evidence (Sackett et al., 2008) tells us exactly the reverse is true. Standardized admission tests (ACT and SAT) have a small, but positive bias *in favor* of minority applicants, meaning that minorities who are admitted with the same test score as non-minorities perform less well in college (see Section 12.3 for details). And of much greater importance, because tests are portable, cheap, and easy to administer, they provide a valuable tool for finding hidden talent that otherwise might be missed. This has been long demonstrated (since 1955) by the success of the Merit Scholarship program that annually searches for 50,000 jewels, some of them well-hidden, among the 1.4 million high school juniors who are tested (see Section 7.3 for more on the Merit Scholarship program)

Admission tests predict college graduation rates quite well (see Figure 10.1). Using 2019 data, correlations between 25th percentile ACT and SAT scores of matriculating students and an institution's graduation rate is about 0.9. A parallel result is the "percentage of students who apply to a university who are accepted." That correlation is -0.7, or that the higher the acceptance rate, the lower the graduation rate (2019 data obtained for 242 universities from the Integrated Postsecondary Education Data System).

Costs of high vs. low graduation rates can be calculated in terms of how much a degree actually costs. Suppose university A admits only 30 percent of its applicants but 70 percent graduate within six years. University B has the same tuition, fees, and housing costs and admits 70 percent of its applicants but only 30 percent graduate within six years (these relationships between percentage accepted and graduation rate are realistic). Suppose each university gets 1,000 applicants in a given year. University A admits 300 and university B admits 700. After six years, both universities graduate exactly the same number of students – 210.

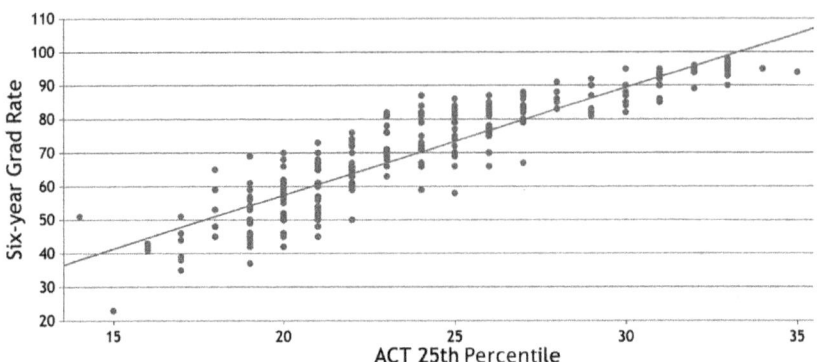

Figure 10.1 Data showing that for every 10 percent increase in the distribution of ACT scores of the entering freshman class, the graduation rate increases by 3 percent.

University A is more cost efficient, but by how much? If C is the cost for a single student to matriculate, the cost per graduate at University A is 300C/210 whereas it is 700C/210 at University B. The ratio of these two costs is 7/3, or that it costs 233 percent more per graduate at University B than at A.[1]

To connect our simple example to reality: The University of Texas at Austin (UT Austin) had a 30 percent acceptance rate in 2019, whereas the University of Texas at Arlington (UT Arlington) had an 83 percent acceptance rate. The six-year graduation rates for UT Austin and UT Arlington are 86 percent and 51 percent, respectively. The estimated costs for tuition and fees for 2022–2023 at both schools are just over $12,000.

If we randomly select 1,000 newly admitted students from each university, we find that eventually about 860 students at UT Austin graduate, compared to 510 at UT Arlington. During their first four years of college, each student spends about $48,000 on tuition and fees. Thus, at UT Austin, the cost per graduate is

$$(1,000 \times 48,000)/860 = \$55,814,$$

whereas at UT Arlington it is

$$(1,000 \times 48,000)/510 = \$94,118.$$

---

[1] This is a simplification and models the unlikely situation that each dropout stays enrolled for the same amount of time at each university. A more true-to-life model would include differential dropouts each year, but this simple model makes the point – false positive rates in admission are likely very expensive, multiplying the cost of higher education. It is easy to argue that the extra money would be better spent increasing financial aid to able students who lack resources.

And so, it costs $38,304 MORE per graduate at UT Arlington than it does at its sister school in Austin. Paraphrasing Senator Everett Dirksen's famous warning about federal spending, "$38,000 here, $38,000 there, and pretty soon you're talking real money."

And this is just tuition and fees: it omits the considerable costs for room, board, books, and all of the other expenses that institutions invest in their students. Such back-of-the-envelope calculations help us to understand what choices universities must make when governments require them to be more efficient. Compared to UT Austin, the students at UT Arlington tend to be poorer. That means that the consequences of spending their limited funds without receiving a degree are even more profound.

While we do not wish to gainsay the costs associated with making inaccurate admissions decisions nor how much the improvement in accuracy and fairness would be yielded due to the inclusion of tests scores in the process, we must highlight the *even more consequential* results of errors in licensing tests.

10.3 Licensing Tests

Some years ago, the *Montreal Gazette* (then called simply, *The Gazette*) carried a story about an event that occurred at a local swimming pool. Apparently, one of the swimmers had gotten into trouble and called for help. The lifeguard, sitting high in his chair, gestured to another swimmer nearby to aid the first swimmer in getting to the edge of the pool. And she did. After the emergency was resolved, she went to the lifeguard and asked why he (the lifeguard) hadn't just jumped in and made the rescue himself. He replied that he would've, but he couldn't swim. The good Samaritan was aghast and exclaimed, "You can't swim! How did you get a job as a lifeguard?" He replied, "I was bilingual."

Unfortunately, this is not the only example of a secondary desideratum getting prioritized in a hiring decision; for example, an "item" in one firefighter's exam required the candidate to carry a heavy hose up a ladder. It was criticized and eventually removed from the test, because it was considered to be "biased" against smaller candidates.

10.3.1 On the Costs of an Incorrect Decision to License

These stories make it clear why for some hiring decisions, the costs of making a false positive error – hiring someone who ought not have the job – are too high to allow secondary skills to dominate the primary ones for that particular decision. We should obviously add the licensing of physicians, airline pilots, teachers, and many other occupations to lifeguards as decisions in which a false positive has serious consequences. Organizations that license some of these professions are well aware of this responsibility and set passing-scores on their exams that explicitly recognize the asymmetrical cost function of a hiring error (see, for example, Clauser & Wainer, 2016; Grabovsky & Wainer, 2017).

10.3.2 On the Costs of an Incorrect Decision to Withhold a License

Tests are not only an instrument to shrink errors and reduce the artifacts associated with decisions based on more subjective criteria, but they also provide a way to correct errors that are made. It is obvious that erroneously denying a candidate permission to practice a profession that they have conceivably spent considerable time and resources preparing for is indeed a serious cost that must be absorbed by the candidate. But this is well recognized by most licensing organizations who usually allow such errors, to the extent that they occur, to be corrected through retesting. Unfortunately, the same method of correction isn't available for incorrect positives, since candidates who are incorrectly classified as "pass" are unlikely to present themselves for retesting.

10.4 Discussion

The idea of an asymmetrical loss function is very old indeed. It was canonized into British law in 1760 as "Blackstone's ratio" – *It is better that ten guilty persons escape than that one innocent suffers*. But Blackstone was not the first to attempt to provide a cost function for legal decisions. In the fifteenth century, Fortescue opined that the ratio should be 20 to 1. This was a relaxation of Moses Maimonides' ratio of 1,000 to 1. And this view of asymmetry is not confined to Judaism; Jami' at-Tirmidhi quotes Mohammed that that "it is better for a judge to err towards leniency than towards punishment."

That such decision-making processes must be asymmetric is clear, but what is required is to gather evidence for the consequences of bad decisions and establish a parallel to Blackstone's ratio for each.

What is the advantage of using objective tests to make decisions instead of the sorts of 'expert judgment' that has recently been proposed as the alternative to tests? In short it is the objectivity that allows the instrument to be studied, any flaws that exist to be detected, and the instrument corrected and refined.

Let us conclude with a true story (the identity of the principals is concealed on advice of counsel) that illuminates the mischief that subjective admissions decisions can cause.[2] There was a medical school that chose its students using the traditional litany of criteria: undergraduate courses taken, the grades obtained in them, MCAT scores, letters of recommendation, and so on. From these measures a list of finalists for admission was chosen. The ultimate choice, made from among these finalists, was decided by a long-time professor at the school who interviewed all of the finalists. The finalists who were then not chosen were placed on a waitlist of alternates to fill in for any openings that occurred when one of those chosen opted not to enroll. At one point, it had begun to be noticed that there seemed to be an overabundance of women candidates among those wait-listed. But that was viewed as just the way things had worked out. Then, one year, at the very last moment, the state legislature allocated an increase in the budget for the medical school, which mandated a substantial expansion of the entering class. So, they dug into the wait-list and classes began. But the school administration was worried about the performance of those students (predominantly women) who were finally admitted, but who had not qualified initially, so their performance in medical school was carefully monitored. Not only did they do well in school, they dominated the top of the student performance ratings. This led to a re-examination of the character of the interview process that led to them being wait-listed. The examining professor was concerned about three characteristics of a good doctor which, he believed, were not represented in the standard admission criteria. Specifically, (i) maturity, (ii) commitment to medicine, and (iii) neuroticism. This seemed sensible, but how were these important characteristics measured? It turned out that if a male candidate was married, he was considered mature; if a woman was married it indicated that she wasn't committed to medicine. If a man was divorced this was evidence of his commitment to medicine, whereas if a woman was divorced, she was neurotic.

Note that the only way that this sex bias (which had been invisibly in place for years) was uncovered was the accident associated with the increase in funding. But had there been a similar sex-bias on a test it would have been

---

[2] There is an especially dramatic second example presented in Chapter 5 in which the lack of objective criteria in licensing led to the murder of an examiner. The crucial importance of having valid criteria was reflected by the jury when the self-confessed murderer was convicted of justifiable homicide.

easily uncovered and promptly corrected. We say "easily" because every credible testing organization has in place a constant process of quality control in which data that would reveal any sort of bias are gathered regularly and their analysis is part of the normal testing process.

Decision errors can still be made when using tests as part of the process, but they can be made more easily without them.

Chapter 11
Evidence in Science: Should We Use Data and What Data Can We Trust?

Evidence may not buy happiness, but it sure does steady the nerves.
— after Leroy Robert (Satchel) Paige

Prologue

Science and policy share many goals, but perhaps the most important one revolves around causal inference. In most of this book's chapters issues of causality underly, either explicitly or implicitly, all discussions, and, moreover, these issues come in pairs. For example:

- In *military testing* (Chapter 3) we might ask "what is the effect on force preparedness of changing the minimal required score on the ASVAB?" And, in parallel, "what was the cause of the observed decline in soldier performance in training?"
- In *K-12 testing* (Chapter 4) it is natural to ask "what was the effect of various programs (e.g., No Child Left Behind, Every Child Succeeds) on subsequent measures of student performance?" And the parallel question: "what was the cause of the decline in standardized test scores?"
- In *Licensing* (Chapter 5) "what is the effect of lowering the passing score on the various licensing exams on medical accidents?" On plane crashes? On student performance? And, again the parallel questions "why has the likelihood of successful completion of air travel (or a medical procedure or a school year) declined?"
- In *College Admissions* testing (Chapter 6) "What are the effects of not requiring an admission test?" And, again, "what was the cause of the change in our graduation rate?"

As we will learn, we can calculate the answer to the first of the two questions – measuring the effect of a possible cause – if suitable data are gathered and are made available. Typically, these data consist of test scores for individuals and the subsequent performance of those same individuals. The second question, finding the cause of an observed effect, is not easy. Indeed, it is often impossible. But as we shall soon see, measuring the effect of a cause is often just what we need to assess the efficacy of our selection processes.

Yet the gathering and dissemination of such data is not widespread. We suspect that the reason for this is related to the reasons we are hesitant to stand on a scale after a long holiday filled with too many good meals and insufficient exercise. It is hard to find the requisite data to answer the sorts of causal questions posed above. More about this shortly.

Anyway, you get the idea; we need not go further to illustrate the essential role that causal inference plays in all aspects of our lives, not limited to testing. But if causal inference is so crucial (and we believe that it is) why did we postpone its discussion until now?

The reasons for our delay are both motivational (we wanted to establish unambiguously the need for such a discussion) and cowardice (the understanding of causal inference requires counterfactuals, which tend to give those who contemplate them for any length of time a pounding headache). But in good conscience we cannot postpone this discussion any longer – so here goes.

Although there were foundational contributions to our understanding of causal inference in the eighteenth century from Scottish philosopher David Hume (1711–1776), and in the twentieth from statisticians Ronald Fisher (1890–1962) and Jerzy Neyman (1894–1981), the modern view was influenced markedly by the work of Harvard statistician Donald Rubin (1943–). Rubin pointed out that trying to find the cause of an effect was a task of insuperable difficulty, but, with the tools of modern experimental design, we could, under carefully defined circumstances, measure the effect of a cause.

In the balance of this chapter we will explain Rubin's model of causal inference and illustrate its use in several different circumstances. Our principal example shows how to estimate the size of the causal effect that fracking (hydraulic fracturing) has on the size and frequency of earthquakes in Oklahoma. At this point it is natural to ask (as has been done repeatedly by the reviewers of this book when it was still in manuscript form) why, in a book on testing, are you discussing earthquakes? The answer is important and revealing. *In order to measure causal effects we must have suitable data and, when it comes to testing, such data are either not gathered, or when they are, are kept hidden from the public view.* Earthquakes, at least those greater than 3 on the Richter scale, have a tendency to make themselves widely known.

To count is modern practice, the ancient method was to guess
Samuel Johnson

Suitable data must be gathered, and they must be made public. To measure the effect of lower entrance test scores on graduation rates, test scores and graduation rates must be recorded *and* made public. If we wish to assess the effect that a test score policy has on minority enrollment, we must know what the minority enrollment was, what were their associated scores, and what are they now. This is true both for all of the problems we have elaborated upon and many others that we have not.

Without such data all we can do is guess.

The chapter comes in two parts. The opening is meant as motivation. We tell a real, but short, tale of a problem in causal inference that emerged during the evaluation of a new admissions policy implemented in the early 1990s at the University of Nebraska, with the goal of improving graduation rates. The outcome was at first gratifying but after a closer look yielded disappointment. The costs of what turned out to be a failed experiment would have been reduced had the fundamental tenets of doing causal inference been applied.

The second part is considerably longer and begins centuries earlier. It lays out the formal issues surrounding the making of causal inferences with an extended exploration of John Snow and William Farr's parallel searches for the cause of London's dreadful 1854 cholera epidemic. It goes on to include the search for the cause of the 1962 decline in SAT scores in the United States. At this point enter Donald Rubin and his clarifying model for causal inference. The model works best when we have the sorts of complete control that normally are only possible within the confines of a full experiment in which treatment conditions are well defined, objects are assigned to treatment according to a specific design, and outcomes are specified and recorded. This set-up is familiar to all who study clinical trials of new medical treatments and the terms "random assignment" and "control group" are old friends. But for many issues such control is not possible, which brings us to the third part of this chapter.

Beginning in Section 11.6 we describe a more complex, and alas, more common situation in which the sorts of control seen in clinical trials are not possible. In the balance of the chapter we illustrate how the tenets of Rubin's Model can be adapted by trying to assess the size of the causal effect that fracking (and in particular, wastewater reinsertion) has on the frequency of earthquakes in Oklahoma. You can judge for yourself how credible are the arguments generated by adhering as closely as possible to the format of Rubin's Model.

Our hope is that you can then reflect on a number of the claims made throughout this book and see how their credibility is boosted by borrowing from the logical structure of this model. We also hope that it becomes obvious how crucial it is that proposed policies have as an integral part plans for gathering *and* making public data that illuminate the efficacy of those policies. We make this explicit in the recommendations in Chapter 13.

11.0 A Tale of Causal Inference from an Observational Study: Full of Sound and Fury but Signifying Very Little Indeed[1]

Consider the following imagined scenario. It is 1991 and a newly hired chancellor at one campus of the University of Nebraska is, among other directives, charged with:

1. improving the unacceptably low four-year graduation rate (14 percent in 1990) – state legislators were loath to continue to appropriate funds to the university when so few students graduate on time;
2. admitting more students to increase enrollment and thus alleviate some budgetary tensions.

On the face of it, addressing both challenges simultaneously is at the very least difficult and might even be impossible, for acceptance rates and graduation rates are typically negatively correlated (as one goes up, the other goes down) (Mulvenon & Robinson, 2014).

A team of researchers and data analysts were recruited and after days of discussion they proposed a bold plan. Admission requirements would be stiffened, increasing the number of required high school courses in math, science, and foreign languages, which would likely accompany a parallel increase in admissions test scores (ACT scores). They anticipated that this would yield an increase in the academic quality of their undergraduate students, and, hopefully, higher graduation rates. While all agreed that a negative short-term effect of this policy would be reduced enrollment, it was hoped that the associated improvement in graduation rates would make the school more attractive to better students and thence, long term, yield increases in enrollment.

---

[1] Our apologies to Macbeth (Act 5, Scene 5) – good manners require that we refrain from identifying the teller of this tale.

11.0 A Tale of Causal Inference from Observational Study

So, the following year, admission standards were raised and over the ensuing 15 years the average ACT scores for entering freshmen increased from 22.5 in 1990 to 24.9 by 2005. As expected, enrollment slipped from 24,453 in 1990 to 22,268 in 2000. But, more importantly, the 4-year graduation rate increased to 32 percent in 2005 and 46 percent in 2023.

Although some details of this scenario grew from our imaginations, the actions we described, and their reported outcomes, are real and characterized the experience of the University of Nebraska-Lincoln.

Although there was a temporary cost in enrollment to be paid, the actions taken by the university in increasing admission standards yielded a concomitant increase in its graduation rates. And, eventually, the immediate hit in enrollment was reversed.

With such convincing results that accompanied the causal chain of actions and outcomes, why haven't all universities faced with disappointing graduation rates opted to follow this same strategy?

Unfortunately, valid causal inference is not so easily accomplished. Was it the increased admission standards that truly *caused* the increased graduation rates? Or was it something else? Alas, the experience in Nebraska parallels that of the nineteenth-century inhabitants of Lower Saxony who discovered that the causal link between the parallel increases in both local birthrates and the number of pairs of nesting storks was more apparent than real (see Section 11.3). An expanded look at Nebraska's good news included the experience of parallel institutions during the same time period, which told a very different story. In all U.S. colleges over the same span of 15 years, the average ACT score for entering freshmen remained essentially the same (21) while over the same period the 4-year graduation rate increased sharply (from 20 to 32 percent). This suggests that something else was going on nationally that was likely unrelated to undergraduate quality. But what?

In Table 11.1 we show mean ACT scores and graduation rates for the University of Nebraska and three neighboring land-grant universities (Colorado State, Iowa State, and Kansas State), as well as national data for the 15 years described plus for the most recent data available. There is no strong evidence available that the happy gains in graduation rates that Nebraska experienced were related to their tightening of admission standards. Although a glance at enrollment figures (Table 11.2) confirms that Nebraska did pay a price for the change in its standards, which was reversed by 2010.

But we are left with a mystery. Why did graduation rates increase so sharply at all institutions apparently regardless of their admissions policy? Could Nebraska have obtained the same gains in graduation without having to pay the price of a temporary decline in enrollment?

Table 11.1 *Graduation rates and mean ACT scores for four Midwest state universities and the U.S. (Source: ACT, 2023; NCES, 2021)*

University	Mean ACT score			4-year graduation rate (Percent)		
	1990	2005	2023	1990	2005	2023
Nebraska	23	25	25	14	32	46
Colorado State	24	24	26	22	36	48
Iowa State	25	25	25	21	32	52
Kansas State	23	24	24	19	30	47
All U.S.	**21**	**21**	**20**	**20**	**32**	**52**

Table 11.2 *The enrollments (in thousands of students) for four Midwest state universities*

	Total enrollment (thousands)			
	1990	2000	2010	2015
Nebraska	24	22	25	25
Colorado State	27	27	30	31
Iowa State	26	27	29	36
Kansas State	21	22	24	24

What happened between 1990 and 2005 that can account for the increased graduation rates above and beyond what Nebraska did with its admission standards?

A plausible answer was proposed by the Texas economist Jeffrey Denning and his colleagues in a 2022 paper that connected grade inflation to rising graduation rates. It has long been known that a student's GPA strongly predicts graduation and in 2021 the *National Center for Education Statistics* reported that the median college GPA increased from 2.7 in 1990 to 3.02 in 2016. By 2020, the first year of the pandemic, it was up to 3.28. The greatest increases were at public 4-year colleges. At Iowa State, for example, the mean GPA for undergraduates increased from 2.78 in 1997 to 3.08 in 2021. This inflation is even visible in high school. The percentage of college freshmen who had a 4.0 high school GPA went from 13 percent in 1985 to 31 percent in 2019 (Eagan et al., 2016).

Is grade inflation the cause of the increase in graduation rates? We don't know what would have happened to graduation rates at the universities if the grades did not inflate over time, but it is a credible candidate. As we will discuss shortly, trying to find causes of effects is a difficult, if not impossible, task. But what is possible is to measure the size of the effect that any possible cause might have on the variable of interest.

This short example was meant to illustrate how important it is to both establish causality and to measure the size of causal effects. It is a topic of profound practical and theoretical significance. Yet it is also one that is shrouded in darkness and misinformation. In the balance of this chapter we try to reduce some of that darkness. Over perhaps the last century (beginning with Fisher's 1925 *Statistical Methods* but certainly since his 1935 *Design of Experiments*) it has been well established that the rigorous study of causality is rooted in randomized controlled experiments. We will elaborate on that shortly. But we also are well aware that the kinds of control required for such research are frequently not practical (indeed, sometimes not even possible), and so we will spend considerable time and pages describing how we can still do effective causal inference when all we have available are observational studies. You will soon learn how, without doing a randomized controlled experiment, we are still able to measure the size of the causal effect that fracking has had on earthquakes in Oklahoma.

11.1 Introduction

The search for truth has been a theme throughout human history. This search comprises two hierarchical categories: Do we use evidence? And, if so, what sorts of evidence have validity for the situation at hand? The exploration of these great questions falls under the purview of epistemology and the philosophy of science; it is usually part of the discussion of methods for gaining knowledge, which might translate into "Scientific Method," which might then be specialized to "procedures used by actual practicing scientists."

The great American physicist Richard Feynman [1918–1988] provided, as only he could, a clear description of the key ideas behind the Scientific Method. In his famous 1964 Messenger Lectures, he said,

> *In general, we look for a new law by the following process. First, we guess it. Then we compute the consequences of the guess to see what would be implied if this law that we guessed is right. Then we compare the result of the computation to nature, with experiment or experience, compare it directly with observation, to see if it works. If it disagrees with experiment it is wrong. In that simple statement is the key to science.*
>
> *It does not make any difference how beautiful your guess is. It does not make any difference how smart you are, who made the guess, or what his name is - if it disagrees with experiment it is wrong. That is all there is to it.*

Feynman answered the philosophic question of how and when evidence should be used by placing it in an exalted position. Evidence vetoed all else. Yet, strangely, this point of view has never been universal.

We hear the term "evidence-based decision making" in many fields: medicine, education, economics, and political policy, to pick four. This implies there is a new and modern way to solve contemporary problems. If what we are doing *now* is evidence based, what were we doing *previously*? How can we consider the use of evidence in science new? Hasn't evidence been at the very core of science for millennia? The short answer is no.

Making decisions evidence based has always been a tough row to hoe. Once you commit to it, no idea – no matter how beautiful, no matter how desirable – can withstand an established contrary fact regardless of how ugly that fact might be. The conflict between evidence-based and belief-based epistemology in the modern world is all around us. So, it is not surprising that using evidence to make decisions has taken a long time to catch on. The formal idea of using evidence as a method for gaining knowledge is often dated (as are so many things) with Aristotle [384 BC–322 BC]. Aristotle diverged from his teacher Plato's purely rational approach by advocating the crucial inclusion of *experience*.[2] Aristotle famously studied the prenatal development of chickens by collecting several freshly laid eggs and then sequentially opening them, one each day, and noting the changes in the development of the chick embryos that he observed within them.

But the path from Aristotle to Feynman was not smooth. Once one commits to using evidence to make decisions, facts take precedence over opinion. And not all supporters of an empirical approach had the muscular support of Alexander the Great. Hence, it took almost 1,500 years before it briefly reappeared with Roger Bacon [1214–1292], who observed, "Reasoning draws a conclusion, but does not make the conclusion certain, unless the mind discovers it by the path of experience."

But once again it slipped away, only to gain a firmer foothold with the work of Francis Bacon [1561–1626] who re-popularized the formal use of evidence, which was subsequently expanded and amplified by the British empiricists John Locke [1632–1704], George Berkeley [1685–1753], and especially the influential Scot David Hume [1711–1776], whose 1738 *Treatise on Human Nature* – as well as his 1741 *Essays, Moral and Political* – had a profound influence on Adam Smith, Jeremy Bentham, and Immanuel Kant. Although it took a very long time, by the late eighteenth century the stage was set for the

---

[2] Aristotle was certainly not the first to advocate the critical advantages provided by empirical evidence. Sun Tzu [544–496 BC] predated Aristotle by two centuries and was the author of the widely cited *The Art of War*. In it he was very clear about the value of direct experiential knowledge. He wrote, "Foreknowledge cannot be gotten from ghosts and spirits, cannot be had by analogy, cannot be found out by calculation. It must be obtained from people; people who know the conditions of the enemy."

beginning of a reasonably broad agreement on what constituted evidence along with the by now well-established Hindu-Arabic number system (which itself provided a workable format for describing quantitative phenomena). And there were important and vexing problems requiring solutions as well as a growing impetus to gather informative data. But what was lacking was the willingness to look at numbers and see *meanings*.

11.2 What Kind of Evidence? What Kind of Claim?

*Evidence is **observable** data related to a claim.* Evidence cannot exist independent of a claim, and so it is natural to begin our discussion of evidence by specifying the two different kinds of claims that can be made: (1) descriptive and (2) causal.

Descriptive claims require only that supporting evidence be reputable. For example, if Mary claims that she no longer has a headache, the support for her claim is just the extent to which she is believable. Her statement gains credibility if we know that historically Mary is honest and that she has no ulterior motives for trying to deceive us.

Causal claims are much more difficult to support. If Mary claimed that she no longer has a headache *because* two hours ago she took two aspirin, the support for her claim must address alternative explanations. Key to these explanations is the question, "Compared to what?" Headaches usually end of their own volition. What would have happened if Mary had not taken the aspirin? Such a causal claim exemplifies one kind of causal inference: *measuring the effects of a cause*. We want to know the extent to which taking two aspirin two hours ago affected a headache. There is a second kind of causal inference that is much more difficult to make – *finding the cause of effects*. This issue might arise if Mary noticed that her headache has suddenly gone away and she wants to know why.

The distinction between measuring the effects of causes versus finding the causes of effects is crucial, and often subtle. Finding causes of effects is a task of insuperable difficulty; measuring the effects of causes can be done, if we are careful. We will explore these two issues sequentially in the next two sections.

11.3 Finding the Causes of Effects – The Cause of Cholera

The iconic example of a careful scientific approach to finding the cause of an effect concerns a London cholera epidemic that raged over St. James Parish in

1854. The first cholera epidemic began in Bengal, India in the 1820s, where tens of thousands died, and reached England in October 1831, apparently on a ship coming from the Baltic states. By 1832, it spread all over the United Kingdom where more than 55,000 perished. A second pandemic, following much the same route, struck the United Kingdom in 1848. In just a two-year period, another 50,000 died.

In 1836, the English Parliament created the General Registry Office (GRO), which compiled a complete database for the entire population of England. This database included every birth, death, and marriage. No dead body could be buried without a certificate of registration. Thus, when the first cases of cholera appeared in London in 1854, it was quickly noted and taken very seriously indeed. Working separately, two young physicians – William Farr [1807–1883] and John Snow [1813–1858] – had by then been trying to track down the causes of cholera for several years (Farr, 1852; Snow, 1849). They hoped its early detection would lead to its control before it became catastrophic.

At that time there were many theories of the factors that caused and spread the disease. In France, it was believed to be associated with poverty; in Russia, they thought it was spread by contagion with an unknown mechanism; in the United States, it was thought to have been brought in by Irish immigrants. Both Farr and Snow used the data provided by the GRO. Both kept meticulous records and made careful tabulations associating cholera deaths with a myriad of independent variables that could be the cause. In 1852, Farr noted: "The elevation of the soil in London has a more constant relation with the mortality from cholera than any other known element. The mortality of cholera is in the inverse ratio of the elevation."Farr showed that the London deaths due to cholera in the 1832 pandemic closely followed this inverse ratio, so that if the fatality rate in areas near the Thames were, say, 1, at successive terraces of rising elevation the rates would be reduced to 1/2, 1/3, 1/4, 1/5, and so on. As the deadliness of contagion was reduced, so too was the smell. This was the basis of Farr's "miasma theory" of the cause of the disease. The diminishing odor matching diminishing fatalities supported his belief that it was airborne.

Snow, on the other hand, believed that cholera's vector of contagion was water, and used the same GRO data to support his theory. Snow plotted the location of all cholera deaths on a map of London. Because of his belief that water carried the disease, he also plotted the location of all the water pumps (marked with Xs on the map). The map he drew (Figure 11.1), now famous as marking the beginning of modern epidemiology, clearly supports his conclusion that the cause of the cholera deaths was drinking from the Broad Street pump.

11.3 Finding the Causes of Effects – The Cause of Cholera

Figure 11.1 A map of the area near the Broad Street pump showing the results of the cholera epidemic. Each death is represented as a point and the area's water pumps are marked by Xs. This revision of John Snow's map was prepared by Edward Tufte and is reprinted from his justly famous 1983 book.

After petitioning the Vestry of St. James for permission, he removed the pump's handle and, within days, the epidemic that had taken more than 500 lives sputtered to an end.

Did John Snow's careful work and ingenious use of a geographic data set allow him to find the cause of the epidemic? If not, what truly was the cause of the 1854 London epidemic? Was it the water drawn from the Broad Street pump? Or perhaps it was Frances Lewis' feces[3] that leaked out of a nearby cesspool? Frances Lewis was a 5-month-old child, who lived at

---

[3] The woman living at 40 Broad Street (Sarah Lewis, wife of police constable Thomas Lewis) lost both her 5-month-old child, Frances, and husband to cholera. In the five-day interval between her child's onset of diarrhea on August 15, 1854 and subsequent death on August 19, 1854, Mrs. Lewis had soaked the diarrhea-soiled diapers in pails of water and thereafter she emptied the pails in the cesspool opening in front of her house.

40 Broad Street and perished from cholera; she is widely considered to be the index case of that epidemic. Or was it the bacteria *Vibrio cholerae* in those feces? The Italian Filippo Pacini is now credited with being the first to identify this bacterium as the proximal cause of cholera in 1854 – ironically, the same year as the London epidemic. Is it really *Vibrio cholerae?* Or is it the enterotoxin that it generates? You get the idea. As we learn more, our judgment of what is the "true cause" keeps shifting. It is likely that at some time in the future, research will reveal that it is some peculiar protein that interacts in an odd way to cause the disease. And even that is unlikely to be the end of it.

Snow's experience, chasing potential causes down a winding road only to find another alternative, is almost always the case when we try to find the cause of an effect. But measuring the effect of a cause is easier (although by no means easy). And more important, once measured, it is eternal. Although what John Snow determined was the cause of the 1854 cholera epidemic has shifted over time, the effect of having drunk from the Broad Street Pump – the end of 570 lives – remains true. A practical orienting attitude is to accept that to some extent, anything can partially cause anything that succeeds it, leaving the crucial question to be answered, "How much of an effect does it have?"

Yet counter-posed to this pessimistic conclusion is John Snow's apparently successful use of this method to find the cause of the epidemic and thence to initiate action that apparently ended it. Importantly, Snow did not simply draw his famous map and declare that the Broad Street pump was contaminated. The map just provided a neat summary of what was a pains-taking investigation. He went to the homes of the families of those who died –but were far from the pump – to see if they had any connection. He found out about the Lewis family's waste disposal practices, and he investigated the drinking habits of brewery workers who worked near the pump but were under-represented among its victims. In short, the map might be considered a brilliant beginning of his investigation, but it was a long way from the end.

However, there is strong evidence that his dramatic removal of the pump handle had little effect on the cholera epidemic. We suspect this because we now know how fragile and short-lived *Vibrio cholerae* is outside of its host's body. Even without this knowledge, there was evidence in Snow's time that the epidemic had run its course. In Figure 11.2[4] we see the start of the epidemic with Francis Lewis' death on August 19th. Then the disease grew slowly until September 2nd when there was a huge increase in deaths, peaking

---

[4] After Tufte (1997), p. 33.

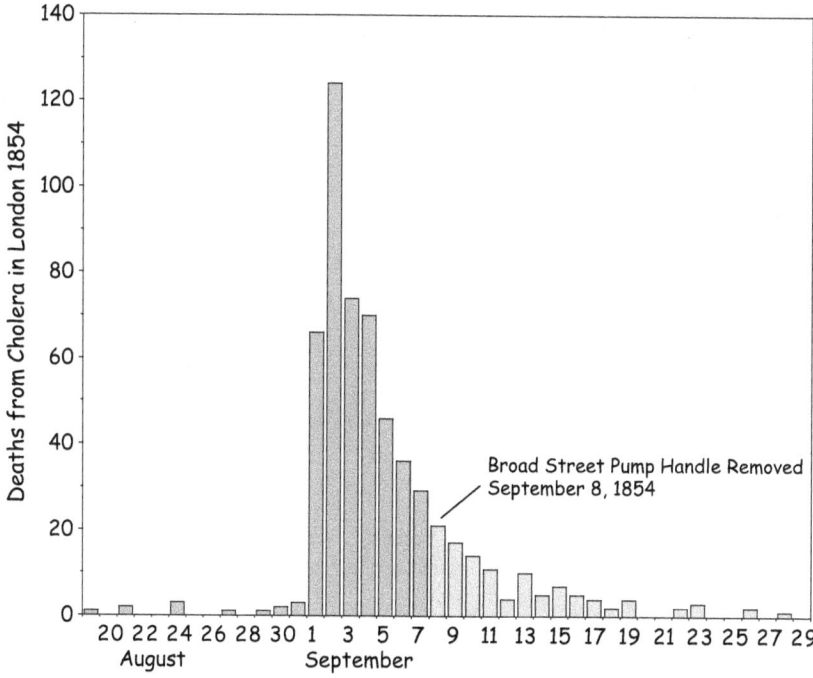

Figure 11.2 The daily number of deaths during the London Cholera epidemic of 1854 showing that the epidemic had already begun to taper off well before the pump handle was removed on September 8th.

the next day when more than 120 died. Then, a decline began with the number of daily deaths shrinking steadily. The shading change in Figure 11.2 illustrates the deaths after the pump handle was removed. But we see no dramatic shift; instead, we see the tapering off that characterizes all epidemics as the number of potential victims diminishes. There is, alas, little evidence that Snow's dramatic action had any profound effect on the outcome of the course of the epidemic.

It is hard to imagine a more careful and thorough search for a cause than the work of Farr and Snow. Yet, in the end, they failed. Their failure was not for lack of motivation, scientific know-how, or intellectual horsepower. The task of finding cause is one of insuperable difficulty. But, with the right tools, measuring the size of an effect is often within our grasp. But we must control hubris and exercise care.

Sadly, we find that few searchers for causal truth exercise the extraordinary care of Farr and Snow. Too often careless investigators employ the logical

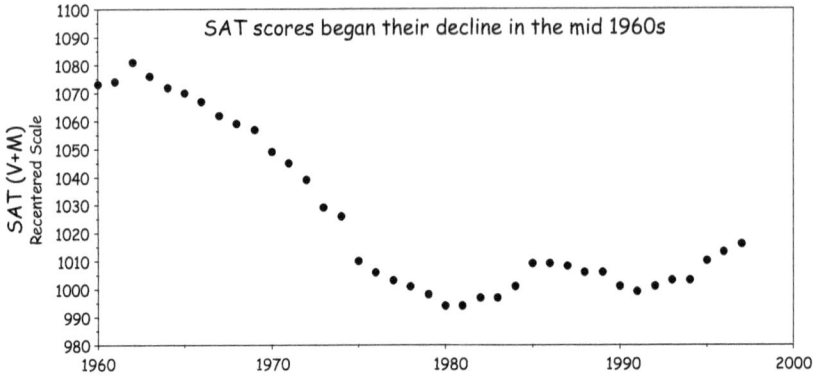

Figure 11.3 Average SAT scores for 27 years, showing a peak in 1962 that is followed by an 18-year decline.

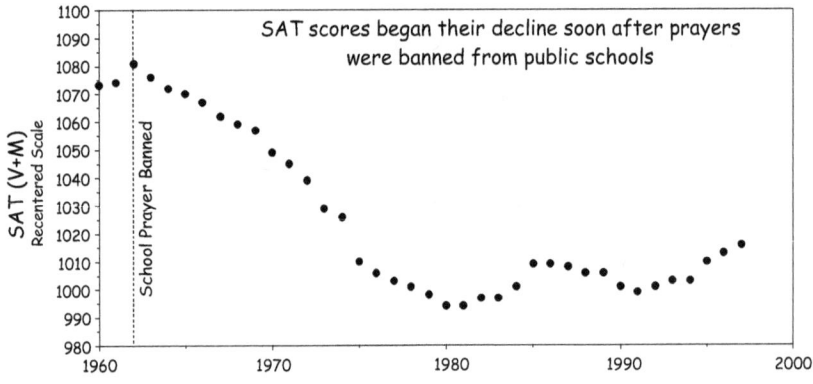

Figure 11.4 An augmentation of the SAT score plot indicating what some believed to be the proximal cause of the score decline.

fallacy expressed by *post hoc ergo propter hoc*[5] as their guiding principle. This notion has been used to argue that the parallel decreases in the number of both storks and human births in the German state of Lower Saxony was evidence of a causal connection.

In the late 1990s, the College Board published data showing a long-term national decline in SAT scores (Figure 11.3), which seemed to signal a parallel decline in the efficacy of American education.

Obviously, before we can remediate the problem it is crucial to uncover the cause of the decline. Many causal candidates were suggested. One (Figure 11.4)

---

[5] After this, therefore because of this.

insisted that it was obviously the 1962 Supreme Court decision to ban prayer in public schools. A debate ensued arguing that if school prayer was indeed the cause of the decline, why did scores stabilize in the late 1970s? The 1977 death of Elvis Presley and lack of scholarship he represented were deemed an obvious candidate for the cause of score stabilization. Other explanations involving changes in funding for education were also proposed and received some professional acceptance. In the next section we will introduce a very powerful tool that makes such measurement possible.

11.4 Measuring the Effects of Causes – Rubin's Model for Causal Inference

We may define a cause to be an object followed by another, and where all the objects, similar to the first, are followed by objects similar to the second, and, where, if the first object had not been, the second would never have existed.

David Hume

Issues of causality have haunted human thinkers for centuries, with the modern view usually ascribed to the Scot David Hume [1711–1776], whose famous discussion of causality we quote above. The opening phrase is but a rewording of *post hoc ergo propter hoc*. The key difference is the second phrase, which introduces counterfactuals.

A signal event in statisticians' modern exploration of this ancient topic was Paul Holland's comprehensive 1986 exposition "Statistics and causal inference" that laid out the foundations of what he named "Rubin's Model for Causal Inference."

A key idea in Rubin's model is that finding the cause of an effect is often an impossible task, and so science can make itself most valuable by measuring the effects of causes. What is the effect of a cause? It is the difference between what happens if some unit is exposed to a treatment of interest versus what would have been the result had it not been. Thus, enters Hume's counterfactuals that are, of course, impossible to observe. Stated in a more general way, *the causal effect is the difference between the actual outcome and some unobserved potential outcome.*

Because counterfactuals can never be observed for an individual unit, we can never calculate the size of a causal effect on a single unit directly. But one thing we can do is calculate the average causal effect for a group of units. This can be done credibly through randomization. If we divide a group of units randomly into a treatment group and a control group (to pick one obvious situation), it is credible to believe that, because there is nothing special about being in the control group, the average result that we observe in the control group is what we would have observed had the treatment group been enrolled in the control condition instead. Thus, the difference between the treatment and the control outcomes is a measure of the size of the average causal effect of the treatment (relative to the control condition). The randomization is the key to making this a credible conclusion. But, in order for randomization to be possible, we must be able to assign either treatment or control to any particular unit. Thus, is derived Rubin's (1975, p. 238) bumper-sticker worthy conclusion that there can be "no causation without manipulation."

This simple result has important consequences. It means that some variables, like gender or race, cannot be fruitfully thought of as causal, since we cannot randomly assign them. Thus, the statement "she did badly on the test because she didn't study" can be causal; we can imagine an experiment in which we randomly assign some people to study and others not (a so-called "encouragement design") and then see how much better those assigned to study performed on the test than those who did not. But the apparently parallel statement "she did badly on the test because she is a woman" is causally meaningless, for to measure the effect of being a woman we would have to know how well she would have done had she been a man. The heroic assumptions required for such a conclusion removes it from the realm of empirical discussion.

Implicit in our discussion so far is the level of control required for this most powerful method of measuring the size of causal effects. We must be able to determine what is to be the treatment, what is the alternative (control), what is the dependent (outcome) variable, and which units get which. Without such control, the credibility of the inferences suffers.

11.5 On the Role of Assumptions in Causal Inference

In the past, a theory could get by on its beauty; but in the modern world a successful theory has to work for a living.

Our apologies to Elmore Leonard

Rubin's Model lays out a path for measuring the effects of causes and it explains the logical background behind what is generally thought of as the gold standard for generating credible evidence for causal claims. The model has three important components:

1. control groups,
2. potential outcomes, and
3. random assignment.

Control groups are critical to answering the question "compared to what?" The outcome in the control group tells us what would have happened had we done something else. A poor, but sometimes necessary, alternative is to replace the results from a control group with an assumption. One common assumption is that of stasis – had we done nothing, things would have continued into the future just as they have in the past. Sometimes this is credible. More often it is not. For example, if we have a treatment for 10-year-olds to help them grow taller we could measure them before and after the treatment and interpret the difference as the causal effect of the treatment. But 10-year-olds usually would have grown anyway, and so assuming they'd stay the same is simply not credible. We really must know what would have happened had they not been treated (Hume's counterfactual again).

The counterfactual of what would have happened had they not been treated represents the second component of Rubin's model – potential outcome. For each unit in the experiment there are two potential outcomes: what happens if they were treated and what happens if they were not. Implicit is the key idea that both potential outcomes have to be possible for the experimenter to get to choose which they observe. We will discuss this in greater detail shortly.

And finally, random assignment makes credible the assumption that what we observed on average in one group is what we would have observed in the other group had they had the other treatment.

When Experiments are Possible

Perhaps the best-known example of a randomized experiment in the field of education is the Tennessee Class Size Experiment, which involved some 6,500 students in 330 classrooms in about 80 schools beginning in 1985 (Mosteller, 1995). How did such a large study come about? Governor Lamar Alexander, the Tennessee legislature, and the educational community were interested in whether spending extra money on reducing class sizes in early (kindergarten through third grade) elementary schools would increase student learning. A 4-year study was authorized and provided a three-million-dollar budget. Class sizes (experimental conditions) were small (13–17), regular (22–25), and regular with a teacher's aide. Within schools, students and teachers were randomly assigned to one of the three conditions each year. Both standardized tests and curriculum-based tests were used as dependent measures.

The results indicated that compared to being in a regular class, when students were in small classes, they scored about a quarter of a standard deviation higher on achievement tests. Also, having a teacher's aide in a regular class led to about a tenth of a standard deviation improvement in test scores. As a result of these findings, Tennessee implemented reduced class sizes for students in the first four grades in the poorest school districts. Such a large-scale experiment is rare and unfortunately, has not occurred in education since then.

When Experiments are not Possible

When we have the control needed to implement Rubin's Model, we can estimate the size of the average effect for whatever possible cause we are interested in. For many situations, this can take us a very long way. But sometimes such control is not practical or ethical. For example, suppose we wanted to estimate the causal effect smoking has on lung cancer. Although it is *possible* to randomly assign some people to smoke and others to not, and then follow them for 30 years and note the differential incidence of cancer, such an experiment is neither practical nor ethical. Yet, the scientific question is important, and we need an answer. What are we to do?

There are at least two approaches, but they both require assumptions, and the credibility of the estimates depends strongly on how heroic the assumptions required must be. One approach is to do animal experiments in which random assignment to smoking is practical, and then make the assumption that what we observe in animals has a human analog. One reason this approach fails is because lab animals typically don't live long enough for the treatment to have its effect and those with long enough life expectancies (e.g., tortoises) haven't yet been induced to smoke.

A second approach uses Rubin's Model to provide a guide on how to go forward – specifically we would start with the ideal, but impractical experiment, and then deviate from it as little as required to bring the resulting observational study into the realm of the possible. In the course of this we must replace control with assumption. And so, to study the causal connection between smoking and cancer, we might collect a large number people who smoke and then match them on the basis of age, gender, education, race, social class, and so on with an equally large number of people who don't smoke, and then follow them for many years to track the incidence of cancer in the two groups.

There are several concerns associated with such a design. What happens if someone in the smoking group decides over time to stop smoking?

Or someone in the non-smoking group takes up the habit? Or if some die in a traffic accident or some other cause unrelated to smoking? Or if the two groups differ on some other crucial characteristics that we didn't measure? All of these diminish the credibility of our causal estimates.

Another approach would be to gather a large group of people who have lung cancer (the "Cases") and another group matched by age, gender, race, social class, and so on to the cases but who do not have cancer (the "Controls"). Then, compare the proportion of smokers among the cases to that among the controls. If that proportion is the same in the two groups, we have no evidence of smoking being a cause of lung cancer. If, however, it is five times larger (a commonly found result) among the cases than the controls, we have evidence of a causal connection. Usually in case/control studies, words describing the result are chosen carefully. Thus, rather than claiming that smoking is a cause of lung cancer, it is claimed that the risk factor of lung cancer associated with smoking is greater than 5. That is, lung cancer occurs more than five times as often among those who smoke than among those who do not.

The exploration of various clever methods like this for doing observational studies with the goal of making credible estimates of causal effects has exploded over the past few decades. The University of Pennsylvania statistician Paul Rosenbaum, a former student of Rubin's, has been a leader in this area and his books (Rosenbaum, 2002; 2009; 2017) are the standard works in the field.

When we have the complete control necessary to apply Rubin's Model, we can unambiguously estimate the size of the causal effect of a particular treatment on a particular outcome for a specific sample of people. As our control diminishes, so does the credibility of our estimates. But, at the end of the day, there remain important causal questions that require answers and real practical limitations. Keep in mind that there are huge fields of intellectual endeavor (history and astronomy among many others) that have successfully estimated causal effects without the remotest possibility of ever doing a randomized, controlled experiment.

In the next section we will examine in detail two critically important causal questions and show how observational studies yielding "only" circumstantial evidence, can still yield credibly convincing and useful causal conclusions if we are careful and try to mimic the character of an experiment.

11.6 A Trout in the Milk

On November 11, 1850, Henry David Thoreau observed, "Some circumstantial evidence is very strong, as when you find a trout in the milk." Thoreau was referring to an 1849 dairyman's strike in which some of the purveyors were suspected of watering down the product. Thoreau is especially relevant when we are faced with trying to estimate a causal effect, but do not have the ability to do a suitable experiment, and so are constrained to using available data for an observational study.

11.6.1 Causal Inferences from Observational Studies 1: The Causal Effects of CO_2 on Global Warming and Violent Weather

The United States National Oceanic and Atmospheric Administration (NOAA) keeps track of the carbon dioxide (CO_2) content of the Earth's atmosphere and reports its findings to the public regularly. On the NOAA website is a plot (Figure 11.5) of the dramatic increases in CO_2 since the industrial age got into full swing. Over the past 75 years or so, the enormous increase in the number of humans on the planet yielded associated increases in fossil fuel burning factories, automobiles, airplanes, and electrical generation. Scientists, through a combination of theory and experiment, presented a compelling case for a physical connection between the amount of CO_2 in the atmosphere and the ease with which heat can escape into space. The inevitable conclusion is that we should expect planetary warming caused by CO_2 emissions. The empirical question is "how much?"

On Thursday, February 7, 2019, the *New York Times* had a front-page article describing the changes in the global temperature over the last 140 years

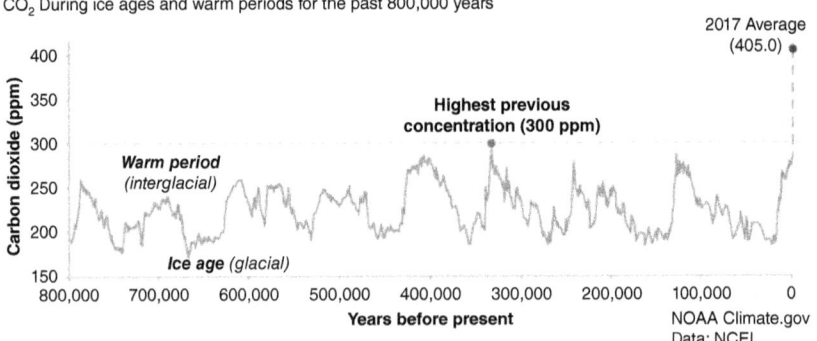

Figure 11.5 A NOAA plot showing the CO_2 content of the Earth's atmosphere for the last 800,000 years. Source: NOAA Climate.gov, National Oceanic and Atmospheric Administration. See
https://www.climate.gov/news-features/understanding-climate/climate-change-atmospheric-carbon-dioxide

11.6 A Trout in the Milk 141

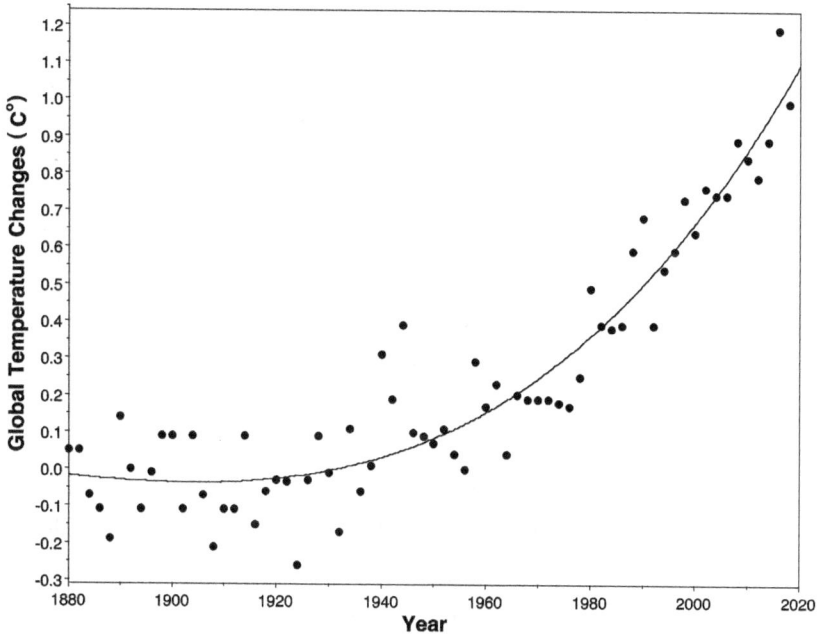

Figure 11.6 Global temperatures since 1880. The zero point represents the average global temperature during the whole of the nineteenth century.

(see Figure 11.6). The dominant feature of the plot was the sharp and steady rise over the last 60 years. The text of the story told us that the geologic record shows that the Earth had not seen such a sharp rise since long ago when the planet was still very much in flux and volcanic eruptions were throwing huge quantities of CO_2 into the atmosphere. The doubling of atmospheric CO_2 over just a few decades due to humankind's emissions has had a parallel increase in global temperature of over 1° C over the same period.

A plausible causal connection between human activities resulting in the release of CO_2 into the atmosphere and the increase in global temperature is apparent. A second level of inference is less clear: specifically, how much of the climate change that we experience directly (e.g., more and stronger hurricanes and typhoons, longer droughts, wilder temperature swings, etc.) are due to global warming and how much is just part of normal climatic fluctuation?

The answer to this question requires probabilistic thinking, which is perhaps best done through analogy. Consider an interstate highway that passes just north of a modest sized town. There are two exits to the interstate, one just to the town's east and another just to its west. At one point a repair was needed to a bridge on the interstate that lay between those two exits. While the repair was taking place, the interstate was closed and the traffic from it was routed through the main street of the town. Ordinarily there were about five traffic accidents a month in the town, but during each month that the detour was in place there averaged twenty traffic accidents in the town. Although it was impossible to ascribe the closing of the road as the cause of any particular accident, it was pretty clear that the effect of the closure was an increase of about fifteen accidents per month.

So, too, it is clear that while we cannot say for sure that any particular drought, storm, and so on is the direct result of global warming, we can credibly calculate the average causal effect on our weather due to global warming that was caused by the release of CO_2 into the atmosphere.

11.7 Causal Inferences from Observational Studies 2: Fracking, Injection Wells, Earthquakes, and Oklahoma

Next we will explore the consequences of the unfortunate combination of using an oil drilling technique called hydraulic fracturing (commonly called "fracking") and the disposal of wastewater by the high-pressure injection of it back into the earth. We believe that the available evidence is, in Thoreau's delicious simile, like a trout in the milk.

11.7.1 Dewatering

An oil well is considered to be exhausted when the amount of oil it yields is no longer sufficient to justify the cost of its extraction. Most of Oklahoma's wells fell into this category by the 1990s because of the immense amount of wastewater that was brought up along with the diminishing amount of oil. But in the twenty-first century, the combination of dewatering technologies and the rising price of oil made many of Oklahoma's abandoned wells economically viable again. The idea was to just pull up the water with the oil – about ten barrels of water for each barrel of oil. This yielded billions of barrels of wastewater annually that had to be disposed of. The current method is to use high-pressure pumps to inject it back into the earth in wastewater wells.

11.7.2 Fracking

Fracking is the process of drilling down into the earth before a high-pressure water mixture is directed at the rock to release the gas inside. Water, sand, and chemicals are injected into the rock at high pressure that allows the gas to flow out to the head of the well. This procedure has been in use for about 60 years. However, horizontal drilling is a new wrinkle introduced by 1990 that could dramatically increase the yield of the well. Horizontal drilling is a horizontal shaft added onto the vertical one after the vertical drilling has reached the desired depth (as deep as two miles). This combination expands the region of the well substantially. The high-pressure liquid mixture injected into the well serves several purposes: It extends the fractures in the rock, adds lubrication, and carries materials (proppants) to hold the fractures open and thus extend the life of the well. Horizontal fracking is especially useful in shale formations that are not sufficiently permeable to be economically viable in a vertical well. The liquid mixture that is used in fracking is disposed of in the same way as the wastewater from dewatering wells.

11.7.3 Concerns

The principal concern about the use of fracking began with the volume of water used in the operation (typically 2 to 8 million gallons per well) and the subsequent possible contamination of drinking water if the chemicals used in fracking leached into the groundwater. Concerns arose about the disposal of wastewater generated from fracking and dewatering causing a substantial increase in seismic activities. Most troubling was a vast increase in earthquakes in areas unaccustomed to them.[6] It is concern that most of these earthquakes are manmade that is the principal focus of this section.

11.7.4 A Possible Experiment to Study the Seismic Effects of Fracking

If we had a free hand to do whatever we wished to estimate the causal effect that the injection of large quantities of wastewater has on earthquakes, all sorts of experimental designs come to mind. One might be to choose a large number of geographic locations and pair them on the basis of a number of geological characteristics, then choose one of each pair at random and institute a program of water injection (the treatment group) and leave the other undisturbed (the control group). Of course, we would have to make sure that all the areas

---

[6] A January 2015 study in *The Bulletin of the Seismological Society of America* indicates that fracking built up subterranean pressures that repeatedly caused slippage in an existing fault as close as a half mile beneath the wells. http://www.seismosoc.org/society/press_releases/BSSA_105-1_Skoumal_et_al_Press_Release.pdf

chosen were sufficiently far from one another that the treatment does not have an effect on a member of the control group. Then, we keep track of the number of earthquakes in the treatment regions and the number of earthquakes in the control regions. It might take some time, but eventually we would have both a measure of the causal effect of such injections and a measure of the variability within each of the two groups.

While it may be pretty to contemplate such a study, it isn't likely to be conducted, and it certainly wouldn't be conducted any time soon. Waiting for such a study before we take action is of little solace to people living in those regions. For example, Prague, Oklahoma resident Sandra Ladra landed in the hospital on November 5, 2011 from injuries she suffered when the chimney of her house collapsed in a 5.7 magnitude earthquake (the largest ever recorded in Oklahoma) in a series of quakes that destroyed fifteen homes in her neighborhood as well as the spire on Benedictine Hall at St. Gregory's University in nearby Shawnee. Subsequently, researchers analyzed the data from that quake[7] and concluded that the quake that injured Ms. Ladra was likely due to injection of fluids associated with oil and gas exploration. The quake was felt in at least seventeen states but "the tip of the initial rupture plane is within ∼200 m of active injection wells."

11.7.5 One Consequence of Not Having Good Estimates of the Causal Effect

It isn't hard to imagine the conflicting interests associated with the finding of a causal effect associated with oil and gas exploration in Oklahoma. Randy Keller, director of the Oklahoma Geological Survey, posted a position paper saying that they believed the increase in earthquakes was the result of natural causes. In 2014, when faced with the increase of seismic activity, Oklahoma Governor Mary Fallin advised Oklahomans to buy earthquake insurance. Unfortunately, many policies specifically exclude coverage for earthquakes induced by human activity.

11.7.6 An Observational Study

So, we are faced with the unlikely event of doing a true random assignment experiment on the causal effects of the combination of fracking and high-volume wastewater injection on seismic activity, and the urgent need to

---

[7] Keranen, K.M., Savage, H.M., Abers, G.A., & Cochran, E.S. (June 2013).

11.7 Causal Inferences from Observational Studies 2

estimate that effect. What can we do? The answer must be an observational study. One way to design an observational study is to first consider what would be the optimal experimental design (like the one just sketched) and try to mimic it within an observational structure like this:

- *Treatment condition*: Oil exploration using fracking and dewatering in which the wastewater generated is injected under pressure into disposal wells. This will be in the state of Oklahoma during the time period 2008 to the present, which is when these techniques became increasingly widespread.
- *Control condition:* No fracking or disposal of wastewater using high-pressure injection into disposal wells. The control condition would be what existed in the state of Oklahoma for the 30 years from 1978 until 2008, and for the same time period in the state of Kansas which abuts Oklahoma to the north. Kansas shares the same topography, climate, and geology, and has had far less gas and oil exploration over the time period 1973–present.
- *Dependent variable*: The number of earthquakes with magnitude of 3.0 or greater. We choose 3.0 because that is an earthquake magnitude that can be felt without any special seismic detection equipment. Since Oklahoma has begun to experience increased seismic activity, the U.S. and Oklahoma Geological Surveys (USGS and OGS) have increased the number of detectors they have deployed in the state. Therefore, some of the increase in detected small quakes could be a function of detection sensitivity and not an increase in incidence.

11.7.7 A Trout in the Milk

In Figure 11.7 (from the USGS) we see Oklahoma's seismic activity summarized over the past 38 years.

The figure ends on September 24, 2014, showing 375 earthquakes of magnitude 3.0 or greater. By the end of 2014, the total reached 585. If smaller earthquakes were to be included the total would be greater than 5,000! More recent data from 2015 (not shown) indicated an average of two earthquakes of magnitude 3.0 or greater *per day*. In the 30 years preceding the expansion of these methods of oil and gas exploration there averaged fewer than two earthquakes of magnitude 3.0 or greater *per year*. To put this in perspective, California, sitting as it does on three major fault lines (e.g., San Andreas on the west, Sierra Nevada on the east, and Garlock on the south) has historically had the most earthquakes, prior to the recent adventures in Oklahoma, in the continental U.S. with about 200/per year.

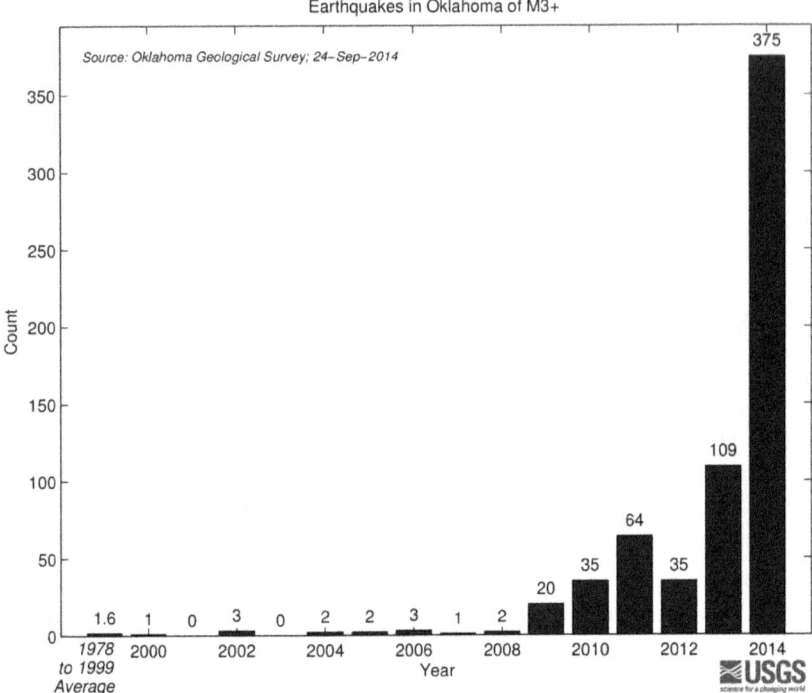

Figure 11.7 The frequency of 3.0+ earthquakes in Oklahoma since 1978 (from the United States Geological Survey).

This 300-fold increase has not gone unnoticed by the general population. Oklahomans receive daily earthquake reports like they do of the local weather. Oklahoma native and *New Yorker* writer Rivka Galchen reports that driving by an electronic billboard outside Oklahoma City in November 2014 he saw, in rotation, "an advertisement for one percent cash back at the Thunderbird Casino, an advertisement for a Cash N Gold pawnshop, a three-day weather forecast, and an announcement of a 3.0 earthquake in Noble County." Driving by next evening, he saw "the display was the same, except that the earthquake was a 3.4 near Pawnee."

The geographic distribution of quakes is shown in Figure 11.8, also from the USGS, with dots showing the 89 earthquakes in the 39 years prior to 2009, the other 960 dots represent the five and a quarter years since then.

Finally, what about the control group? What was the seismic activity in Kansas during this same period? Figure 11.9 is a similar map, although the coding of the plotted points is different than in the Oklahoma map there are but four quakes shown for the period 1973 to 2014 of 3.5–4.0 magnitude.

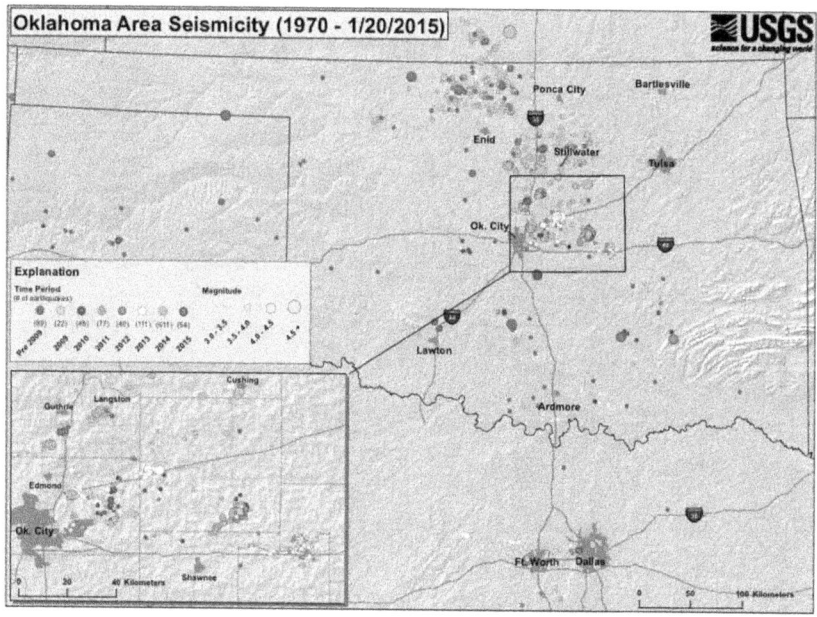

Figure 11.8 The geographic distribution of 3.0+ earthquakes in Oklahoma 1970–2014. The clusters surround injection wells for the disposal of wastewater (from the United States Geological Survey).

Concluding Thoughts on Inferences from Observational Studies

The inferences that can credibly be drawn from observational studies do have limitations. Consider the well-established fact that among elementary school children there is a strong positive relation between scores on reading tests and shoe size. Do large feet help you read better? Or does reading help stimulate the growth of one's feet? Sadly, neither. Instead, there is a third variable, age, that generates the observed relation. Older children are typically both bigger and better readers. An observational study that does not adjust for this variable would draw the wrong inference. And there is always the possibility of such a missing third variable unless there is random assignment to the treatment and control groups. For it is through randomization that all missing third variables, known or unknown, are balanced on average.

The evidence we presented in this chapter makes it clear there is a strong positive association between wastewater injection and earthquakes, as there is between admission test scores and graduation rates. But, because these

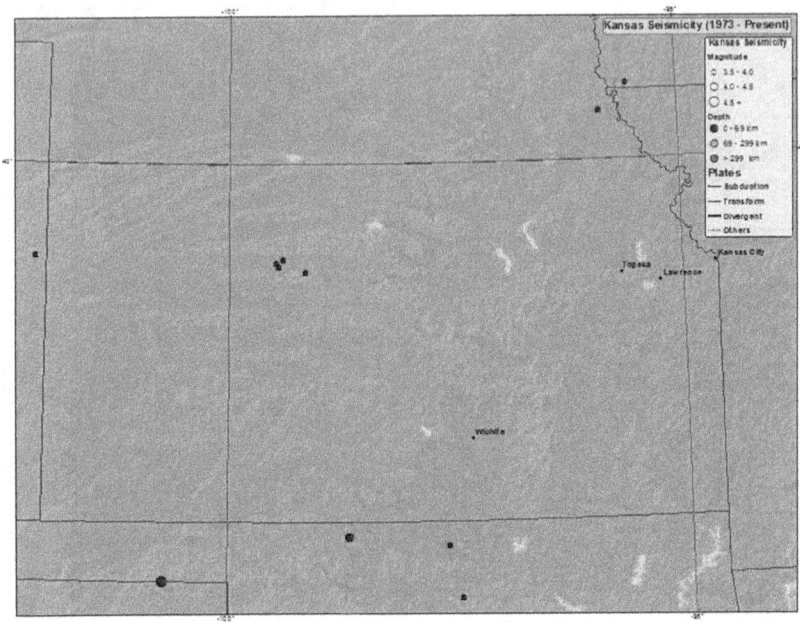

Figure 11.9 The geographic distribution of 3.5+ earthquakes in Kansas since 1973 (from the United States Geological Survey).

are observational studies, we don't know for sure whether or not there is some missing third variable that would explain the observed phenomenon and the size of the apparent causal connection could shrink, or even disappear.

However, no one would believe that foot size has any direct causal connection with reading proficiency because we know about reading (and feet). Similarly, we (or at least trained geologists) know about the structure of earthquakes and the character of the rock substrata that lies beneath the state of Oklahoma, and thus can draw credible causal conclusions about the evidence presented here.

The inferences to be drawn from these results seem straightforward to us. It is hard to imagine what missing third variable might account for what was observed. What other plausible explanation could there be for the huge increase in seismic activity?

The evidence presented here is certainly circumstantial but compelling none-the-less. There have been a substantial number of studies published by the foremost of authorities in the most prestigious peer-reviewed journals supporting the close causal relation between fracking and its associated wastewater disposal to the onslaught of earthquakes that have besieged Oklahoma.[8] We have not been able to find any credible reports to the contrary.

The evidence described here is the very incarnation of Thoreau's fish. When faced with such arguments some will assuredly point out how easy it is to lie with statistics. Certainly true, but it is far easier to lie without them.[9]

11.8 Lessons Learned

The truth is rarely pure and never simple.

Oscar Wilde

Science's principal goal is the understanding of the universe in both the large and the small. A crucial step toward achieving this goal is understanding the causal relationships among events and the kinds of evidence that facilitate such understanding. We have seen that description of phenomena is a necessary and relatively easy step toward this understanding in which the supporting evidence for valid and reliable description must be publicly available and replicable. Understanding causality is more difficult.

The goal of finding the causes of effects is usually a never-ending journey and was illustrated by John Snow's earnest search for the cause of cholera in nineteenth-century London. Recognizing this difficulty led to the shifting of attention away from finding causes to instead measuring effects; this shift was an important step toward wisdom. Finding causes is akin to the eternal sharpening of theories as new facts and understandings present themselves. Measuring effects is the place where the tools of quantitative science can be most effectively employed. We merely assume the possibility of anything can be a cause of anything that succeeds it.[10] The question that matters is "how large an effect does it have?"

Rubin's Model gives us a logical and practical way to measure causal effects, at least on average. The logic surrounding Rubin's Model is what supports and justifies the widespread use of randomized controlled experiments. This model provides a start toward the collection of evidence

---

[8] To cite three recent studies see Hand, E. (July 4, 2014); Keranen, K.M., Savage, H.M., Abers, G.A., & Cochran, E.S. (June 2013); Keranen, K.M., Weingarten, M. Abers, G.A., Bekins, B.A., & Ge, S. (July 25, 2014).

[9] Harvard's Fred Mosteller was the first statistician we know of to make this observation explicitly.

[10] Even Hume's requirement of order can be relaxed, if we are to believe particle physicists about the strange behavior of antimatter in quantum formulations.

supporting causal claims in all situations, and, of particular interest to us, in the evaluation of proposed educational policies: a start, but not the whole story.

11.9 Sample Size Requirements

When we divide the sample up into a treatment group and a control group, we want the only difference between the two groups to be the treatment or lack thereof. If there are any other systematic differences, we can't know whether any differences we observe are due to the treatment or to this other factor on which the two groups differ. Even if we measure all sorts of other characteristics about the sample, there is always the possibility that there is some unmeasured other factor on which the two groups differ. The key element of Rubin's Model that deals with equalizing all such "missing third factors" is randomization. As an example, suppose we are testing the efficacy of some new drug, where the control treatment is an older drug. Our results would be compromised if all the subjects in the treatment group were male and all in the control group female. But it would be very unlikely, if group membership was determined randomly, for that to occur – equivalent for all coin tosses to determine membership in the treatment group to come up heads and all those corresponding to the control group to come up tails. Importantly, the likelihood of such an event decreases with the sample size. So, if we had but a single unit in each group randomization couldn't work. But with 100, it is very likely that *all* missing third factors would be equalized.

Thus, one component of valid evidentiary claims is sample size. The larger the better; but unfortunately, the law of diminishing returns operates. Each additional subject of the experiment counts less than the one that just preceded it,[11] so if we wish to double the precision of the experiment, we must increase the size by a factor of four. Hence, we want to use a sample only big enough to yield the precision required, for making it only moderately larger yields only limited benefits.[12]

11.10 But What If Something Unplanned Happens?

All experiments are observational studies waiting to happen
                                                    Paul Holland (2023a)

---

[11] Stated more carefully, the precision goes as one over the square root of the sample size.
[12] Costs of studies usually increase linearly with sample size, but benefits (precision) increase only as its square root.

11.10 But What If Something Unplanned Happens?

Inexperienced researchers soon learn that it is not enough to merely carefully plan an experiment with the intention of allowing the randomization to take care of all concerns about balancing the various experimental groups. Wisdom, borne of long experience, has taught us to gather a broad range of background data of the sort used in observational studies to match the groups on everything but the treatment. Why is this necessary?

> *Man plans and God laughs*
>
> Ancient Yiddish expression[13]

Consider the following situation. We are trying to measure the size of the causal effect of a new treatment, relative to an existing one, on some horrible disease. We choose a large enough sample of subjects and divide them in half randomly; half get the new treatment; half get the old treatment. The dependent variable is the average score on some sort of health inventory one year after treatment. We run the experiment and at the end of the year round up the subjects. We then discover that in the interim some died, some moved away, and some just disappeared. What do we do?

The short answer is that we use the ancillary information that we were wise enough to gather about each participant and do some post hoc matching, so it is still credible that the only difference between the two groups is which treatment they received. Sadly, the supporting evidence is weaker than it would have been had not some of the observations gone missing. The issue that remains is the determination of whether the evidence that remains is strong enough for the purposes at hand. If the study began with two samples of 500 in each and at the end of the year we had lost two subjects in one group and three in the other, we would usually be content to interpret the results as having almost as much validity as they would have without any dropouts. But if we lost, say, 90 percent of each, we would be much more likely to interpret any differences observed as being due more to the dropouts than to the treatment.[14]

Whenever there are missing data, it is always sensible to estimate how much the missingness affects the outcome. One way to do this is called multiple imputations. What this means is to make up numbers (impute) where there aren't any and then calculate the outcome as if they were real. Then do it again, and again, and again (the multiple part of the imputation). And keep doing this until the entire range of possible values the missing data might have taken has

---

[13] *Der mentsh trakht und got lakht*

[14] Recent election polls were notoriously inaccurate due to the *nonresponse* rates that went as high as 92 percent. This figure was only rarely mentioned by the media, perhaps because pollsters are loathe to declare that large nonresponse can make the accuracy of their products roughly equal to that of predictions made from reading the entrails of dead goats.

been tried out. So, one (admittedly extreme) imputation might be that all the subjects getting the treatment who didn't show up would've had very high scores on the outcome, another that they all would've had very low scores: the same with the missing observations in the control group. Then, we look at the distribution of the outcome variable including the imputations. If the variation is very small, we can conclude that the missingness has not had a profound effect on the outcome. If it is so large that the missingness effect dwarfs the treatment effect, the experiment has not provided supporting evidence for the claim being considered.

The lesson to be taken home from this is that the magic of statistics cannot put numbers where there are no data. The best that can be managed is to estimate how much the precision of our estimates is affected by the missingness.

Data with uncontrolled dropouts violate one of the fundamental conditions for Rubin's Model, specifically that each subject in the experiment has two potential outcomes: one is what would happen under the treatment condition and the second what would happen under the control condition. Only one of these is observable because the subject gets either the treatment or the control, but not both. If a subject dies, the potential outcomes do not exist. Using this insight leads to a subtle solution (to learn more about dealing with missing data in this context see chapter 4 in Wainer, 2016).

11.11 What If We Can't Do an Experiment?

Only a subset of important questions lends themselves to the power obtained from the control available in a true experiment. Must we simply abandon those other questions? Of course not. But we can be guided by what the experiment would have been had we been able to do it and see how close we can come to that ideal before we must replace some of the data with assumptions. The more plausible the assumptions, the closer we get to the evidentiary support of a true experiment. Let us discuss some typical modifications.

11.11.1 Self-Control.

Sometimes having a separate control group poses practical problems. When this occurs an often-used alternative is to use historical data from each group as its own control. We have shown two examples of this earlier in this chapter. We saw that the state of Oklahoma experienced only two or three substantial (magnitude 3.0 or greater) earthquakes *per year* in each of the 30 years prior to the widespread use of fracking. Then, as the use of fracking increased so too did the incidence of earthquakes, until by 2015 Oklahoma averaged three such earthquakes *per day*. The assumption such an approach substitutes for a control group is that had fracking not occurred (Hume's counterfactual again), Oklahoma's seismic activity of the past would have continued into the future. Supporting this assumption is the observation showing that prior to fracking, Oklahoma's seismic activity was essentially flat. Had this not been the case – had it, for example, been steadily increasing – the evidentiary case against fracking would be weaker. Thus, we use the earlier activity to predict later activity, and the difference between what we observe and this predicted amount is the estimated causal effect of fracking.

The same approach is used in Figure 11.5 where it is not possible to find a control planet into whose atmosphere we do not spew CO_2. Instead we use the Earth, prior to the industrial age, as its own control. We noted that the average worldwide temperature stayed within relatively tight bounds for hundreds of thousands of years. It does not seem illogical to assume that *ceteris paribus* it would continue that way. Thus, it is credible to estimate the effect of the striking increase in atmospheric CO_2 as the difference between the temperature ranges that are currently observed and those which existed in the past (which we project to be what would have happened had we not injected CO_2).

Using historical data as a substitute for a control group is often a credible alternative when a true control is either impossible or impractical. The evidence thus provided may not be quite as strong as a true control with random assignment, but often (as in these two cases) it is strong enough.

11.11.2 Matching

Random assignment is the powerful tool used to assure that the only difference between the treatment and control groups is the treatment. When sample sizes are large enough, randomization balances all other factors automatically. But what happens when randomization is not possible or not practical? Again, we must substitute assumptions. Some assumptions, like "don't worry, everything is ok" are too heroic for most people. We can make them more reasonable if we have collected lots of additional information and then design the experimental and control groups intelligently. So if we are stuck with the membership of the treatment group (a common occurrence in the real world) but we have recorded gender, age, race, and so on (known collectively as covariates) we can construct a control group that is matched on all of those covariates. Thus, the control group has the same age distribution as the treatment group, the same proportion of males and females, the same mixture of races, and so on. After matching, we assume that the treatment and control groups are so similar that the only difference between them is that one received the treatment and the other didn't. Such an assumption is more credible than nakedly saying "don't worry" but still leaves open the possibility that some variables that were uncollected or unthought-of not only are unbalanced, but in fact are one cause of the observed effect that we chalk up to the treatment.

An infamous example of this manifested itself in early studies on the effect of obesity on life expectancy. Obviously, there was no practical way to randomly assign some people to be obese and others slender before following them for many years to measure how long they lived. It had to be an observational study in which the two groups were matched on all the usual covariates. Surprisingly, it turned out that modest[15] obesity yielded little or no effect on life expectancy. Only later was it discovered that there was a confounding effect due to smoking, which was not among the matching variables. Smokers tended to be both slimmer than nonsmokers and have shorter life expectancy. By not adjusting for smoking, the life expectancy estimates had a bias against more slender people. Only when smokers were removed from the analyses did the negative effect of obesity manifest itself.

In the study of the seismic effects of fracking in Oklahoma, we used Oklahoma's past as a control. But as convincing as this was, it still left open the possibility that there was a general regional trend toward increased seismic activity. To answer this, the immediately adjacent state of Kansas was used to represent a control condition. We noted that the seismic activity in Kansas was the same as that in Oklahoma prior to the onset of widespread fracking (about 3 per year). As time went on, there was little fracking in Kansas, and the seismic activity there stayed the same while, at the same time, it exploded apace with fracking activity in Oklahoma. The use of two different kinds of controls, temporal and geographic, both provided supporting evidence in the assessment of the causal effect of fracking. Of course, the places where fracking took place were not randomly assigned, yet still the results are credible.

11.11.3 Convergence of Evidence

In any inference task our evidence is always incomplete, rarely conclusive, and often imprecise or vague; it comes from sources having variable credibility. As a result, conclusions reached from evidence having these attributes can only be probabilistic in nature.

David Schum, 1994, p. 1

---

[15] "Modest" as differentiated from "morbid" obesity, which had a profound effect on life expectancy.

11.11 What If We Can't Do an Experiment?

In view of the necessarily incompleteness of our evidence, a valuable path toward increasing the likelihood of the validity of our conclusions is through multiple different sources. If they are independent but all point in the same direction, we are reassured. One example of how this can work (described previously, in Section 11.3) was John Snow's search for the cause of cholera. His search began by plotting the location of all cholera deaths during the epidemic and noting their proximity to the Broad Street pump. But it didn't end there. He went to the homes of people who died that lived closer to another pump to ascertain what their drinking habits were. He found in one case that the dead man preferred the taste of the water from Broad Street and so went out of his way to retrieve his drinking water from there. There were very few cholera cases for workers at a local brewery almost adjacent to the Broad Street pump; Snow discovered that one of the benefits of working at the brewery was free access to the product. We now know that *Vibrio cholerae* does not prosper in alcoholic solutions. The conclusion being that there is a convergence of information that all pointed in the same direction, supporting the hypothesis that cholera is water borne and the center of the epidemic was the Broad Street pump. This confluence increases the credibility of our conclusions.

The conclusion of our study of the causal connection between fracking (and in particular, the reinjection of wastewater back into the earth near to where it had been extracted) is strengthened with newer data. Despite the gigantic increases in the number of magnitude 3+ earthquakes shown in Figure 11.7, which culminated in the more-than-daily earthquakes in 2014, representatives of the politically powerful gas and oil industry steadfastly denied any causal connection with their activities. So things continued to get worse. In 2015 there were more than two magnitude 3+ earthquakes a day in Oklahoma. Princeton Professor of Geosciences Alan Rubin writes

> *The oil and gas industry employ about 20 percent of workers in Oklahoma, so the state legislature refused to accept the (obvious, uncontroversial) USGS conclusion that the increase in earthquake rate in OK was due to increased deep wastewater injection. Until earthquakes damaged some homes in the suburb in which some of those legislators lived. So then they asked (by law they couldn't require) that the injection rates be reduced, and the earthquake rate went down with a lag of some months. The oil industry relented, but without conceding any culpability, and began to find other places to distribute at least some of the wastewater. The more of the wastewater that was disposed of elsewhere the greater the diminution of the number of earthquakes.*

This remarkable turnaround is shown in Figure 11.10 (which also contains updated estimates of the number of earthquakes in earlier years.

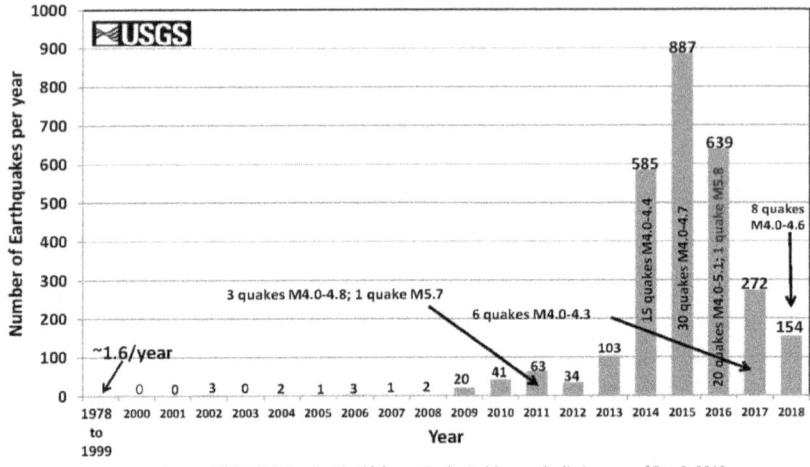

Figure 11.10 Oklahoma earthquakes magnitude 3.0+ over 40 years (1978–2018) (from the United States Geological Survey).

The overall decline in the frequency of earthquakes paired with the reduction of wastewater disposal provides compelling ancillary evidence in support of the causal connection between the two. A more detailed analysis shows that the decline of seismic activity was greatest in the areas where the wastewater disposal had ceased and was unchanged where the disposal practice remained the same. The connection between the two is made explicit in Figure 11.11 (figure 3 in Langenbruch & Zoback, 2016).

The evidence is primarily circumstantial, but as Thoreau pointed out more than a century earlier – sometimes circumstantial evidence can be like a trout in the milk.

11.12 Application to Social Science Research

The principal goal of this chapter is to argue for empiricism, above all else, as the arbiter of the validity of scientific claims. The balance of this book focuses on the role of testing. Over the past century evidence has been gathered on the efficacy of mental testing to improve the quality of selection in an amazingly broad range of applications including personnel selection and professional licensing.

Causal evidence to support claims in these critical applications spans many sources. Principal among these sources are randomized controlled experiments that allow us to estimate the size of the causal effect of the intervention with

11.12 Application to Social Science Research

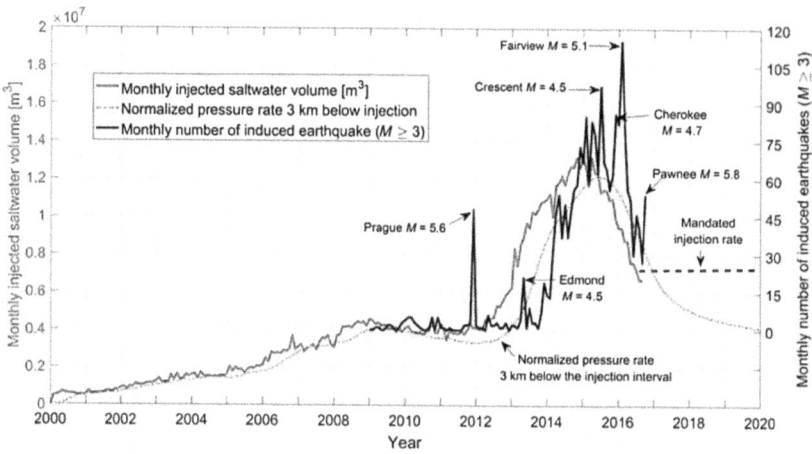

Figure 11.11 (Langenbruch & Zoback, 2016, figure 3). Combined monthly saltwater injection and induced earthquake rate in central and western Oklahoma.[16]

minimal assumptions. Although these experiments always start out as pure as the driven snow, the realities of the world often lead them to drift. In this chapter we have tried, through real-world examples, to show how this drift might occur and how they can be accommodated and still yield credible estimates of the size of the causal effect of the training.

But the sweetness of the elegance of randomized/controlled studies lingers on. The elegance and efficacy of randomized/control studies is so powerful and so attractive that the breadth of its use is sometimes shocking. One especially shocking use was a "sham surgery" experiment performed in 1959 by Dr. Leonard A. Cobb under the auspices of the National Institutes of Health. Twenty years earlier an Italian surgeon named Antonio Fieschi reported spectacular success in relieving angina with a surgical technique known as internal mammary artery ligation. But he had no control group and no random assignment. Cobb tested Fieschi's technique with a real experiment. Seventeen patients with angina were rolled into the operating room, anesthetized and their chests opened. The surgeon then opened an envelope, which randomly assigned them to either the experimental group (their arteries were ligated)

---

[16] Monthly saltwater injection (2000 to July 2016) and earthquake rate (2009 to September 2016). Earthquake rate changes follow changes of the injection rate with a time delay of several months. Aftershock sequences are visible in the monthly earthquake rates for the largest magnitudes. The dashed line shows the normalized pressure rate, which arrives delayed at a depth of 3 km below injection (the average depth of the earthquake hypocenters)

or the control (their incisions were closed). There was no difference in outcome in the two groups.

The employment of sham surgery has, since the beginning of the era of "informed consent" of experimental subjects, become ethically unthinkable[17] (Hubert & Wainer, 2013). Although everyone recognizes that true randomized controlled studies provide a powerful tool for estimating the size of causal effects, the ethical and practical limitations to its use require alternative approaches; fortunately, we now have alternatives that typically cost little or nothing in terms of their power or the validity of their conclusions. The extended examples of global warming and fracking that we discussed previously illustrate how convincing these approaches can be.

One factor that determines how rigorous the evidence-gathering schemes need to be is the size of the effect of the treatment. Treatments whose effects are "interocular" (they hit you between the eyes) require evidence gathering of only modest power to engender widespread belief. No one would require a rigorous control group in the testing of parachutes (although they would likely be needed to establish how much better a modified design is). Treatments whose effects are subtler require more powerful techniques to expose.

Often the evidentiary basis supporting a claim uses ancillary material. As is described in Chapter 6 some users of test scores for admission use graduation rates to demonstrate its efficacy. But validity is strengthened by ancillary information (e.g., school grades improve, or families report improved behavior).

So, while conclusive evidence is often impossible to obtain – in any area of scientific inquiry – we must make judgments with probabilistic reasoning, asking ourselves if the evidence we have is relevant, credible, and convergent. If it is, we can make intelligent inferences from it and, thus, informed decisions. But while evidence can help to cure ignorance, it is sometimes insufficient to dissuade "true believers." In Chapter 12 we describe three different ideas about testing that are still roaming the Earth despite evidence that ought to have slain them had they not had such fervent believers. The famed physicist Wolfgang Pauli upon observing this phenomenon deduced that "science advances one funeral at a time," echoing Einstein who pointed out that "old theories never die, just the people who believe them."

---

[17] The value of sham surgery as an efficacious placebo is still being debated. The obvious question is, "If phony operations can help people, why not do them?"

Chapter 12
Three Cautionary Tales of Zombie Ideas about Testing

That's one of those ideas that only makes sense if you say it fast.
Donald B. Rubin

12.1 Introduction

A zombie idea is policy or action that, despite having been slain with data long ago, still walks the Earth, continuing to influence people who are unaware of its earlier demise. Testing, as a field, seems to attract an especially resilient species of zombies, for numerous such zombies have refused to die. This chapter tells of three.

12.2 Coaching for the SAT

Our first zombie concerns the value of coaching in improving a candidate's score on a college admissions test (e.g., the SAT or ACT). In the past, extravagant claims about the efficacy of coaching for the SAT were made by coaching schools (Princeton Review guaranteed at least 150 points) and in the polemical booklet *The SAT Coaching Coverup* (Stockwell et al., 1991), it was claimed that expected gains were over 100 points. As we will discuss shortly, the weakness of such claims was exposed by extensive data collected and analyzed by the most reputable of scientific sources. But over the last decade or so arguments touting the value of coaching have been revivified:

> *We've had ... the growth of a tremendous testing and test prep industry in New York, which has been accompanied by a massive rise in inequality. It has produced a system in which the school is now admitting only three, four, five black and Latino students, and the students they are admitting are almost entirely affluent white kids*

> *with tutors or second-generation immigrants from Queens and other places where the parents pay for test prep. You end up with a system where who you are really letting in are the kids with access to test prep, the kids with access to resources.* (Blumgart, 2012).

It would be a surprise that any coaching program that involves spending time on both the subject of the test and on test-taking skills in general doesn't show some effect. What is crucial is the quantitative question, "how big is the effect?" Are such gains large enough to confer an overwhelming advantage to those who could afford such special programs? Or are they so minor that in the grand scheme of things in admissions decisions they would be overwhelmed by some other asset of an applicant (e.g., was recording secretary of the audio-visual club in high school or played the oboe in the school orchestra)?

Happily, a straightforward study can allow us to determine how much of an advantage is conferred by having taken such a course of coaching. Stated in more precise terms, we are interested in what is the size of the average causal effect of coaching on SAT/ACT score.

12.2.1 Measuring the Causal Effect of Coaching

There is a generally accepted method for measuring the size of causal effects (see, for example, Chapter 11 and Paul Holland's justly famous 1986 paper in the prestigious *Journal of the American Statistical Association*) – this method consists of five steps that we denote **Method I**.

1. Draw a sample of suitable individuals from the population of individuals about whom you want to make inferences. This sample should be as large as your budget allows. Have them all take the admissions test of interest (e.g., SAT or ACT). These are the pre-scores.
2. Randomly divide the sample into two equal groups, commonly denoted treatment (coaching) and control (no coaching) and calculate the average test score in each of the two groups. If the randomization worked properly, they should be statistically equal.
3. Provide coaching for the treatment group, do nothing for the control group.
4. Have them all retake the admissions test of interest. These are the post-scores.
5. Subtract the pre-scores from the post-scores for each group. These are the gain scores. The difference between the gain scores of the treatment group and the control group is the average causal effect of the treatment (coaching).

12.2 Coaching for the SAT

The structure of this experiment is neither revolutionary (its structure has become well established in the century since Fisher described it), nor complex (a two-group design with random assignment has been the gold standard of all medical research for decades). But Fisher (and Rubin and Holland more recently) have made it clear that it does require a control group. Happily, there have been a fair number of studies that have followed this format (see Messick et al., 1980 for citations) and one major meta-analysis (DerSimonian & Laird,1983).

Unsurprisingly, there have been an even larger number of other studies of the efficacy of coaching done (often by coaching schools themselves, but by other researchers as well) using a simple "before and after" design in which the heroic assumption of stasis was substituted for a control group. We shall denote the approach to estimating the causal effect of a treatment using "*After MINUS Before*" as **Method II.**

As an analogy, suppose we were to use Method II to study the efficacy of a height counselling service in which children were advised on the importance of height and were encouraged to grow taller. Suppose we studied the efficacy of this treatment by measuring the heights of a group of 5-year-old children, who were then subjected to monthly counselling for the subsequent 5 years. Then their heights were remeasured when they were 10 years old and the difference in their heights was attributed to the counselling they received.

Could this be one of those rapid ideas that Rubin was referring to in the initial quotation?

Studies that use Method II are the ones that have found the effect of coaching to be in the range of 100–120 points (on the 400–1600 SAT scale), although occasionally one turns up that reports gains as high as 220 points (Powers & Rock, 1999).

If the assumption of stasis that is crucial for the validity of Method II was found to be empirically true the estimates of both methods should be essentially the same – that is there should be no gains shown in Method I's control group (Powers & Rock, 1999).

But alas, this assumption is not true. Studies that use Method I typically find the same 100–120-point gains in the treatment group but also 80–100-point gains in the control group (Briggs, 2005; DerSimonian & Laird,1983).

Thus, the causal effect of coaching is estimated to be in the range of 10–20 points. This is similar to the conclusion of the Federal Trade Commission's investigation 45 years ago regarding claims by test prep companies that they could raise scores by 100 points. The FTC found that the average increase was only 25 points (Sullivan, 2009).

> *We didn't have a control because it was <u>only</u> an experiment.*
> *(anonymous educational researcher)*

12.2.2 So What's a Person to Do?

What's going on? It seems that examinees get a gain of 80–100 points just from practice taking the test – it is hypothesized that practice familiarizes the examinee with the character the test and how to time their efforts to match the time allocated for the exam. Moreover, taking a practice test is not expensive. Yes, a student could sign up and take the actual test twice (or even three or more times) but that isn't necessary. Instead a student could take one of the practice tests available for free on the College Board website (e.g., https://satsuite.collegeboard.org/practice/practice-tests), or go to the library and take a practice test contained in any one of several books that provide copies of previously used SATs; for example,

> *10 Practice Tests for the SAT, 2023: Extra Prep to Help Achieve an Excellent Score*
> Or
> *10 SATs: Plus Advice from the College Board on How to Prepare for Them.*

Research has shown (Messick & Jungeblut, 1981) that simply sitting down at home and taking a practice test under standard test conditions (including timing) yields the same gain as actually taking the test multiple times.

Having established that the gains due to expensive coaching (over just taking a free practice test) are only 10–20 points we must now ask is such a modest gain still putting those who do not opt for (or cannot afford) coaching at a significant disadvantage? Derek Briggs (2009), who has studied the fairness issues of coaching for many years writes that "I changed my mind about the effects of coaching not being practically significant. At highly competitive schools with a restricted range of scores among applicants, a 10 to 20-point difference could make a difference to a person's chances of admissions."

We can certainly imagine the possibility of two candidates for admission who are so closely matched on all criteria that instead of just choosing between them at random an admissions committee would seize on a very small difference in their SAT scores (10–20 points) to tip the scales. And, in doing so the committee would be giving an advantage (albeit a small one) to candidates whose family circumstances gave them access to coaching. Yet, it would seem hypocritical for an institution that claims that it wants to diminish (nowadays to the point of elimination) those admission measures (e.g., test scores) that give any advantage to candidates based not on their abilities, but instead on their family circumstances, and yet to adopt policies that give huge advantages to those same students. Let us end this zombie example with a discussion of one such policy.

12.2.3 Cherry-picking Scores to Be Submitted

The genesis of this problem began more than two decades ago during a visit to a well-known, highly competitive institution in Cambridge, Massachusetts. During a campus tour we were told by someone from the admissions office that the previous year they had ~1,500 applicants with perfect 800 math/800 verbal SAT scores. This was about the same as the total number of students in their freshman class and so if they accepted them all it would leave little or no room for applicants who played the cello or who were all-American swimmers or those applicants whose surnames were on the new Science Center). Hence, if this claim was correct, a substantial number of 800/800 applicants would be rejected.

After the tour we discussed the claim she made that they had ~1,500 applicants with perfect (800/800) SAT scores. We pointed out to her that in that same year there had been only 396 high school seniors in the U.S. who had 800/800 scores and that the previous year there were 473 HS juniors who had perfect scores – so, assuming that they all applied the maximum could only be 869. So how did she get 1,500? She explained that students could submit scores piecewise – a math score taken in March and a verbal score from last June (this policy now bears the euphonious appellation of "Superscoring"). At the time we didn't have any relevant figures at our fingertips, but it seemed plausible with such a policy they would be able to piece together a much larger number of 800/800 of submissions. The irony was that she had prefaced her earlier remarks with the complaint that "the SAT didn't have enough top for their purposes."

The issue is this – it is clear that if a candidate is allowed to cherry-pick the scores that are to be sent to a particular school those who have taken the test more often (at $60 a pop) would have a greater choice and thus an opportunity to capitalize on chance and so be able to send in higher scores than someone of equal (or maybe even greater) ability who, for whatever reason, opted to only take the test once. The question is how much does a person's SAT score improve as the number of times the person has taken the test increases? And how does this advantage compare to the 10–20-point advantage that accrued from coaching?

We investigated two situations. The first was assuming that an applicant simply takes and retakes the SAT some number of times but does not learn

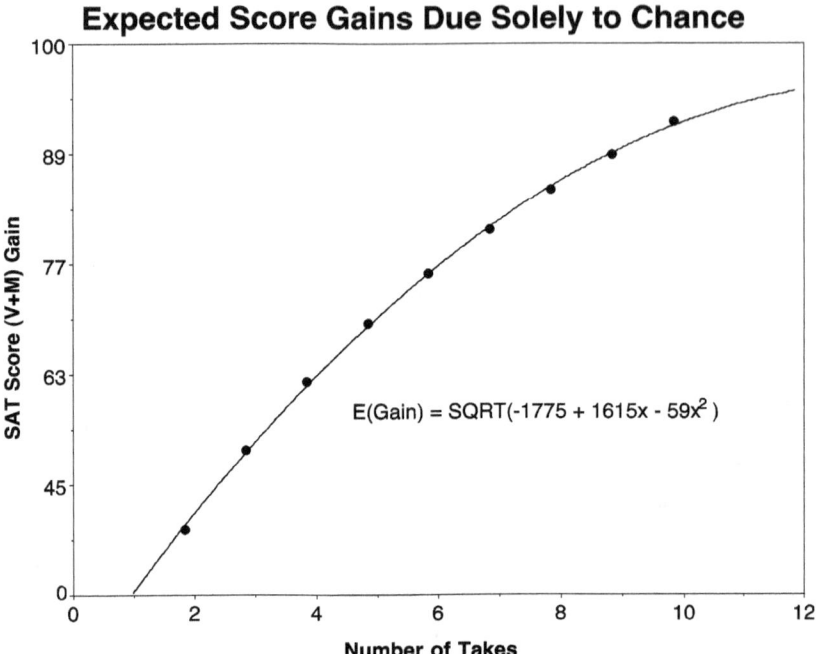

Figure 12.1 Expected gain in the total SAT (V+M) reported if the examinee is able to report only the maximum score for each (V and M) from among *n* takes of the exam.

anything in between. Thus, any advantage gained from being able to cherry pick which scores to report is based solely on the vagaries of chance. Which is what we focus on here. If we posit that there is some change in the examinee's ability (the second situation), then there will be additional gains attributable to the examinee's ability to pick and choose what will be reported.[1]

What we found is shown in Figure 12.1, where we see that the effects of a superscoring policy allowing students to choose which scores are reported yields gains that quickly dwarf the 10–20-point marginal gain due to coaching. Clearly, any schools who are concerned about the excess influence of family wealth can easily shrink it by changing their policy and insisting that all scores must come from the same administration. It does not eliminate the advantage of taking the test multiple times, but it does reduce it.

---

[1] We examined the situation of just one repeat with improvement and found for one test section that with an expected improvement of 30, the expected gain by reporting the best of two is 40; for a 15-point learning gain final total gain is 25; and for a learning effect of 10, the expected gain is 23. We must add that no really clean estimate of what a plausible learning effect might be exists (Wainer et al., 2024).

Also note the closed-form equation shown in Figure 12.1, which will allow anyone to immediately calculate how much of an advantage we can expect by allowing a person to retake the exam any specific number of times.

The assumption of *no improvement in ability between test administrations* that was key to generating the curve shown in Figure 12.1 is conservative in that we would expect the curve's slope to be much steeper if we added the gains due to improved ability with those of the capitalization on chance. Keeping that in mind note that taking the SAT ten times (at $60 each) would cost $600, which pales in comparison the $100/hour commonly charged for coaching[2] and is likely to yield score gains of about 90 points.

Research results from a variety of neutral parties (e.g., Harvard's Nan Laird and the Federal Trade Commission, to pick two) drove an empirical stake through the heart of excessive claims from test coaching schools more than 40 years ago. Yet here we are, and the zombie of "coaching advantage" is still walking the Earth. We hope the reminder of those old results and more recent replications of them combined with the greater gains available by taking advantage of the dopey policy of superscoring will inter "the coaching advantage" for good. But alas, experience suggests that we ought not be sanguine.

12.3 Strivers and its Kin

Twenty-five years ago, "Strivers" emerged from a swamp of bad ideas and stalked the Earth. In the August 31, 1999, issue of the *Wall Street Journal* an article appeared about a research project done under the auspices of the Educational Testing Service called "Strivers." The goal of Strivers was to aid colleges in identifying applicants (usually minority applicants) who have a better chance of succeeding in college than their test scores and high school grades might otherwise suggest. The basic idea was to predict a student's SAT score from a set of background variables (e.g., ethnicity, SES, mother's education, etc.) and identify students who score much higher than their predicted value. These students, designated as Strivers, might then become special targets for college admission officers. In the newspaper interview, the project's director, Anthony Carnevale, said, "When you look at a Striver who gets a score of 1000, you're looking at someone who really performs at 1200."

---

[2] Kaplan charges $799 for an online or Bootcamp course; $1,999 for tutoring + online course; and $1,999 for unlimited prep (https://www.kaptest.com/sat). There is an analysis of score choice from an econometric perspective that does note the advantage of score choice but does not exploit psychometrics (Goodman et al., 2020).

12. Three Cautionary Tales of Zombie Ideas about Testing

Harvard emeritus professor Nathan Glazer, in an article on Strivers in the September 27, 1999, *New Republic*, indicated that he shared this point of view when he said (p. 28), "It stands to reason that a student from a materially and educationally impoverished environment who does fairly well on the SAT and better than other students who come from a similar environment is probably stronger than the unadjusted score indicates."

This idea suddenly gained strength from the prevailing romantic *zeitgeist*:

> *Surely everyone can agree, as one college official told the Journal, 'A 1200 SAT score from a student in Beverly Hills means something totally different than a 1200 from a student in a school in South Central Los Angeles.' The data have long shown that SAT scores are predicted, lockstep, by parents' income; that at each $10,000 incremental increase in family income, average SAT scores rise.* <u>When kids score well despite numerous economic obstacles, they are likely to perform much better in the long run than their raw scores suggest.</u>
>
> Kahlenberg, R.D. (1999)

As we will elaborate shortly, the predicted Strivers outcome does not match what would be predicted from statistical theory nor what was actually observed empirically. We expected that the union of both theory and scientific data would drive a stake through the heart of this claim, dispatching it forever. Silly naïve us, for 20 years later, the Striver idea was reanimated in zombie form in 2019, when Cynthia Weissblum, President and CEO of the Edwin Gould Foundation, called for highly selective schools to accept more Strivers.

> *It is up to elite colleges and universities to open the doors and admit these deserving students in greater numbers. They are knocking at the front door prepared, voracious and ready to succeed. Wake up and let them in, let a true meritocracy reign.*
>
> (Weissblum, 2019)

Weissblum was not alone in her effort to breathe life once again into the Striver corpse. William R. Fitzsimmons, Dean of Admissions at Harvard University, also contributed to the zombie awakening: "Rewarding Strivers presents provocative research and analysis that provides a blueprint for the way forward."[3]

As with most bad ideas that seem immune to common sense and are quickly embraced, we once again must return to Donald B. Rubin's wise epigram:

> *This is another of those ideas that only make sense if you say it fast.*

To craft a better stake to be driven into the heart of this modern zombie, it is best if we begin at the beginning.

---

[3] https://www.semanticscholar.org/paper/Rewarding-strivers-%3A-helping-low-income-students-in-Kahlenberg/79405cfbaa6302ae98cd3bf4bad3d0781375bd77

12.3.1 Some Theory and Some History

A frequently observed phenomenon is that when we obtain a relatively extreme result in a random sample from a population the next sample would very likely be less extreme – the sampling process regresses inward. In 1889, Francis Galton pointed out that this always occurred whenever measurements were taken with imperfect precision and was what he called "regression toward the mean."

What does 'regression to the mean' mean? To answer this, we must go a little out of the way to come back a short distance correctly. Bear with us.

Suppose you are asked to predict how tall some unborn and unnamed American child will be at adulthood. Other than knowing that they will be born and raised in the U.S. you have no knowledge and so the best you can do is to predict that it will be of average stature, which in the U.S. is 66.5". Predicting the average (or mean) minimizes the expected error.[4] But if you were then to learn that the child would be male you could improve your estimate by predicting the mean adult height for men: 69". You can continue to improve your estimate as you accumulate more information; for example, if the parents were both taller than average you would increase your predicted height for their unborn son a bit. How much of an increase depends directly, but not completely, on how closely related parents' heights are to their children's heights. So when we have a lot of relevant information our predictions can be dragged away from the maximal ignorance estimate of the overall mean, but if we were to lose some of that information, our best guess will regress back toward the mean – the extent of that regression back depends on how valuable was the information that we have given up. Because the connection between parent's and children's heights is not perfect, we will find that tall parents will have tall children, but, on average, not as tall as they are. In parallel, short parents will have short children, but not as short as they are. It is the imperfection of the relationship between predictor and outcome that yields the shrinkage of those predictions toward the mean.

Thus, we always find that with imperfect prediction the variability of the predictions will be less than the variability of the actual data – the predicted heights will vary less than the true heights turn out to be because the predictions have all been regressed inward toward the mean, and the extent of that regression is exactly parallel to the imprecision of the information used to make the prediction.

---

[4] Actually, the expected squared error, but no need to be persnickety here.

Although regression has been well understood by mathematical statisticians for more than a century, the terminology among appliers of statistical methods suggests that they either thought of it as a description of a statistical method or as only applying to biological processes. In 1924, Frederick C. Mills, an economic statistician, wrote that "the original meaning has no significance in most of its applications" (p. 394).

Famed Chicago statistician Stephen Stigler (1997, p. 12) pointed out that this was "a trap waiting for the unwary, who were legion." The trap has been sprung many times. One spectacular instance of a statistician getting caught was

> in 1933, when a Northwestern University professor named Horace Secrist unwittingly wrote a whole book on the subject, The Triumph of Mediocrity in Business. In over 200 charts and tables, Secrist 'demonstrated' what he took to be an important economic phenomenon, one that likely lay at the root of The Great Depression: a tendency for firms to grow more mediocre over time.

Secrist showed that the firms with the highest earnings a decade earlier were currently performing only a little better than average; moreover, a collection of the more poorly performing firms had improved to only slightly below average. These results formed the evidence supporting the title of the book. Harold Hotelling, in a devastating review published the same year, pointed out that the seeming convergence Secrist obtained was a "statistical fallacy, resulting from the method of grouping." He concluded that Secrist's results "prove nothing more than that the ratios in question have a tendency to wander about."

It is remarkable, especially considering how old and well-known regression effects are, how often these effects are mistaken for something substantive. Although Secrist himself was a professor of statistics, Willford I. King, who, in 1934 wrote a glowing review of Secrist's book, was president of the American Statistical Association! This error was repeated in 1985 by W.E. Sharpe, a Nobel laureate in economics (p, 430) who ascribed the same regression effect Secrist described to economic forces. His explanation of the convergence, between 1966 and 1980, of the most profitable and least profitable companies was that "ultimately economic forces will force the convergence of profitability and growth rates of different firms." The explanation is statistical, not economic. Apparently, this led Milton Friedman (in 1992), yet another Nobel laureate in economics, to try to set his colleagues straight.

12.3.2 Kelley's Paradox

In 1927, Truman Kelley described a specific instance of a regression formula of great importance in many fields, although it was proposed for use in

12.3 Strivers and its Kin

educational testing. It shows how you can estimate an examinee's true score from their observed score on a test. "True score" is psychometric shorthand for the mean of the distribution of observed scores that someone would get if parallel forms of the same test were repeated infinitely. Kelley's equation relates the estimated true score ($\hat{\tau}$) to the observed score (x), It tells us that the best estimate is obtained by regressing the observed score in the direction of the mean score (μ) of the group that the examinee came from. The amount of the regression is determined by the reliability (ρ) of the test. Kelley's equation is:

$$\hat{\tau} = \rho x + (1 - \rho)\mu$$

Note how Kelley's equation works. If a test is completely unreliable ($\rho = 0$), as would be the case if each examinee's score was just a random number, the observed score would not count at all and the estimated true score is merely the group mean. If the test scores were perfectly reliable, ($\rho = 1$), there would be no regression effect at all, and the true score would be the same as the observed score. The reliability of virtually all tests lies between these two extremes, so the estimated true score will be somewhere between the observed score and the group's mean.

Intuition about how Kelley's equation works when there are multiple groups is aided by a diagram. Figure 12.2 shows the distributions of scores

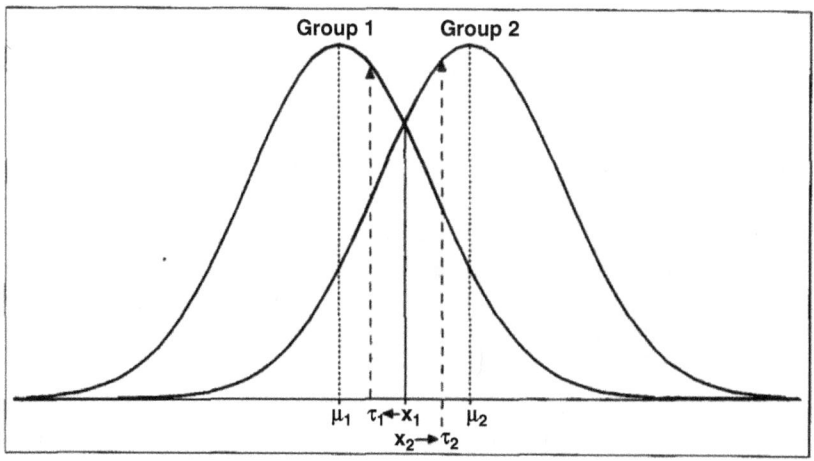

Figure 12.2 A graphical depiction of Kelley's equation for two groups. The two distributions and their means are shown. How the true scores are regressed when two identical observed scores come from each of the two different score distributions is also indicated.

for two groups of individuals, here called Group 1 (lower scoring group) and Group 2 (higher scoring group). If we observed a score x midway between the means of the two groups, the best estimate of the true score of the individual who generated that score depends on which group that person belonged to. If that person came from Group 1, we should regress the score downward. If from Group 2, we should regress it upward. The regression effect is because we know that there is some error in the score. The average error is considered to be 0, so some errors will be positive and some negative. Thus, if someone from a low-scoring group has a high score we can believe that to some extent that person is the recipient of some positive error that is not likely to reappear on retesting, so we regress their score downward. Similarly, if someone from a high-scoring group has an unusually low score, we regress that score upward.

So far this is merely an equation. What is the paradox? Webster defines a paradox as a statement that is opposed to common sense and yet is true. So long as Kelley's equation deals solely with abstract groups named 1 and 2, no paradox emerges. But suppose we call Group 1 the "Low SES Group" and Group 2 the "High SES Group." Now when we see someone from Group 1 with a high score, despite their coming from an environment of intellectual and material deprivation, we suspect that they must be very talented indeed and their true ability ought to be considered somewhat higher. Similarly, someone who comes from a more privileged background but who scores low leads us to suspect a real lack of talent and hence ought to be rated lower still.

12.3.3 Conclusions

Do people truly make this sort of mistake? We began this second zombie example with a description of Strivers and the public reception that greeted it. But now that we have in hand a little of the regression machinery needed to examine the claims made by advocates of Strivers, we must conclude that neither Mr. Carnevale nor Mr. Glazer were correct. When you look at a Striver who gets a score of 1,000, you're probably looking at someone who really performs at 950. And, alas, a Striver is probably weaker than the unadjusted score indicates.

O'Neill (2003) confirmed this theoretical prediction empirically when she assessed the first-year academic performance of both Strivers (students whose SAT score was in the top 5 percent according to their expected score, given demographic variables) and another category she created called Underachievers (those whose score was in the bottom 5 percent of what would be expected. She found that Strivers were more likely to leave college than non-Strivers with the same SAT score and that Underachievers were more likely to stay in school than matched non-underachievers.

The results reported by O'Neill are accurately described by Kelley's equation. The Strivers' SAT scores were likely higher than their SAT true score, whereas the Underachievers experienced the opposite – their SAT scores were likely lower than their SAT true scores. Thus, the fact that Strivers are less likely to stay in school is not surprising. At the same time, students from the upper distribution who scored lower than expected on the SAT are at a smaller risk of dropping out at least partially because they are likely to score higher on the SAT if they were to take it again, and hence our estimate of their future performance is higher than their initial score would've indicated; exactly the opposite of what proponents of Strivers have contended.

In this example, we tried to follow Rubin's advice and say things more slowly in the hopes that we finally put a stake in the heart of the bad idea that Ms. Weissblum, Ms. Kahlenberg, and others have chosen to revivify. Unfortunately, Einstein's observation about the life span of bad ideas ("Old theories never die, just the people who believe them") doesn't breed optimism.[5]

12.4 The Test-Optional Zombie

For fools rush in where angels fear to tread.

Alexander Pope (1711)

In 1969, Bowdoin College, a small, selective liberal arts college in Maine became the first college to adopt a test-optional admissions policy. Such a policy simply means that applicants can choose whether to submit their test scores or not. For the applicant a test-optional seems like a good idea.[6] Why submit a test score if you don't think it will help your chances for admission? If you have a poor test score, don't submit it. If you have a good test score, then by all means, send it in. But what effect does this policy have on the quality of the admissions decisions?

In 1969, because this was a new policy, virtually all of Bowdoin's applicants took the SAT. For even if they did not intend to submit their scores to Bowdoin, they would likely need to submit them to any other school to which

---

[5] This was further amplified in 1950 by Max Planck who declared "science advances one funeral at a time." He went to elaborate that "a new scientific truth does not triumph by convincing its opponents and making them see the light, but rather because its opponents die, and a new generation grows up that is familiar with it."

[6] But, as it turns out, only if you say it fast.

they might apply. This meant that it was possible, through a special data gathering effort at the ETS, to obtain the SAT scores for all applicants to Bowdoin – for both those that chose to submit and those who chose not to. This rare trove of data allowed us (Wainer, 2011) to compare the performance of those two groups of students who matriculated at Bowdoin on both the SAT and their subsequent grades at Bowdoin. What we found was that the applicants, on average, behaved sensibly, for the 72 percent who had submitted their SAT scores scored about a standard deviation higher than those who withheld their scores. Moreover, freshman college grades at Bowdoin were accurately predicted by SAT scores, with the lower-scoring SAT withholders averaging a fifth of a grade point lower than those who submitted them. Given this evidence, why would an admissions committee, whose principal goal was to construct a class that would have its best chance of success at Bowdoin, purposely choose to ignore information that would be helpful? Although this was a small study at a single school, the evidence was certainly strong enough to encourage other researchers to repeat the Bowdoin study at other schools. But they didn't. Why not? Perhaps because the study would have been too hard to do, or perhaps because its results, which matched both professional and lay expectations, conflicted with a policy that was desired for other reasons than bolstering the efficacy of admissions decisions.

Had this information been made public and replicated, these results might have constituted sufficient evidence to slay the test optional idea. Unfortunately, it took 40 years (Wainer, 2011) for anyone outside Bowdoin or ETS to know of the findings. In the absence of, and even in the presence of, evidence, popular opinion can still rule the day. In this case, issues of fairness fanned the test optional flames. A common public opinion is that admission test scores such as the SAT and ACT serve as a barrier for underrepresented minorities, keeping them out of prestigious colleges. Thus, giving applicants the option of whether to submit test scores removes this barrier. Or does it?

This popular opinion, absent evidence, likely influenced other colleges to implement similar test optional policies, albeit very slowly, with a total of only 280 colleges doing so by 2000. The test optional movement gradually picked up steam during the next two decades, despite the publication of the Wainer (2011) study, and over a thousand colleges adopted it by 2019 (fairtest.org/test-optional). In 2008 even the National Association of College Admission Counseling recommended that colleges adopt a test-optional policy.

The trickle of schools that adopted this policy turned into a raging river in 2020, with changes in testing, education, and general behavior forced upon us by the requirements of dealing with the COVID epidemic. Across the country, the test optional policy, which should have been long dead and buried, pushed its way from beneath the soil and lurched across the landscape, as many colleges and universities reconsidered their admissions policies concerning ACT/SAT scores. By 2022–2023, only 43 percent of applicants included entrance exam scores, compared to 75 percent in 2019–2020 (Bauer-Wolf, 2023). The number of high school students in the U.S. who took the ACT or SAT was down considerably from before the pandemic. In California, about 273,000 students took the SAT in 2019. In 2022, there were only 102,000. By 2024, there were over 1,800 colleges that were officially test optional.

Thus, the test-optional zombie not only came back to life, but for the first few years, it appeared that it would thrive due to three immediate, and positively viewed, results. First, there was a record number of applications, including those from minorities, to selective universities (Jaschik, 2023). Second, there was an increase in most institutions' average SAT/ACT scores as the applicants who chose to submit them scored higher than those who did not – similar to what was found in the Wainer (2011) study. And third, an increase in applications resulted in lower acceptance rates for the elite colleges who have limited space. UCLA now admits only 9 percent – down from 21 percent in 2010. Having a lower acceptance rate and higher average test scores meant higher rankings among colleges and universities in *U.S. News and World Report*.

But it did not take long to discover that these impressive numbers were accompanied by an increase in the rejection of minority applicants. Institutions can also get higher rankings by having higher graduation rates. But with test-optional policies, it is less clear that admitted students who do not submit test scores will graduate given that important predictive information (test scores) is missing. Thus, the *U.S. News'* ranking algorithms have yielded a disincentive for admitting minority students and more colleges are withdrawing from the rankings (Diep, 2023).

For Akil Bello, senior director of advocacy at FairTest and a longtime rankings critic, bowing out of *U.S. News* is a start toward correcting the overwhelming income imbalances among who attends America's "top" colleges. "It's a positive first step," he said. But by itself, it's not enough. He emphasized that real transformation could come only from changing admissions policies so more low- and middle-income and other historically underrepresented students get in.

But does having a test-optional policy really benefit low-income students (i.e., can the zombie stay sentient)? Recently, a few highly selective universities (e.g., Harvard, Yale, Dartmouth, NYU, Johns Hopkins, Cal Tech, and MIT) reversed their test-optional policies introduced during the pandemic. Why the sudden reversal from test-optional? Evidence, often absent or ignored, resurfaced. Another unique data-gathering effort, this time through the Academic Research Committee – an organization involving over fifty colleges and the College Board – permitted participating colleges to ascertain the SAT scores of applicants who had not submitted them as part of the test-optional policy. These data revealed similar findings to the 50-year-old Bowdoin study. Not surprisingly, students who did not submit test scores scored lower than students who did. More importantly, test scores still predicted success in college better than high school grades.

Admission officials from Dartmouth and Yale said that they were more likely to take a chance on non-White, low-income applicants if they included a test score. Further, there is some evidence to indicate that having a test-optional policy discourages some minority students who tested well enough to be admitted from submitting their scores. Abandoning entrance exams has had the opposite effect that was intended. Rather than increasing the numbers of diverse students that could succeed in college, going test-optional lowered the numbers of college-ready underrepresented candidates admitted (https://home.dartmouth.edu/sites/home/files/2024-02/sat-undergrad-admissions.pdf).

This predictive power of test scores over other metrics influenced UT Austin to reverse their test-optional policy and begin requiring applicants to submit scores for the 2025–2026 school year. UT Austin officials said their decision was simply based on evidence. In 2023–2024, 73,000 high school students applied. Most applicants took the SAT regardless of whether they planned to submit the scores. Again, similar to the Bowdoin findings 55 years earlier, UT Austin found that of the 42 percent who included test scores as part of their application, their median SAT score (V+M) was 1,420. The remaining applicants who chose not to submit scores had a median SAT score of 1,160. The admitted students who included test scores had first-semester GPA that was about a letter grade higher than those who were admitted without test scores (McArdle, 2024). Another stake in the heart of the "test-optional" zombie.

UT Austin had already employed an admissions policy designed to enroll a diverse student body. Public high school students in the state of Texas who graduate in the top 6 percent of their class are offered automatic admission. But this policy does not ensure that all admitted students are ready to succeed at the selective school. For example, some students might rank near the top of their class but also score low on the ACT or SAT. Simply placing such students in the highly competitive engineering program has proven to be a bad idea. Knowing their test scores allows the university to provide wiser counsel on choosing which programs and courses are most suitable to increasing the likelihood of their graduation in four years. UT Austin said that having an applicant's test scores provides vital information for these decisions, and more importantly, for identifying which and how many admitted students would likely be needing extra help.

This use of test scores serves a similar purpose at colleges with open enrollment admission policies – like many community colleges and some for-profits like the University of Phoenix. Even though almost all applicants are accepted, college advisors can use the test scores to decide on a curriculum that best serves the applicant. Someone with a low SAT math score would not be well advised to pursue a career that is math heavy (e.g., accounting, etc.). Is the zombie yet slain? Unfortunately, we conclude with yet one more example of zombie revival.

Despite the wooden stakes of evidence and in direct contrast to other highly selective universities like Yale, Dartmouth, MIT, NYU, and UT Austin, the University of Michigan recently formally adopted a test-optional policy after relying on other admission metrics during the pandemic. This move is even more surprising given the history of admission testing in the state. In 2007, Michigan began requiring all high school juniors to take the ACT. Prior to this policy, only 54 percent of the state's high school students took a college entrance exam (and only 35 percent of women) (Dynarski, 2018). As a result of the new policy, for every 1,000 low-income students who took the test before 2007, another 480 were discovered by the test (Hyman, 2017). More low-income students attended and graduated from 4-year colleges. Given these data, why would the University of Michigan go test-optional and risk having some low-income students not submit scores that would otherwise be good enough to get admitted? Michael Bastedo, an education professor at Michigan, said that among the reasons why the university came to their decision was that the test-optional policy had proved to be very popular with students and families (Knox, 2024). Perhaps colleges need to base decisions on evidence rather than on misinformation and popularity contests whose principal outcome is likely to be keeping zombies roaming the Earth among us.

A little ignorance may be a dangerous thing.

after Alexander Pope (1711)

Chapter 13
Coda

To count is modern practice, the ancient method was to guess
                                            Samuel Johnson[1]

13.1 Introduction

At a 1935 London dinner party Winston Churchill told the hostess," Madam, take away this pudding, it has no theme." To prevent this same concern to manifest itself here it seems wise for us to reiterate the theme (or more properly, themes) while there is still time, and then review how the various aspects of our presentation support those themes.

This book has focused on the issues surrounding the efficient utilization of human resources in all of its many aspects. These include, for example, selecting people in a climate of limited physical resources, as occurs when admissions committees try to fill the slots in the freshman class of highly competitive universities. They also occur when employers try to choose among all job candidates those who are most likely to satisfy the requirements of both the job at hand and more complex jobs that are likely to arise in the future. Or they are used to protect the public by screening applicants for licensing candidates for impactful professions like pilots, physicians, or teachers. The history of testing, summarized in Chapter 1, stretched over thousands of years from the employment testing pioneered in Xia dynasty China and evolved into a more modern form in the civil service testing during the British Raj (1858–1947) in India. The mortal threats faced by the U.S. military during World War I awakened leadership to the need for the more efficient use of

---

[1] He was paraphrasing Seneca (*Epistulae* 88.27) – "*Magnum esse solem philosophus probabit, quantus sit mathematicus*".

manpower to improve national defense. They utilized a large-scale testing program and were remarkably successful. A key innovation of this program was shifting the test away from measuring specific skills and instead measuring what has turned out to be a surprisingly general underlying trait – Intelligence. The pathways of testing in the U.S. military were recounted in greater detail in Chapter 3.

After its successes in helping with issues of selection encountered in various civil services and militaries, testing's use exploded, evaluating students' proficiencies in grades k-12 (Chapter 4), in licensing (Chapter 5), in educational admissions (Chapter 6), and for use in awarding scholarships (Chapter 7).

But problems emerged when tests were used in situations for which they were not designed and were too often ill-suited. Changes in student scores during the course of a school year tempted administrators to use those changes as a measure of teacher effectiveness. This ill-fated application is discussed in Chapter 8. And, when a single score, based on the entire test, proved to be broadly useful, breaking up that score into its component pieces was, unfortunately, irresistible. In Chapter 9 we provide a brief discussion of the perils and pitfalls in the use of subscores.

As tests' use broadened, the accumulating data associated with their use provided illumination of the vast darkness of our ignorance that was associated with the many arcane aspects of this complex field. One key area of crucial importance is the cost of not testing. When we make decisions based on test scores how much better are those decisions than what we would have done without them? In Chapter 10 we explored this issue in greater depth.

Throughout these discussions our overall thrust has leaned heavily on the great epistemological theme of empiricism – specifically how all claims should be based on observable evidence. In Chapter 11 of this account we have traced how this one method of gathering evidence to understand the world grew in fits and starts from Aristotle to Roger Bacon to David Hume to Richard Feynman. Empirical evidence has formed the basis of the modern world and its most basic characteristic is that it must be observable. But the story of evidence is just the beginning of the tale told in Chapter 11 – it also lays out how evidence can be used to make causal inferences. Most specifically, it describes how we can use evidence to measure the size of a causal effect. In the end, the most important use of tests is to make causal inferences. Remember how issues of causality dominated the validity of the value-added models discussed in Chapter 8. When we say that after a school adopted a policy that preferred admitting applicants who scored high on an entrance exam and that the subsequent graduation rates improved, implicit is the causal inference that their graduation rates went up *because* they had higher scores. The implication of a causal link between graduation rates and test scores is not a given. If instead of graduation rates we measured the student's heights at graduation, the inference of greater stature *because* of their higher test scores would not be especially credible.

All arguments supporting the efficacy of testing rely on a mixture of a modest amount of reasoning and a large helping of data-based evidence. But this is not unique to the study of testing and applies broadly almost everywhere. This was pointed out famously on June 25, 1891 when Sherlock Holmes expounded on this general issue explaining that he had no theory yet because,

> *I have no data. It is a capital mistake to theorize before one has data.*
> *Insensibly one begins to twist facts to suit theories,*
> *instead of theories to suit facts.*

Alas, not all modern investigators are as wise and careful as the master.

13.2 When there is a Conflict Between Facts and Values

In Chapter 2 we made the unsurprising observation that tests are often disliked by those who don't do well on them. This animus is for at least two reasons:

1. The examinee's score was insufficient to get the job or be admitted to the desired school or get the scholarship or be licensed for the profession.
2. The score made the examinee feel bad/inadequate, even if it was unrelated to any specific consequence.

For as long as tests have been widely used collectors of test data have seen that there were group differences in performance. Sometimes there were sex differences in which women did better than men on tests of verbal skills, while men did better on more mathematical skills (spatial visualizing became an especially intriguing ability after strong evidence emerged of it being a sex-linked genetic trait (Bock & Kolakowski, 1973)). There is also undeniable evidence of a strong link between children's test performance and their families' wealth. It is not hard to construct a credible causal chain connecting wealth, and hence better schools and more resources within the home, with stronger test performance.

As test use expanded, spanning both school and work, the consequences for students who did not do as well, quickly went beyond feeling bad about it to having profound consequences on their ability to make a living. And, because

13.2 When there is a Conflict Between Facts and Values 179

there has long been an intimate connection between race and income, a *zeitgeist* began to emerge that testing (and, indeed, any system that stratifies the population based on race or sex or any other characteristic that is not under the control of the examinee) was unfair.

The question that naturally arose at this point was how could we ameliorate this unfairness? One obvious pathway to answering this question involves causal inference: finding the cause of the unequal performance on tests and fixing it. But, as we illustrated in Chapter 11, finding the cause of an effect is a task of insuperable difficulty. Was the poorer performance of students caused by poorer schools? Or were the poorly performing schools simply those that were unfortunate in the make-up of their student bodies? Chapter 4 discusses the decades-long parade of programs to improve schools. More than 50 years ago there were many court decisions (e.g., *Serrano vs. Priest, McInnis vs. Ogilvie , Rodriguez vs. San Antonio*) that declared that funding schools based on local property taxes was a denial of equal protection, for poorer districts had fewer taxable assets per pupil than wealthier districts (often by a factor of more than two to one) and simultaneously had greater educational needs (see Wise, 1968). And while there were some gains made in the academic performance of children from needier districts the gaps remained stubbornly large (Wainer, 2012). This is illustrated in Figure 13.1 which displays performance of fourth-graders on a standardized test of mathematics from the National Assessment of Educational Progress over a 20-year period for each state. Each dot represents a single state for the year indicated. We have emphasized one state (New Jersey) to provide a clear view of the pattern of gains. We see that fourth-grade Black students lagged behind White students in their performance in 1992. But in 2011, 19 years later, the Black students' performance had caught up to the level at which White students had been performing in 1992. Good news by any measure. But White students had not been sitting on their laurels, and they too had improved. Although the Black students' performance in math still lagged behind that of Whites, the gap had diminished.

NAEP results on other subjects and for other age groups showed gains similar to these; but despite this clear indication of progress many advocates were impatient. They wanted a rapid solution to this problem that most agree had been caused by centuries of neglect. One ill-considered proposed solution to unequal test scores was to shoot the messenger – get rid of the tests.

Let us consider these two proposed 'solutions': one involves the slow, difficult and expensive pathway of improving the lives of all children and thence, as a side benefit, improving their performance on both the tests and the

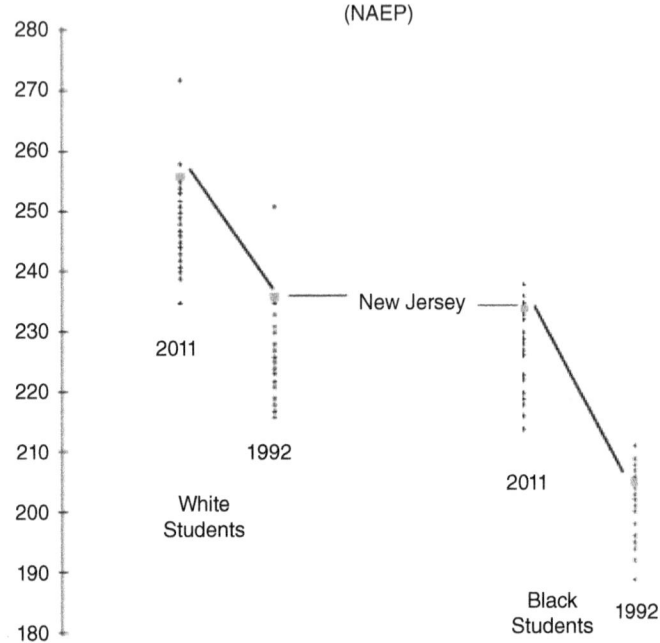

Figure 13.1 Average fourth-grade mathematics scores for each state on the National Assessment of Educational Progress (NAEP).

activities the tests are being used to screen for. The second, cut to the quick, and stop using tests (and, indeed any other measures which show any differences among groups) that generate information predictive of future behavior and substitute instead the assumption that everyone is equal.

If we gather suitable data, we can measure the benefits (predictive validity) of using test scores, or any other measures. So, for example, we can determine subsequent college graduation rates if we screen prospective students with a suitable test, as well as what would be those rates without such screening. This could be done with a designed experiment (e.g., admit half a class using test scores and admit the other half ignoring those scores entirely and see what happens), or with an observational study in which, for whatever reason, test scores were not used and compare graduation rates with an earlier time (or a later one) in which they were used. Data we cited in the Preface showing that without the use of GRE scores one department's failure rate among graduate students quadrupled (from 8 to 32 percent) are typical. The university calculated that this meant that the cost to the department of producing one Ph.D. increased by 20 percent. And this doesn't include the costs to individual students in lost time and/or student loans that have to be repaid without the benefit of an advanced degree and its associated increased earning power.

But how can we estimate the value of attending a school with a more diverse student body? Or, conversely, the cost of attending a school without diversity? Few doubt that there is such a cost, and that it is substantial (see Chapter 2's discussion of the value of inclusion) but how can we balance it against the very real costs associated with not choosing the most able candidates? How do we assess the importance of values? And, once we do, how can we put such an assessment on the same scale as the effects of ability?

The short answer to this question is that we cannot. Noted statistician Mel Novick wrote a letter to the American Psychological Association (drawing from the prescient 1976 paper he wrote with Nancy Petersen) in which he pointed out that "If preferences are to be given subgroups, then this must be done openly and on the basis of explicit agreement and public debate. *It simply is not possible to provide a psychometric rationale for this*" (Novick, M.R. Letter to N.S. Cole, November 11, 1974, p. 78) (emphasis ours). So, what's to be done?

13.3 What's to be Done?

The race is not always to the swift, nor the battle to the strong, but that's the way to bet.

Franklin P. Adams[2]

Predictions of future merit are imperfect. Some students with high SAT scores will flunk out of college and others with low scores will do well. But such results are an anomaly and could never be the basis of a successful policy. How much ought a policy aimed at rewarding merit bend to accommodate social values? Seeking a balance between policies that make decisions solely on predicted merit and policies that try to ameliorate social injustices that were centuries in the making is not a task for small children nor the faint of heart. But serious investigations spanning decades have provided the broad outlines of the principles for a policy to incorporate the desires for diversity at all levels and the need to select people most likely to perform well in the positions for which they were selected. The elements for such a policy are:

---

[2] Adams published this in the February 8, 1919 Collier's magazine and attributed it to the prominent sportswriter Hugh E. Keough.

1. Before deciding to buy into any policy, policy makers must know the costs of the alternatives. To be able to provide those costs, data gathering must take place. Sometimes this is easy (e.g., keeping track of what proportion of an entering class of students graduate within a reasonable time), sometimes it is harder (what proportion of licensed physicians become good doctors, what proportion of licensed airline pilots crash their planes, what proportion of elementary school teachers – and hence their pupils – don't understand fractions).
2. In addition, once those costs are known they must be made publicly available. Available both to those who get to decide on policy and also to those who have to pay those costs. When the news is good, making the results public is easy, but when it is bad (graduation rates drop, number of malpractice suits skyrocket, number of aviation accidents increase or, more subtly, when there are more "near misses"[3]) the desire to keep things secret may be irresistible.
3. The causal connection between those outcomes and the various predictors must be calculated and made public. This is not always easy. For example, how are we to learn how effective SAT scores are in predicting college performance at schools in which their use is optional? We have the SAT scores for those who submit them but not everyone else. There have been some studies (described in chapter 1 of Wainer, 2011) done under special circumstances in which all applicants took the test but only a subset submitted them. This data set allows us to calculate how accurately the unsubmitted score reflects the students' actual performance at the school. Without somehow gathering such data, estimating the value of test scores for those who didn't submit them is likely to involve heroic assumptions.
4. Proponents of ignoring objective information on merit and basing decisions instead on other characteristics should make their arguments in support of that policy public and engage in debate justifying them. Public arguments on diversity must include what kinds of diversity. Almost a half century ago Peterson and Novick (1976) argued persuasively that, "In our judgment, preference generally should not be given on the basis of race or ethnicity".

---

[3] Near misses occur in other areas than aviation. In health care Atul Gawande (2009) has told us of surgical apparatus unintendedly left in a surgical patient but were noticed and removed before the final sutures. Less dramatic is when a hospital pharmacy sends the wrong prescription, but before it is administered to the patient it is spotted by the nurse and returned. Keeping track of near misses is crucial for quality control because they provide a measure of weaknesses in the system that need to be remediated. Unfortunately, lawyers rarely advise their clients to publicize how often they only barely avoided catastrophe.

Rather, "the distinction should be made on the basis of advantage or disadvantage" (p. 83).

13.4 The Plural of "Anecdote" is not "Data"

And, finally, let us briefly discuss the difference between anecdote and data, especially in the context of diversity vs. merit. In 1973 Patrick Chavis enrolled in the University of California-Davis Medical school under a special program that enrolled five Black applicants who had lower scores (college GPA and MCAT) than Allan Bakke, a white male, who was denied admission (twice). Bakke challenged the admissions program and in 1978 the U.S. Supreme Court ruled in Bakke's favor stating that the rigid use of racial quotas as employed at the school violated the Equal Protection Clause of the Fourteenth Amendment. In 1978 Bakke was finally admitted to UC- Davis Medical school, graduating in 1982, and went on to a successful career as an anesthesiologist at the Mayo Clinic and at the Olmsted Medical Group in Rochester Minnesota.

But what happened to Patrick Chavis? Upon completion of his residency in 1981 at Long Beach Memorial Hospital, he was hired there as an associate staff physician. In 1988 a panel of physicians and administrators issued a reprimand based on his professional performance.

Chavis then switched his practice to focus on abortion and liposuction. He was sued for malpractice 27 times, had medical board complaints filed in seven liposuction cases and was accused of causing the death of one liposuction patient. A judge suspended his license in 1997, writing in an eleven-page opinion that Chavis "demonstrates an inability to perform some of the most basic duties required of a physician." The Medical Board of California revoked his license in 1998 for "gross negligence, incompetence and repeated negligent acts." In 2002 Dr. Chavis was fatally shot as he returned to his car after buying an ice cream cone in Hawthorne, California.

Dr. Chavis' tragic story has been used as an indictment of affirmative action. We do not agree. This is an anecdote; it is not data. Obvious questions arise immediately. What happened to the other four Black students admitted ahead of Dr. Bakke? What is the relation between admission qualifications to medical school and later license revocation? Debates about how to make decisions which mix both measured merit and societal values require data not anecdotes.[4]

---

[4] See Cuddy et al. (2017) and references therein for data showing a positive relation between performance on medical licensing exams and subsequent success as a physician.

13.5 Fairness is Compromised by Darkness Surrounding Process

In Chapter 10 we provided a chilling example of the costs of secrecy. The details of the final admission decisions to a medical school were shrouded in secrecy and hence a grievous bias was allowed to survive until discovered through happenstance. It showed the dangers of unstandardized and secret criteria for decision making. The use of interviews, especially unstructured ones, has a long and unhappy history. It provides too many opportunities for latent biases to manifest themselves. Objectivity and sunlight on the process are important. But this does not necessarily apply in all aspects. Usually, fairness requires that the examinee's identity, as well as many of their characteristics, be kept private. This is especially true for those characteristics unrelated to whatever position the selection process is being used for. Modern auditions for musicians are one clear example, which is a variation of the interview format, and is now commonly modified by keeping musicians anonymous as they play from behind a curtain. This is a linear descendent of ancient test scoring practices in which the name of the examinee is not known to the person scoring.

13.6 Costs of Errors Vary by Situation

The costs of an error made in college admission are smaller than those made in licensing. If a student is admitted who is unlikely to succeed in that college, the costs to the student involve lost time that might have been spent on something more productive, money spent without receiving full value in return, and whatever (often substantial) psychic distress such failure engenders. The school suffers the opportunity cost of using up a space that might have been better allocated to someone else. Conversely, if a student who likely would have succeeded is rejected, the loss all around is smaller, for such students simply go somewhere else and proceed to follow their dreams elsewhere.

But the story of testing for licensure is very different. A negative error, in which a competent candidate is failed, is initially painful, but can be easily corrected with judicious[5] retesting and the costs of such errors are smaller than the costs of a false positive. In this case an incompetent person is loosed upon

---

[5] Commonly a candidate seeking licensure cannot retake very quickly nor an unlimited number of times, and sometimes, to adjust for the vagaries of chance, licensing organizations insist that the passing score increases a small amount with each repetition.

the public and the damage that is thus done depends on (i) what the profession is, and (ii) how rigorous is professional supervision. But the prospect of an incompetent surgeon, or airline pilot, or tractor-trailer driver, or teacher is terrifying.

Thus, although the current zeitgeist to limit the use of testing in college admission is likely to be wasteful of both physical and human assets, the errors created can be corrected and, if efficacy data are collected, the faulty policy will be spotted and amended.

But if that policy is extended to licensing, the effects are not likely to be benign. The best hope of limiting damage from such a misplaced policy is to gather data on the efficacy of such licensing policies and make them public (despite the likely embarrassment they will cause) and hope that evidence of a failed policy will be noted, and the policy changed. Note that it has long been known that in many situations in which test results are consequential there are always easily accessed remediations for false negatives (someone who failed but should have passed). The most common one is to allow examinees who failed to retake an exam, and if they pass, to immediately enter the category of 'licensed.' Unfortunately, a parallel situation doesn't exist for false positives (some who passed but should not have) – it is hard to imagine the circumstances that would cause happily surprised candidates who unexpectedly passed to present themselves for reexamination to correct what they suspect to be a likely error. The closest policy that professional organizations have to remediate such circumstances, is the requirement for periodic recertification. A public safeguard for sure, but it may be too late for some who fall victim to an incompetent practitioner.

13.7 Zombies Revisited

Chapter 12 described three procedures/policies that are currently being seriously discussed as either solutions for existing inequities (i and ii) or a cause of some of those inequities (iii). These are: (i) making admissions tests optional, (ii) giving an admissions boost to "Strivers," and (iii) claiming unearned efficacy for test-coaching. All of these are flawed and, at best, do not contribute to the goal of the fair and efficient utilization of human resources, and, at worst, work against either fairness or efficiency, or both. Specifically,

(i) Making admissions tests optional just gives away information that would likely have proved useful, and by discouraging some from submitting their scores, effectively removes a trustworthy indicator of talent used by university recruiters to find hidden jewels.

(ii) Boosting the likelihood of admission to Strivers with the anticipation that they will do even better than their scores predict runs counter to both what is expected theoretically and what actually turns out to be true in practice. In fact, on average such students do worse than expected.

(iii) Coaching for admissions testing has long gotten more credit than it deserves. Coaching helps, but only a little. Indeed, it helps about as much as studying the subject itself for the same amount of time would help. As our eyes became adapted to the dim light surrounding the value of coaching most now agree that coaching helps only a little (10-20 SAT points on a scale of 400–1600). But some argue that for some competitive schools even a boost that small might prove decisive. Unfortunately, many of those making such an argument also support reporting only the best performance of a student, what've come to be called "super-scores." This is to encourage students to take the admissions tests early and often, and then only reporting the highest scores, arguing that this represents the students at their best. Unfortunately, it represents a capitalization on chance that benefits those with the grit and wherewithal to retake the exams often. Once again we must conclude that fairness is best served by reporting everything[6] – hiding nothing.

13.8 Quo Vadis?

Mental testing has been around for a long time. As a tool for improving the efficiency with which we utilize human resources it has proven its worth so often that even its most skeptical critics must agree with its predictive value. But testing was born from a belief in empiricism – in facts and evidence – and its existence can only continue so long as we continue to believe in evidence. But empiricism is not an easy god to live with – for by its lights one ugly fact, if it is proven and reliable, can overturn even the most beautiful of theories. Testing is currently enduring hard times, not because its empirical value of predicting future merit has declined, but because we are unhappy with who its results sometimes point to as the best choice. Yet just as we cannot cure obesity by banning scales, we cannot remediate the unfairness of centuries by declaring that the unfairness has left no lasting scars. The power of testing

---

[6] Including, for example, how many times a candidate needed to take the exam before achieving a passing score.

can be used for many purposes – in the present situation it can be used to measure the gains that are made by various approaches that society utilizes to remediate those historical sins (the results shown in Figure 13.1 is a small example of how we can use test scores to evaluate social programs). Yet there are many who propose what they believe are credible arguments in support of ignorance. How can they, in good faith, propose ignorance when there is a bomb under the table?

In 2023, when we began writing this book, we were under the (retrospectively naïve) expectation that truth, merely as truth, has some inherent power, denied to error, of prevailing against policies that ignore the bomb under the table. We soon learned that people are no more zealous for truth than they often are for error. We hoped that a sufficient application of logic and evidence would succeed in stopping the propagation of the ill-advised policies that now seem rampant. We shall see.

One hundred and sixty-six years ago John Stuart Mill wrote that

> *The real advantage which truth has consists in this, that when an opinion is true, it may be extinguished once, twice or many times, but in the course of ages there will generally be found persons to rediscover it, until some one of its reappearances fall on a time when from favorable circumstances it escapes persecution until it has made such headway as to withstand all subsequent attempts to suppress it.*
>
> John Stuart Mill, On Liberty (chapter 2), 1859

We hope that now is that time.

References

American Academy of Orthopaedic Surgeons (AAOS) Department of Research Quality and Scientific Affairs. (2017). *Orthopaedic Practice in the U.S. 2016*. Rosemont, IL: American Academy of Orthopaedic Surgeons.

ACT. (2023). Fewer high school seniors ready for college as ACT scores continue to decline. *ACT Newsroom and Blog*. October 23. https://leadershipblog.act.org/2023/10/act-scores-decline.html

Almond R.G., Steinberg, L.S., and Mislevy, R.J. (2002). Enhancing the design and delivery of assessment systems: a four-process architecture. *Journal of Technology, Learning and Assessment* 1 (5), 1–63.

American Association of Colleges for Teacher Education (AACTE). (1988). Minority recruitment and retention: A public policy issue. *AACTE Wingspread Proceedings 1987*. Washington, DC: AACTE.

American Educational Research Association, American Psychological Association, & National Council on Measurement in Education, & Joint Committee on Standards for Educational and Psychological Testing (AERA, APA, & NCME). (2014). *Standards for Educational and Psychological Testing*. Washington, DC: AERA.

Amrein-Beardsley, A., Collins, C., Holloway-Libell, J., and Paufler, N. (2016). Everything is bigger (and badder) in Texas: Houston's teacher value-added system. *Teachers College Record*, January 5. http://www.tcrecord.org/Content.asp?ContentId=18983

Amy, J. (2023). Georgia won't demand tests to enter 23 of 26 public colleges. *AP News*. April 20. https://apnews.com/article/georgia-universities-act-sat-test-optional-admissions-5b88c7bb5cb8ff3875d4a2bf3e55f3a5

Angelou, M. (1993). *On the Pulse of Morning*. New York: Random House.

Assefa, M., Stamm, K., Page, C., Polk, T., and Williams, W. (2024, June). Shifting admission criteria for graduate psychology programs. *Monitor on Psychology* 55 (4), 23.

Associated Press (1997). St. Mary's copes with poor exam scores. *Lubbock Avalanche-Journal*.

Baker v. Columbus Municipal Separate School District, 329 F. Supp. 706 (N.D. Miss. 1971). https://law.justia.com/cases/federal/district-courts/FSupp/329/706/2596231/ https://www.ncbi.nlm.nih.gov/pmc/articles/PMC5785537 /

Baker, S. (1995). Testing equality: The National Teacher Examination and the NAACP's legal campaign to equalize teachers' salaries in the South, 1936–63. *History of Education Quarterly* 35 (1), 49–64.

Baldwin, P., Bernstein, J., and Wainer, H. (2009). Hip psychometrics. *Statistics in Medicine* 28 (17), 2277–2292.

Barshay, J. (2024). Proof points: Tracing Black–white achievement gaps since the Brown decision. *The Hechinger Report.* May 13. https://hechingerreport.org/proof-points-black-white-achievement-gaps-since-brown/

Bauer-Wolf, J. (2023). College applicants still aren't submitting SAT, ACT scores at pre-pandemic levels. *Higher Ed Dive.* March 30. https://www.highereddive.com/news/college-applicants-still-arent-submitting-sat-act-scores-at-pre-pandemic/646328/

Beardsley, N. (February 23, 2005). The Kalenjins: A look at why they are so good at long-distance running. *Human Adaptability.*

Behrens, J.T., Mislevy, R.J., DiCerbo, K.E., and Levy, R. (2012). An evidence centered design for learning and assessment in the digital world. In M.C. Mayrath, J. Clarke-Midura, and D. Robinson (Eds.), *Technology-based Assessments for 21st Century Skills: Theoretical and Practical Implications from Modern Research* (pp. 13–54). Charlotte, NC: Information Age.

Beran, M.K. (2021). WASPs, Jews, and elite failure. *City Journal.* September 13. https://www.city-journal.org/article/wasps-jews-and-elite-failure

Berry, S. (2002). One modern man or 15 Tarzans? *Chance* 15 (2), 49–53.

Bjorkman, E. (2023). White men have ruled the sky as airline pilots, but that's finally changing. *Chicago Sun Times.* September 19. Retrieved on March 15, 2024. https://chicago.suntimes.com/2023/9/19/23879313/airline-pilots-white-men-diversity-race-gender-training-eileen-bjorkman

Blumgart, J. (2012). The age of illusion: An interview with Chris Hayes. *Jacobin.* https://jacobin.com/2012/06/meritocracy-chris-hayes

Board of Admissions and Relations with Schools (BOARS). (2005). Letter to University of California System schools from Michael T. Brown (Chair) concerning divestment from the National Merit Scholarship Program. Assembly of the Academic Senate, March 1, 2005.

Bock, R.D. and Kolakowski, D. (1973). Further evidence of sex-linked major-gene influence on human spatial visualizing ability. *American Journal of Human Genetics* 25, 1–14.

Bock, R.D. (1991). "The California Assessment." A talk given at the Educational Testing Service, Princeton, N.J. on June 17, 1991.

Braun, H.I., and Wainer, H. (2007). Value-added modeling. In R. Rao and S. Sinharay (Eds.), *Handbook of Statistics (volume 27) Psychometrics* (pp. 867–892). Amsterdam: Elsevier Science.

Bressler, M. (1992). A teacher reflects. *Princeton Alumni Weekly* 93 (5), 11–14.

Bridgeman, B. and Wendler, C. (2005). *Characteristics of Minority Students Who Excel on the SAT and in the Classroom.* Educational Testing Service. https://www.ets.org/Media/Research/pdf/PICMINSAT.pdf

Briggs, D.C. (2005) Meta-analysis: a case study. *Evaluation Review* 29 (2), 87–127. https://doi.org/10.1177/0193841x04272555

(2009). *Preparation for College Admission Exams*. Arlington, VA: National Association for College Admission Counseling.

Brinton, W.C. (1939). *Graphic Presentation*. New York: Brinton Associates.

Brown, O., Mou, T., Lim, S., Jones, S., Sade, S., Kwasny, M.J., Mueller, M.G., and Kenton, K. (2021). Do gender and racial differences exist in letters of recommendation for obstetrics and gynecology residency applicants? *American Journal of Obstetrics and Gynecology* 225 (5), 554.e1–554.e11. https://doi.org/10.1016/j.ajog.2021.08.033

Byrne, C.L., and Broach, D. (2014). An evaluation of the utility of the AT-SAT for the placement of new controllers by option. Federal Aviation Administration Final Report. October. https://apps.dtic.mil/sti/tr/pdf/AD1050296.pdf

Calder, R., Edelman, S., and Bardolf, D. (2023). Black, Hispanic NYers who failed teacher's test strike $1.8B in NYC settlement. *New York Post*. July 15. https://nypost.com/2023/07/15/nyc-bias-suit-black-hispanic-teachers-and-ex-teachers-rich/

Caldwell, O.W. and Courtis, S.A. (1923). *Then and Now in education, 1845–1923: A Message of encouragement From the Past to the Present*. New York: World Book Co.

Campbell, J.P. (1990). An overview of the Army Selection and Classification Project (Project A). *Personnel Psychology* 43, 231–239.

Carleton, D. (2009). Horace Mann. *Free Speech Center*. January 1. https://firstamendment.mtsu.edu/article/horace-mann/#:~:text=via%20Wikimedia%20Commons)-,Known%20as%20the%20%E2%80%9Cfather%20of%20American%20education%2C%E2%80%9D%20Horace%20Mann,curriculum%20that%20excluded%20sectarian%20instruction.

Carroll, J.B. (1993). *Human Cognitive Abilities: A Survey of Factor-analytic Studies*. New York: Cambridge University Press.

Case, S.M., Becker, D.F., and Swanson, D.B. (1993). Performances of men and women on NBME Part I and Part II: The more things change. *Academic Medicine* 68 (10), 25–27.

Council of Chief State School Officers and State Department of Education (CCSSO) (2006) *Educational Leadership Policy Standards*. https://wallacefoundation.org/sites/default/files/2023-09/Educational-Leadership-Policy-Standards-ISLLC-2008.pdf (accessed April 15, 2025).

Chait, J. (2015, August 24). How New Orleans proved urban education reform can work. *Daily Intelligencer*. http://nymag.com/daily/intelligencer/2015/08/how-new-orleans-proved-education-reform-can-work.html

Clauser, A. and Wainer, H. (2016). A tale of two tests (and of two examinees), *Educational Measurement: Issues and Practice* 35 (2), 19–28.

Cobb, L.A., Thomas, G.I., Dillard, D.H., Merendino, K.A., and Bruce, R.A. (1959). An evaluation of internal-mammary-artery ligation by a double-blind technique. *New England Journal of Medicine* 260 (22), 1115–1118.

Cole, T.J. and Mori, H. (2018). Fifty years of child height and weight in Japan and South Korea: Contrasting secular trend patterns analyzed by SITAR. *American Journal of Human Biology* 30 (1), e23054.

Coleman, J.S., Campbell, E.Q., Hobson, C.J., McPartland, J., Mood, A.M., Weinfeld, F.D., et al. (1966). *Equality of Educational Opportunity* (NCES. No. OE-38001).

Washington, D.C.: U. S. Department of Health, Education, and Welfare, Office of Education.

College Board. (2017). *Scores on PSAT-related assessments increase across demographics*. September 26. https://newsroom.collegeboard.org/scores-psat-related-assessments-increase-across-demographics

College Board. (2023). How did pandemic disruptions impact applications, enrollment, and outcomes at selective institutions? New findings and implications for long-term policy and practice.

Cordero, K. (2023). SUNY drops SAT standards. *Politico*. April 13. https://www.politico.com/newsletters/new-york-playbook-pm/2023/04/13/suny-drops-sat-standards-00091957

Cronbach, L.J. (1976). Equity in selection: Where psychometrics and political philosophy meet. *Journal of Educational Measurement* 13 (1), 31–41.

Cuddy, M., Young, A., Gelman, A., Swanson, D.B., Johnson, D.A., Dillon, G.F., and Clauser, B.E. (2017). Exploring the relationships between USMLE performance and disciplinary action in practice: A validity study of score inferences from a licensure examination. *Academic Medicine* 92 (12):1780–1785.

Davis, D., Dorsey, J.K., Franks, R.D., Sackett, P.R., Searcy, C.A., and Zhao, X. (2013). Do racial and ethnic group differences in performance on the MCAT exam reflect test bias? *Academic Medicine* 88 (5), 593–602. doi: 10.1097/ACM.0b013e31828 6803a. PMID: 23478636.

Deary, I.J., Batty, D., and Gottfredson, L.S. (2005, July 29). Human hierarchies, health, and IQ (letter). *Science* 309, 703–703.

Deming, W. Edwards (2012). *The Essential Deming: Leadership Principles from the Father of Quality*. New York: McGraw Hill Professional.

Denning, J.T., Eide, E.R., Mumford, K.J., Patterson, R.W., and Warnick, M. (2022). Why have college completion rates increased? *American Economic Journal: Applied Economics* 14 (3), 1–29. https://doi.org/10.1257/app.20200525

Dershowitz, A. (1992). *Chutzpah*. New York: Simon & Schuster.

DerSimonian, S. and Laird, N. (1983). Evaluating the effect of coaching on SAT Scores: a meta-analysis. *Harvard Education Review* 53, 1–15. https://doi.org/10.17763/haer.53.1.n06j5h5356217648

Detterman, D.K. (2016). Education and intelligence: Pity the poor teacher because student characteristics are more significant than teachers or schools. *The Spanish Journal of Psychology* 19, e93. https://doi.org/10.1017/sjp.2016.88

DiBase, R.W. (2005, September). ECS Policy Brief: State involvement in school restructuring under No Child Left Behind in the 2004–2005 school year. p. 2. https://www.ecs.org/clearinghouse/64/28/6428.pdf

Diep, F. (2023). Colleges protesting 'U.S. News' rankings say they're doing it for low-income students. Do they mean it? *Chronicle of Higher Education*. March 1. https://www.chronicle.com/article/colleges-protesting-u-s-news-rankings-say-theyre-doing-it-for-low-income-students-do-they-mean-it

Dockser, A. (1999). New weights can alter SAT scores as family factors determine 'Strivers'. *The Wall Street Journal* https://www.wsj.com/articles/SB9360612652 07782969

Doyle, Arthur Conan (1891). A scandal in Bohemia. *The Strand Magazine*.

DuBois, P.H. (1970). *A History of Psychological Testing*. Boston: Allyn & Bacon.

Dynarski, S.M. (2018). ACT/SAT for all: A cheap, effective way to narrow income gaps in college. Brookings. February 8. *Brookings.* https://www.brookings.edu/articles/act-sat-for-all–a-cheap-effective-way-to-narrow-income-gaps-in-college/

Eagan, K., Stolzenberg, E.B., Ramirez, J.J., et al. (2016). *The American Freshman: Fifty-Year Trends 1966–2015.* Higher Education Research Institute, UCLA. https://www.heri.ucla.edu/monographs/50YearTrendsMonograph2016.pdf

Editor. (2001). New and views: The racial insult built into the National Merit Scholarship Program. *The Journal of Blacks in Higher Education* 32, 30–32. https://doi.org/10.2307/2678755

Edmond, M.B., Deschenes, J.L., Eckler, M., and Wenzel, R.P. (2001). Racial bias in using USMLE Step 1 scores to grant internal medicine residency interviews. *Academic Medicine* 76 (12), 1253–1256.

Embretson, S. (1985). *Test Design: Developments in Psychology and Psychometrics.* New York: Academic Press.

FairTest. (2007). *University testing: Scholarships.* August 22. https://fairtest.org/university-testing-scholarships/

Farr, W. (1852). Influence of elevation on the fatality of cholera. *Journal of the Statistical Society of London* 15, 155–183.

Federal Aviation Administration (FAA) (11 January 2023a). *"FAA has taken steps to validate its air traffic skills assessment test but lacks a plan to evaluate its effectiveness".* Federal Aviation Administration. Retrieved March 16, 2024. https://www.oig.dot.gov/sites/default/files/FAA%20Air%20Traffic%20Controller%20Hiring%20Final%20Report%5E1.11.2023.pdf

Federal Aviation Administration (19 January 2023b). *U.S. Civil Airmen Statistics.* Federal Aviation Administration. Retrieved March 15, 2024. https://www.faa.gov/data_research/aviation_data_statistics/civil_airmen_statistics

Feller, S.E. (2023). Ivy League isn't everything. Here's what we get wrong about getting a good education. *USA Today.* March 6. https://www.usatoday.com/story/opinion/2023/03/06/college-decisions-higher-education-beyond-ivy-league/11381304002/

Fenwick, L. (2022). *Jim Crow's Pink Slip: The Untold Story of Black Principal and Teacher Leadership.* Harvard Education Press.

Fisher, R.A. (1925). *Statistical Methods for Research Workers.* Edinburgh: Oliver & Boyd.

(1935). *The Design of Experiments.* Edinburgh: Oliver & Boyd.

Flanagan, J.C. (1941). An analysis of the results from the First Annual Edition of the National Teacher Examinations. *The Journal of Experimental Education* 9 (3), 237-250.

(1948). *The Aviation Psychology Program in the Army Air Forces* (Report #1) Washington, D.C.: U.S. Government Printing Office. (Chapter 4, p. 69).

Foley, M. (2003). *Confronting the War Machine: Draft Resistance during the Vietnam War.* University of North Carolina Press, ISBN 978-0-8078-5436-5, archived from the original on October 16, 2015.

Friedman, M. (1992). Do old fallacies ever die? *Journal of Economic Literature* 30, 2129–2132.

Frontline interview with Henry Chauncey. https://www.pbs.org/wgbh/pages/frontline/shows/sats/interviews/chauncey.html

Galchen, R. (April 13, 2015). Letter from Oklahoma, Weather Underground: The arrival of man-made earthquakes. *The New Yorker* 34–40.
Galton, F. (1889). *Natural Inheritance*. London: Macmillan.
Gawande, A. (2009). *The Checklist Manifesto*. New York: Metropolitan Books.
Geisinger, K.F. (2022). College admissions: What our goals should be and what works to get us there. In K.F. Geisinger (Ed.), *College Admissions and Testing in a Time of Transformational Change*. Routledge. https://doi.org/10.1080/08957347.2023.2201705
Gitomer, D.H., Martínez, J.F., Battey, D., and Hyland, N.E. (2019). Assessing the assessment: Evidence of reliability and validity in the edTPA. *American Educational Research Journal* 58 (1), 3–31. https://doi.org/10.3102/0002831219890608
Goddard, H.H. (1919). *Psychology of the Normal and Subnormal*. Dodd.
Goertz, M.E., Duffy, M.C., and Le Floch, K.C. (2001, March). *Assessment and Accountability Systems in the 50 states: 1999–2000*. Consortium for Policy Research in Education Research Report Series, RR-046.
Goodman, J., Gurantz, O., and Smith, J. (2020). Take two: SAT retaking and college enrollment gaps. *American Economic Journal: Economic Policy* 12 (2), 115–158. https://www.aeaweb.org/articles?id=10.1257/pol.20170503
Gottfredson, L.S. (2003). g, jobs, and life. In H. Nyborg (Ed.), *The Scientific Study of General Intelligence: Tribute to Arthur R. Jensen* (pp. 293–342). New York: Pergamon.
  (2005). Implications of cognitive differences for schooling within diverse societies. In C.L. Frisby and C R. Reynolds (Eds.), *Comprehensive Handbook of Multicultural School Psychology* (pp. 517–554). New York: Wiley.
Grabovsky, I. and Wainer, H. (2017). A Guide for setting the cut-scores to minimize weighted classification errors in test batteries. *Journal of Educational and Behavioral Statistics* 42 (3), 264–281.
Grantham, C. (2015). With college sports at crossroads, unspoken problem facing NCAA is race. *Sports Illustrated*. May 19. https://www.si.com/college/2015/05/19/ncaa-problems-race
Gulliksen, H. (October 26, 1965). Personal communication, Princeton, NJ.
Gulliksen, H.O. (1950). *Theory of Mental Tests,* New York: Wiley. (Reprinted in 1987 by Lawrence Erlbaum Associates; Hillsdale, NJ).
Gunn, L.H., ter Horst, E., Markossian, T., and Molina, G. (2020). Associations between majors of graduating seniors and average SATs of incoming students within higher education in the U.S. *Heliyon* 6 (5). https://doi.org/10.1016/j.heliyon.2020.e03956
Haberman, S., Sinharay, S., Feinberg, R. and Wainer, H. (2024). *Subscores: A Practical Guide for Their Producers and Consumers*. New York: Cambridge University Press
Hand, E. (4 July 2014). Injection wells blamed in Oklahoma earthquakes. *Science* 345 (6192), 13–14.
Hanson, F.A. (1993). *Testing Testing: Social Consequences of the Examined life*. University of California Press.
Hanson, M. (2024). Average cost of college & tuition. *Education Data Initiative*. May 28. https://educationdata.org/average-cost-of-college

Hanushek, E.A. (1997). Assessing the effects of school resources on student performance: An update. *Educational Evaluation and Policy Analysis* 19 (2), 141–164. https://doi.org/10.2307/1164207

(2016). What matters for student achievement. *Education Next* 16 (2). https://www.educationnext.org/what-matters-for-student-achievement/

Hayes, I.N. (2005). *Epidemics and Pandemics: Their Impact on Human History*, Santa Barbara, Calif.: ABC-CLIO

Heissel, J.A., and Ladd, H.F. (2018). School turnaround in North Carolina: A regression discontinuity analysis. *Economics of Education Review* 62, 302–320. https://doi.org/10.1016/j.econedurev.2017.08.001

Heller, D.E. (2004). The devil is in the details: An analysis of eligibility criteria for merit scholarships in Massachusetts. In D.E. Heller and P. Marin (Eds.), *State Merit Scholarship Programs and Racial Inequality*. The Civil Rights Project. Harvard University.

Hess, A. (July 13, 2017). "Here's how much it costs to go to college in the US compared to other countries". *CNBC*. Retrieved March 14, 2024.

Higgins, B., Langworthy, N., Morelle, J., and Tenney, C. (2023). Putting public safety over politics and preserving the 1,500 hour pilot training rule. Air Line Pilot. August. Retrieved on March 15, 2024. https://www.alpa.org/news-and-events/airline-pilot-magazine/public-safety-over-politics

Hitchens, C. (2009). *God is Not Great: How Religion Poisons Everything* (Kindle edn). Twelve Books.

Hobbes, T. (1651). Leviathan. Rogers, G.A.J., Schuhmann, K. (A critical ed.). London: Bloomsbury Publishing.

Holland, P.W. (2023a). Personal Communication. April 25.

(2023b). Personal Communication. October 26.

(1986). Statistics and causal inference. *Journal of the American Statistical Association* 81, 945–970. https://doi.org/10.2307/2289064

Hotelling, H. (1933). Review of the triumph of mediocrity in business by Secrist H. *Journal of the American Statistical Association* 28, 463–465.

Hubert, L. and Wainer, H. (2013). *A Statistical Guide for the Ethically Perplexed*. New York: Chapman and Hall, 2013.

Hume, D. (1748). *An Enquiry Concerning Human Understanding*. Tom L. Beauchamp (Ed.), New York: Oxford University Press, 2000.

Hyman, J. (2017). ACT for all: The effect of mandatory college entrance exams on postsecondary attainment and choice. *Education Finance and Policy* 12 (3), 281–311. http://www.mitpressjournals.org/doi/full/10.1162/EDFP_a_00206

Jackson, D.Z. (2022). Black college students: An endangered species, unless they play ball. *The American Prospect*. December 23. https://prospect.org/education/black-college-student-athletes-supreme-court-affirmative-action/

Jamison, P. and Nirappil, F. (2018, February 2). Once a national model, now D.C. public school target of FBI investigation. *Washington Post*. https://www.washingtonpost.com/local/dc-politics/dc-public-schools-were-once-a-success-story-are-they-now-an-embarrassment/2018/02/01/fb15dd4c-069d-11e8-b48c-b07fea957bd5_story.html?noredirect=on&utm_term=.cab33c05ccad

Jaschik, S. (2023). Cardona vs. 'U.S. News.' *Inside Higher Ed*. March 2.

Jaynes, J. (1966). The routes of science. *American Scientist* 54 (1), 94–102.

Johnson, D.A. and Chaudhry, H.J. (2012). *Medical Licensing and Discipline in America: A History of the Federation of State Medical Boards.* Lanham, MD: Lexington Books.

Johnson, S. (2006). *The Ghost Map: The Story of London's Most Terrifying Epidemic – and How It Changed Science, Cities, and the Modern World.* New York: Riverhead Books.

Kahlenberg, R.D. (1999). Opinion: The colleges, the poor and the SATs. *The Washington Post.* September 20. https://www.washingtonpost.com/archive/opinions/1999/09/21/the-colleges-the-poor-and-the-sats/9f707187-4b98-45dc-924e-8fb1cb237831/

(Ed.). (2010). *Rewarding Strivers: Helping Low-income Students Succeed in College.* The Century Foundation Press.

Kelley, T.L. (1927). *The Interpretation of Educational Measurements.* New York: World Book.

Keranen, K.M., Savage, H.M., Abers, G.A., and Cochran, E.S. (June 2013). Potentially induced earthquakes in Oklahoma, USA: Links between wastewater injection and the 2011 M_w 5.7 earthquake sequence. *Geology* (41), 699–702.

Keranen, K.M., Weingarten, M. Abers, G.A., Bekins, B.A., and Ge, S. (July 25, 2014). Sharp increase in central Oklahoma seismicity since 2008 induced by massive wastewater injection. *Science* 345 (6195), 448–451. Published online July 3, 2014.

Kerr, E., and Wood, S. (2023). See the average college tuition in 2023–2024. *U.S. News & World Report.* September 20. https://www.usnews.com/education/best-colleges/paying-for-college/articles/paying-for-college-infographic

King, R.E., Manning, C.A., and Herndon, G. (2007). Operational use of the air traffic selection and training battery. Federal Aviation Administration Final Report. May. https://www.researchgate.net/publication/235018159_Operational_Use_of_the_Air_Traffic_Selection_and_Training_Battery

King, W.I. (1934). Review of the triumph of mediocrity in business by Secrist H. *Journal of Political Economy* 42, 398–400.

Knox, L. (2024). The future of testing is anything but standardized. *Inside Higher Education.* February 26. https://www.insidehighered.com/news/admissions/traditional-age/2024/02/26/no-emerging-consensus-standardized-test-policies

Koretz, D., McCaffrey, D., Klein, S., Bell, R., and Stecher, B. (1992). The reliability of scores from the 1992 Vermont Portfolio Assessment Program: Interim Report. December 4. https://files.eric.ed.gov/fulltext/ED355284.pdf

Lacour, M. and Tissington, L.D. (2011). The effects of poverty on academic achievement. *Educational Research and Reviews* 6 (7), 522–527. https://academicjournals.org/article/article1379765941_Lacour%20and%20Tissington.pdf

Langenbruch, C. and Zoback, M.D. (2016). How will induced seismicity in *Oklahoma respond to decreased saltwater injection rates? Science Advances* 2 (11) DOI: 10.1126/sciadv.16015

Laurence, J.H. *et al.* (December 1989). "Effects of military experience on the post-service lives of low-aptitude recruits: Project 100,000 and the ASVAB Misnorming". Archived from the original on 2014-03-02. Retrieved November 22, 2009.

Learned, W.S. and Wood, B.D. (1938). The student and his knowledge: A report to the Carnegie Foundation on the results of the high school and college examinations of

1928, 1930, and 1932. *Carnegie Foundation for the Advancement of Teaching Bulletin No. 29.* New York: Updike.
Lord, F.M. and Novick, M.R. (1968). *Statistical Theories of Mental Test Scores.* Reading, MA: Addison-Wesley.
Low, D., Pollack, S.W., Liao, Z.C., Maestas, R., Kirven, L.E., Eacker, A.M., and MacPherson, M. (2002). McNamara's 'Moron Corps'. *Salon.* May 30. Retrieved August 23, 2014.
Marini, J.P., Westrick, P.A., Young, L., Ng, H., Shmueli, D., and Shaw, E.J. (2019). *Differential Validity and Prediction of the SAT: Examining First-Year Grades and retention to the Second Year.* College Board: https://files.eric.ed.gov/fulltext/ED597325.pdf
McArdle, M. (2024). Colleges are realizing they can't ignore the truth [about test scores], even if it hurts. *Washington Post.* March 18. https://www.washingtonpost.com/opinions/2024/03/18/sat-score-requirement-ut-data/
McGee, K. (2023). With race-based admissions no longer an option, states may imitate Texas top 10% plan. *The Texas Tribune.* June 29. https://www.texastribune.org/2023/06/29/texas-college-top-ten-percent-plan-supreme-court/
McGucken, W. J. (1932). *The Jesuits and Education.* Milwaukee: Bruce.
McPhee, J. (2018). *Draft No. 4: On the Writing Process.* New York: Farrar, Straus and Giroux.
Messick, S. (1995). Validity of psychological assessment: Validation of inferences from persons' responses and performances as scientific inquiry into score meaning. *American Psychologist* 50 (9), 741–749. https://doi.org/10.1037/0003-066X.50.9.741
Messick, S. in collaboration with Alderman, D., Powers, D.E., Rock, D., Rubin, D., and Stroud, T.W.F. (1980). *The Effectiveness of Coaching for the SAT; Review and Reanalysis of Research from the Fifties to the FTC.* Princeton, NJ: Educational Testing Service.
Messick, S. and Jungeblut, A. (1981). Time and method in coaching for the SAT. *Psychological Bulletin* 89, 191–216. https://doi.org/10.1037/0033-2909.89.2.191
Military.com. (2020). What your ASVAB scores mean. August 21. https://www.military.com/join-armed-forces/asvab/what-your-asvab-scores-mean.html
Mill, J.S. (1859). *On Liberty.* MobileReference.
Mills, F.C. (1924). *Statistical Methods Applied to Economics and Business*, New York: Henry Holt.
Mislevy, R.J. and Levy, R. (2007). Bayesian psychometric modeling from an evidence-centered design perspective. In C.R. Rao and S. Sinharay (Eds.), *Handbook of Statistics*, Vol. 26 (pp 839–865). North-Holland, Elsevier.
Mislevy, R.J., Steinberg, L.S., and Almond, R.A. (2003). On the structure of educational assessments. *Measurement: Interdisciplinary Research and Perspectives* 1, 3–67.
Mohr, J.C. (2013). *Licensed to Practice: The Supreme Court Defines the American Medical Profession.* Baltimore: Johns Hopkins University Press.
Moravcik, A. (February 25, 2017). Commentary in the panel discussion "Perspectives on the Global Refugee Crisis" presented at Princeton Alumni Day, Princeton, NJ.
Mosteller, F. (1995). The Tennessee study of class size in the early school grades. *The Future of Children* 5 (2), 113–127. https://edsource.org/wp-content/uploads/old/STAR.pdf

References

Moynihan, D.P. (March 1965). *The Negro Family: The Case for National Action.* Washington, DC: The Office of Policy Planning and Research, U.S. Department of Labor. https://web.stanford.edu/~mrosenfe/Moynihan%27s%20The%20Negro%20Family.pdf

Mulvenon, S.W. and Robinson, D.H. (2014). The paradox of increasing both enrollments and graduation rates: Acknowledging elephants in the ivory tower. *International Journal of Higher Education 3,* 66–70. http://www.sciedu.ca/journal/index.php/ijhe/article/view/3567

Nankervis, B. (2013). Gender inequity in the National Merit Scholarship Program. *Journal of College Admission* 20–25. https://files.eric.ed.gov/fulltext/EJ1011761.pdf

National Center for Education Statistics (NCES). (2021). *Digest of education statistics.* https://nces.ed.gov/programs/digest/d21/tables/dt21_326.10.asp

National Educational Association (1895). *Report of the Committee of Fifteen on elementary education: With the reports of the sub-committees; on the training of teachers; on the correlation of studies in elementary education; on the organization of city school systems.* New York: American Book Company.

National Research Council. (2010). *Getting Value Out of Value-Added.* In H. Braun, N. Chudowsky, and J. Koenig (Eds.). Washington, DC: National Academy Press.

National Association of Student Financial Aid Administrators (NASFAA) (2022) *National Student Aid Profile: Overview of 2022 federal programs.* NASFAA. October. https://www.nasfaa.org/uploads/documents/2022_National_Profile.pdf

Nettles, M.T., Scatton, L.H., Steinberg, J.H., and Tyler, L.L. (2011). *Performance and passing rate differences of African American and White prospective teachers on Praxis examinations.* Research report ETS RR-11-08. Retrieved from https://eric.ed.gov/?id=ED523733

Neyman, J. (1923). On the application of probability theory to agricultural experiments. Translation of excerpts by D. Dabrowska and T. Speed. *Statistical Science* 5 (1990), 462–472.

National Merit Scholarship Corporation (NMSC) (2019). *NMSC 2018-19 Annual Report.* National Merit Scholarship Corporation. October 31, 2019. p. 38–40.

Nolen, L.T. (2020). Why pass/fail Step 1 is really only Step 1. The Harvard Crimson. February 18, 2020. https://www.thecrimson.com/article/2020/2/18/nolen-pass-fail-step-1/

Nova, A. (June 30, 2021). "Student loan bills are set to restart in October. But another extension is still possible". *CNBC.* Retrieved March 14, 2024.

Novick, M.R. and Petersen, N.S. (1976) Towards equalizing educational and employment opportunity, *Journal of Educational Measurement* 13 (1), 77–88.

O'Neill, H.M. (2003). Strivers and underachievers: Effects on first year college grades and retention. *Business and Economics Faculty Publications* 4. https://digitalcommons.ursinus.edu/bus_econ_fac/4

Petersen, N.S. and Novick, M.R. (1976). An evaluation of some models for culture-fair selection. *Journal of Educational Measurement,* 13, 3–29.

Peterson, B., Bligh, R., and Robinson, D.H. (2022). Consistent federal educational reform failure: A case study of Nebraska from 2010–2019. *Midwestern Educational Researcher* 34 (3), 316–327. https://www.mwera.org/MWER/volumes/v34/issue3/MWER-V34n3-Peterson-COMMENTARY.pdf

Peterson, J. (1983). *The Iowa Testing Programs*. University of Iowa Press: Iowa City.
Planck, M.K. (1950). *Scientific Autobiography and Other Papers*. New York: Philosophical Library.
Plomin, R., DeFries, J.C., McClearn, G E., and McGuffin, P. (2001). *Behavioral Genetics* (4th edn). New York: Worth.
Pope, A. (1711). *An Essay on Criticism*. London: Henry Lintot.
Powers, D.E., and Rock, D.A. (1999). Effects of coaching on the SAT I: Reasoning test scores. *Journal of Educational Measurement* 36, 93–118. https://doi.org/10.1111/j.1745-3984.1999.tb00549.x
Rasch, G. (1960). *Probabilistic Models for Some Intelligence and Attainment Tests*. Copenhagen: Denmarks Paedagogiske Institut. (Republished in 1980 by the University of Chicago Press of Chicago).
Ree, M. and Earles, J. (1990). *Differential Validity of a Differential Aptitude Test*. (AFHRL-TR-89-59). Brooks AFB, TX: Manpower and Personnel Division, Air Force Human Resources Laboratory.
Ree, M.J. and Earles, J.A. (1991). Predicting training success: Not much more than g. *Personnel Psychology* 44, 321–332.
 (1991). The stability of convergent estimates of g. *Intelligence* 15, 271–278.
 (1992). Intelligence is the best predictor of job performance. *Current Directions in Psychological Science* 1, 86–89.
 (1993). g is to psychology what carbon is to chemistry: A reply to Sternberg and Wagner, McClelland, and Calfee. *Current Directions in Psychological Science* 2, 11–12.
Ree, M.J., Earles, J.A., and Teachout, M.S. (1994). Predicting job performance; Not much more than g. *Journal of Applied Psychology* 79, 518–524.
Reese, W.J. (2013). The first race to the top. *The New York Times*. April 20. https://www.nytimes.com/2013/04/21/opinion/sunday/the-first-testing-race-to-the-top.html
Riconscente, M.M., Mislevy, R.J., and Corrigan, S. (2015). Evidence-centered assessment design. In S. Lane, T.M. Haladyna, and M. Raymond (Eds.), *Handbook of Test Development* (2nd edn). (pp. 40–63). Informa / Taylor and Francis / Routledge.
Robinson, D.H.,and Bligh, R.A. (2019). Educational muckrakers, watchdogs, and whistleblowers. In P. Kendeou, D.H. Robinson, and M. McCrudden (Eds.), *Misinformation and Fake News in Education* (pp. 123–131). Information Age Publishing. https://www.infoagepub.com/products/Misinformation-and-Fake-News-in-Education
Romney, M. (2004). *Romney opens door to college for top scoring students* (press release).
Rosenbaum, P. (2002). *Observational Studies*. New York: Springer-Verlag.
 (2009). *Design of Observational Studies*. New York: Springer-Verlag.
 (2017). *Observation and Experiment: An Introduction to Causal Inference*. Cambridge: Harvard University Press.
Rubin, A.M. (2024). Personal communication.
Rubin, D.B. (1974). Estimating causal effects of treatments in randomized and non-randomized studies. *Journal of Educational Psychology* 66, 688–701.
Rubin, D.B (1975). Bayesian inference for causality: The importance of randomization. In *Social Statistics Section, Proceedings of the American Statistical Association* (pp. 233–239).

Rubin, D.B.,.Stuart, E.A., and Zanutto, E.L. (2004). A potential outcomes view of value-added assessment in education. *Journal of Educational and Behavioral Statistics* 289 (1), 103–116.

Rushay, S.W. (2009). Harry Truman's history lessons. *Prologue Magazine* 41 (1). https://www.archives.gov/publications/prologue/2009/spring/truman-history.html#:~:text=The%20only%20thing%20new%20in,representative%20nature%20of%20American%20government.

Sackett, P.R., Borneman, M.J., and Connelly, B.S. (2008). High stakes testing in higher education and employment: Appraising the evidence for validity and fairness. *American Psychologist* 63 (4), 215–227. https://doi.org/10.1037/0003-066X.63.4.215

Sagan, C. (1997). *The Demon-Haunted World: Science as a Candle in the Dark* (Reprint ed.). Ballantine Books. ISBN 978-0345409461.

Sanchez, E. and Moore, R. (2022). *Grade Inflation Continues to grow in the Past Decade*. ACT Research Report: https://www.act.org/content/dam/act/unsecured/documents/2022/R2134-Grade-Inflation-Continues-to-Grow-in-the-Past-Decade-Final-Accessible.pdf

Sands, W.A., Waters, B.K., and McBride, J.R. (1997). *Computerized Adaptive Testing: From Inquiry to Operation*. Washington, D.C.: American Psychological Association.

SAT Suite (n.d.) *Test Development*. https://satsuite.collegeboard.org/higher-ed-professionals/test-validity/test-development

Saunders, P. (2022). Why does everyone lie about social mobility? A sociologist explains the history of a much contested truth... *Aporia Magazine*. August 1. https://www.aporiamagazine.com/p/peter-saunders-why-does-everybody?utm_source=%2Fsearch%2Fsaundersandutm_medium=reader2

Schmidt, W.H. Houang, T.D., McKnight, C.C. (2005). Value-added research: Right ideas but wrong solution? In R. Lissitz (Ed.), *Value-Added Models in Education: Theory and Applications*. JAM Press, Maple Grove, MN, pp. 145–165.

Schulker, D., Yeung, D., Keller, K.M., Payne, L.A., Saum-Manning, L., Hall, K.C., and Zavislan, S. (2018). Understanding demographic differences in undergraduate pilot training attrition. RAND Corporation. Retrieved March 15, 2024. https://apps.dtic.mil/sti/pdfs/AD1057350.pdf

Schum, D.A. (1994). *The Evidential Foundations of Probabilistic Reasoning*. New York: Wiley.

Schwartz, S. (2023). States have soured on the high school exit exam. Here's why. Education Week. January 26. https://www.edweek.org/teaching-learning/states-have-soured-on-the-high-school-exit-exam-heres-why/2023/01

Secrist, H. (1933). *The Triumph of Mediocrity in Business*, Evanston, IL: Bureau of Business Research, Northwestern University.

Sharpe, W.E (1985). *Investments* (3rd edn), Englewood Cliffs, NJ: Prentice-Hall.

Sigerist, H.E. (1935). *A History of Medicine*. Oxford University Press; Oxford.

Sinharay, S. (2010). How often do subscores have added value? Results from operational and simulated data. *Journal of Educational Measurement* 47, 150–174.

Smedley, B.D., Stith, A.Y., and Nelson, A. R. (Eds.). (2003). *Unequal Treatment: Confronting Racial and Ethnic Disparities in Health care*. The National Academies Press. DOI: 10.17226/12875

Snow J. (1849). *On the Mode of the Communication of Cholera*. London: John Churchill.
Snow, J. (1855). *On the Mode of Communication of Cholera* (2nd edn). London: John Churchill.
Spitalniak, L. (2023). Two New York institutions permanently shift to test-optional admissions. *Higher Ed Dive*. April 14. https://www.highereddive.com/news/suny-vassar-permanently-shift-to-test-optional-admissions/647724/
Stigler, S. (1997). Regression toward the mean, historically considered. *Statistical Methods in Medical Research* 6, 103–114.
Stockwell, S., Schaeffer, R., and Lowenstein, J. (1991). *The SAT Coaching Coverup*. New York: Fairtest.
Sullivan, P. (August 25, 2009). Test-preparation pioneer Kaplan, 90, dies. *The Washington Post*.
Tahir, I. (2022). The UK education system preserves inequality. *Inequality: The IFS Deaton Review*. September 13. https://ifs.org.uk/inequality/the-uk-education-system-preserves-inequality/
Teng, Ssu-yu (1943). Chinese influence on the western examination system. *Harvard Journal of Asiatic Studies* 7, 267–312.
Terman, L. (1916). *The Measurement of Intelligence*. Riverside: Cambridge, MA.
 (1939). An important contribution. *Journal of Higher Education* 50. February.
The Chronicle of Higher Education (2009). University of Texas at Austin won't sponsor National Merit Scholars anymore. September 1, 2009.
Thernstrom, A. and Glazer, A. (1999) The end of meritocracy – a debate on affirmative action, the SAT and the future of American excellence. *The New Republic*, September 27, pp. 26–29.
Thissen, D. and Wainer, H. (2001). *Test Scoring*. Hillsdale, NJ: Lawrence Erlbaum Associates.
Thompson, D.W. (1942). *On Growth and Form* (2nd edn). Cambridge: Cambridge University Press.
Truman, H.S. https://www.truman.edu/about/history/our-namesake/truman-quotes/
Tucker, C. (2006). Katrina students struggle with Texas school tests. National Public Radio. May 22. https://www.npr.org/2006/05/22/5421332/katrina-students-struggle-with-texas-school-tests
Tufte, E.R. (1983). *The Visual Display of Quantitative Information*. Cheshire, CT: Graphics Press.
 (1997). *Visual Explanations*. Cheshire, CT: Graphics Press.
Vaishnav, A., and Dedman, B. (2004, March 7). Romney's scholarship plan favors richer school
Wai, J., Lubinski, D., and Benbow, C.P. (2009). Spatial ability for STEM domains: Aligning over 50 years of cumulative psychological knowledge solidifies its importance. *Journal of Educational Psychology* 101 (4), 817–835. https://doi.org/10.1037/a0016127
Wainer, H. (1990/2000). *Computerized Adaptive Testing: A Primer*. Erlbaum: Hillsdale, NJ.
 (2011). *Uneducated Guesses: Using Evidence to Uncover Misguided Education Policies*. Princeton: Princeton University Press.
 (2012). Waiting for Achilles. *Chance* 25 (4), 50–51.

(2014). *Medical Illuminations: Using Evidence, Visualization and Statistical thinking to Improve Healthcare*. London: Oxford University Press.

(2016). *Truth or Truthiness: Distinguishing Fact from Fiction by Learning to Think like a Data Scientist*. New York: Cambridge University Press.

Wainer, H., and Robinson, D. (2023). Why testing? Why should it cost you? *Chance* 36 (1), 48–52. https://doi.org/10.1080/09332480.2023.2179281

Wainer, H. and Sakworawich, A. (2020). Scoring tests with contaminated response vectors *Journal of Educational and Behavioral Statistics* 45 (2), 209–226, 2020 (published on-line on October 23, 2019) https://journals.sagepub.com/eprint/QQFSXHYDJVMARKMA5Z7E/full

Wainer, H., Bradlow, E.T., and Wang, X. (2007). *Testlet Response Theory and its Applications*. New York: Cambridge University Press.

Wainer, H., Haberman, S., and Robinson, D. H. (2024). Zombie Research Results: 1. Coaching for the SAT/ACT, *Chance* 37 (4), 43–47, 2024.

Wainer, H., Lukele, R., and Thissen, D. (1994). On the relative value of multiple-choice, constructed response, and examinee selected items on two achievement tests. *Journal of Educational Measurement* 31, 234–250.

Watson, G. (1938). How good are our colleges? *Public Affairs Pamphlet, No. 26*. New York: Public Affairs Committee.

Weissblum, C.R. (2019). If elite colleges want to address the college admissions bribery scandal – accept more low- and middle-income strivers. Philanthropy New York. March 18. https://philanthropynewyork.org/news/if-elite-colleges-want-address-college-admissions-bribery-scandal-accept-more-low-and-middle

Westfall, L. (2011). Athletic scholarships – who gets them and how many are there? *Fastweb*. July 15. https://www.fastweb.com/student-news/articles/athletic-scholarships-who-gets-them-and-how-many-are-there

Westrick, P.A., Marini, J.P., and Shaw, E.J. (2022). *An Updated Look at SAT Score Relationships with College Degree Completion* (College Board Research Report). New York, NY: College Board. https://research.collegeboard.org/media/pdf/SAT_Score_Relationships_with_College_Degree_Completion.pdf

Wignall, A. (2021, August 12). Between a full-ride and a full-tuition scholarship? *CollegeRaptor*. Retrieved from https://www.collegeraptor.com/paying-for-college/articles/questions-answers/whats-difference-full-ride-full-tuition-scholarship/

Williams, M., Kim, E.J., Pappas, K., Uwemedimo, O., Marrast, L., Pekmezaris, R., and Martinez, J. (2020). The impact of United States Medical Licensing Exam (USMLE) step 1 cutoff scores on recruitment of underrepresented minorities in medicine: A retrospective cross-sectional study. *Health Science Reports* 3 (2), 2161. doi: 10.1002/hsr2.161. PMID: 32318628; PMCID: PMC7170452.

Wilson, A.J. (1985, April). Knowledge for teachers: The origin of the national teacher examinations program. Paper presented at the annual meeting of the American Educational Research Association, Chicago, Il. https://files.eric.ed.gov/fulltext/ED262049.pdf

Wise, A.E. (1968). *Rich Schools Poor Schools: The Promise of Equal Educational Opportunity*. Chicago and London: University of Chicago Press.

Women in Aviation Advisory Board Report (WIAAB). (2022). Breaking barriers for women in aviation: Flight plan for the future. Retrieved on March 15, 2024.

https://www.faa.gov/regulations_policies/rulemaking/committees/documents/media/WIAAB_Recommendations_Report_March_2022.pdf

Wood, B.D. (1940a). Ten years of the Cooperative Test Service. *Educational Record*, 25 July.

Wood, B D. (1940b). *Making Use of the Objective Examination as a Phase of Teacher Selection. American Association of Teachers Colleges, Nineteenth Yearbook.* Menasha, WI: Banta.

Zanderland, L. (1998). *Measuring Minds*. Cambridge University Press.

Zwick, R., and Dorans, N.J. (2016). Philosophical perspectives on fairness in educational assessment. In N.J. Dorans and L.L. Cook (Eds.), *Fairness in Educational Assessment and Measurement* (pp. 267–282). Taylor and Francis.

Index

ACP (Achievement Capstone Program) *see* merit-based scholarship testing
ACT (American College Testing) test. *See also* SAT test
  bias, 75–8
  role in college admission and graduation rate, 115–17
  usage, 74
admission testing, costs
  incorrect acceptance, 113–15
  incorrect rejection, 112–13
  role of ACT and SAT, 115–17
  subjective admission decision, 119–20
admission testing, higher education
  bias, 75–8
  Graduate Record Examination (GRE), 73
  graduation rates, 78–81
  poor students, 73
  problems, 177
  standardized testing, 73
  state differences, 72–3
  success rate, 183
  usage history, 74–5
air traffic controller licensing
  Air Traffic Selection and Training (AT-SAT), 62
  Air Traffic Skills Assessment (ATSA), 62–3
Air Traffic Selection and Training (AT-SAT), 62
airline licensing
  air traffic controller, 62–3
  pilot, 61–2
Airline Safety and Federal Aviation Administration Extension Act (2010), 62
American College Testing test *see* ACT Test
anecdote versus data, 183

Armed Services Vocational Aptitude Battery (ASVAB)
  Cassius Clay example, 32–3
  computerized administration, 107
  informed decision making, 31–2
  military mental testing, 28
  Project 100000, 33
  specificity, 106–7
  subscore reliability, 104–5
  success rate, 105–6
  test computerization, 55–6
Army General Classification Test (AGCT), 27–8, 30
assumptions, causal inference
  Rubin's model of causal inference, 136–7
  when experiments are not possible, 138–9
  when experiments are possible, 137–8
ASVAB *see* Armed Services Vocational Aptitude Battery
athletic scholarships
  history, 83–4
  race and, 84
Atlanta Miracle, 43
ATSA (Air Traffic Skills Assessment) *see* air traffic controller licensing
bias, testing
  errors and, 6–7
  ethnicity and, 22
  fairness and, 184
  gender and, 21–2
  higher education admission testing, 75–8
  multi-part multiple-choice exam, 7
  physician licensing, 52–3, 59–60
  subjective college admission, 119–20
  testing dislike, 14

carbon dioxide and global warming study, 140–2
CAT *see* computerized adaptive test
causal inference
  circumstantial evidence, 152–6
  measurement, 149–50
  observational studies, 140–9
  role of assumptions, 136–9
  Rubin's model of causal inference, 135–7, 149–50
  SAT test coaching zombie idea, 160–1
  scientific evidence and, 127–58
  social science research application, 156–8
  testing policy, 181–3
  unexplained events, 151–2
  value-added models, 92
causes of effects, scientific evidence
  cholera epidemic, 129–33
  SAT score decline, 134
cholera epidemic, 129–33
Clay, Cassius, 32–3
Coleman Report, 38–9, 91
college admissions testing
  ACT and SAT tests, 115–17
  bias, 119–20
  fairness and, 16–17
  incorrect acceptance, 113–15
  incorrect rejection, 112, 113
  MCAT test, 59
  multi-part multiple-choice exam, 5
  testing dislike, 13
computerized adaptive test (CAT)
  Armed Services Vocational Aptitude Battery (ASVAB), 55–6
  costs, 56
  future of, 56–7
  history, 56
  instructional diagnosis, 9
  large-scale tests, 8–9
  multi-part multiple-choice exam, 8
  problems, 9–10
costs
  admission testing, 112–17
  computerized adaptive test (CAT), 56
  licensing examinations, 117–18
  not testing, 177
  policy makers knowledge of alternatives, 181–3
  situation variation, 184–5

District of Columbia Miracle, 42–3

Educator Teacher Performance Assessment (edTPA), 70
Elementary and Secondary Education Act (ESEA), 38–9
errors, objective scoring
  bias, 6–7, 52–3
  judge unreliability, 54
  rater variation, 6
ethnicity, testing, 22
Every Student Succeeds Act (ESSA), 43–4
evidence-based decision making, 127–9

fairness
  college admissions testing, 16–17
  compromised by bias, 184
  merit-based scholarship testing, 87–9
  testing dislike, 21–2
  1500-hour rule, 62
fracking
  concerns, 143
  definition, 142–3
  dewatering, 142
  observational earthquake study, 143–8

g (general intelligence), military testing, 30–1
gender, testing, 21–2
General Certificate of Secondary Education (GCSE), 45
Graduate Record Examination (GRE), 73
Grade Point Average (GPA), 18

Hitchen's Razor, 22–3
Hubbard, John, 53–4

inclusion, testing
  fears of, 14
  musical proficiency testing, 14–15, 16
  running, 15–16
  social factors, 16
incorrect acceptance, college admissions, 113–15
incorrect rejection, college admission
  cost to school, 113
  cost to student, 112
IQ (Intelligence Quotient) testing, 36–7
item response theory (IRT), 4

K-12 teacher licensing
  Educator Teacher Performance Assessment (edTPA), 70
  exam requirements, 64

history, 64–5
national exam, 64
National Teacher Examination (NTE), 66–9
problems, 69
standardized test development, 65–6
standards, 63–4
state differences, 63
Kelleys paradox regression, 168–70

licensing examinations
  airline, 60–3
  background, 48–9
  K-12 teacher, 63–70
  physician, 49–60
licensing examinations, costs
  incorrect decision to license, 117–18
  incorrect decision to withhold license, 118

Medical College Admissions Test (MCAT), 59
mental testing
  fundamental change in testing, 4
  IQ testing, 36–7
mental testing, military
  Armed Services Vocational Aptitude Battery (ASVAB), 28, 31–4
  birth of modern, 25–8
  differences between tests, 28–30
  First World War, 6
  g (general intelligence), 30–1
  Project 100,000, 24–5
  recruit, 24–5
merit-based scholarship testing
  academic, 84–5
  Achievement Capstone Program (ACP), 86
  athletic, 83–4
  fairness and, 87–9
  National Merit Scholarship (NMS), 85–7
  overview, 82–3
  testing policy, 181–3
military mental testing
  Armed Services Vocational Aptitude Battery (ASVAB), 28, 31–4
  birth of modern, 25–8
  differences between, 28–30
  First World War, 6
  g (general intelligence), 30–1
  recruit, 24–5
minority inclusion
  National Merit Scholarship (NMS), 86
  physician licensing, 59

public education testing, 37–8
testing policy, 181–3
miracle
  Atlanta, 43
  defined, 41
  District of Columbia Miracle, 42–3
  New Orleans, 42
  Texas, 41–2
multi-part multiple-choice exam. *See also* standardized testing
  benefits, 7–8, 180–1
  bias and, 7
  college admissions testing, 5
  Computerized Adaptive Tests (CAT), 8
  First World War, 6, 25–7
  group differences, 17–18
  many questions, 7
  physician licensing, 51–3, 55
  Second World War, 27–8
  Vineland Committee, 5

Nation at Risk, A, 40, 90
National Board of Medical Examiners (NBME), 52–6, 109
National Merit Scholarship (NMS), 85–7
National Merit Scholarship Qualifying Test (NMSQT), 84–7, 89
National Teacher Examination (NTE), 66–9
National Assessment of Educational Progress (NAEP) *see* Nation's Report Card
Nation's Report Card, 90
New Orleans Miracle, 42
No Child Left Behind (NCLB), 41–2, 90–1, 107–8

objective scoring
  errors, 6–7, 52–3
  history, 3–4
  importance, 6–10
observational studies and scientific evidence
  carbon dioxide and global warming study, 140–2
  fracking study, 142–8
  overview, 124–7, 177–8

physician licensing, history
  inception, 49
  John Hubbard, 53–4
  lack of standardization and objectivity, 50–1
  multiple-choice exam, 51–3, 55
  oral exams, 50
  reason for, 49–50

physician licensing, history (cont.)
  state, 50
  test customization, 55
  test flexibility, 54–5
  true score theory, 55
  United States Medical License Examination (USMLE), 54, 58, 59–60
  Wheeling shooting, 51
physician licensing, minority inclusion, 59
physician licensing, modern
  increased scrutiny, 57–8
  knowledgeable versus good, 58–9
  lessons from the past, 58
pilot licensing
  1500-hour rule, 62
  costs, 62
  demographics, 61
  flight training, 61
  inception, 61
  post WWII, 61
poor students
  admission testing, 73
  merit-based scholarship testing, 82–9
Project 100000,
  higher education, 34
  military mental testing, 33
PSAT *see* National Merit Scholarship Qualifying Test
public education testing
  achievement gaps, 40–1
  Every Student Succeeds Act (ESSA), 43–4
  history, 35–6
  IQ, 36–7
  minority reforms, 37–8
  A Nation at Risk, 40, 90
  poverty reforms, 38–9
  reform effectiveness, 44–6
public education testing, failure
  effects causes, 46
  social inequities, 46–7
  truth, 46
public education testing, miracles
  Atlanta Miracle, 43
  District of Columbia Miracle, 42–3
  New Orleans Miracle, 42

Race to the Top, 91
reliability, test, 19
Rubin's model of causal inference
  effect measurement, 149–50
  scientific assumptions and, 136–9
  scientific evidence and, 135–6
  unexplained events, 151–2

sampling's theoretical role in regression to the mean, 167–8
SAT (Scholastic Assessment Test) test. *See also* ACT test
  bias, 75–8
  role in college admission and graduation rate, 115–17
  score decline study, 134
  usage, 74
SAT test, Strivers zombie idea
  background, 165–6
  Kelleys paradox regression, 168–70
  sampling to the mean regression theory, 167–8
  score and graduation rate conclusion, 170–1
SAT test, test-optional admissions zombie idea, 171–5
SAT test, zombie coaching value
  background, 159–60
  causal inference, 160–1
  versus practice test taking, 162–3
  superscoring effects, 163–5
Scholastic Assessment Test or Scholastic Aptitude Test *see* SAT test
scientific evidence and causal inference
  causes of effects, 129–34
  circumstantial evidence, 152–6
  evidence-based decision making, 127–9
  importance of, 121–2
  kinds of evidence, 129
  measurement, 149–50
  observational studies, 140–9
  observational study, 124–7
  role of assumptions, 136–9
  Rubin's model, 135–6
  social science research application, 156–8
  unexplained events, 151–2
standardized testing. *See also* multi-part multiple-choice exam
standardized testing, subcomponents
  Armed Services Vocational Aptitude Battery (AVSAB), 104–7
  definition, 101
  history, 102–4
  K-12 testing, 107–8
  reliability, 97–8, 104–5

specificity, 106–7
US Census example, 98–100
uses, 101–2
value, 108–10

Tennessee Class Size Experiment, 137–8
testing dislike
   college admissions testing, 13
   construction bias, 14
   fairness and, 21–2
   Hitchen's Razor, 22–3
   inclusion prevention, 14
   options, 18–19
   reasons for, 11–12, 178–9
   solutions for, 179–80
   test construction, 19–20
   test quality, 18–19
testing history
   Chinese inception, 2–3
   Indian, 3
   IQ, 36–7
   lasting problems, 1
   Middle Eastern, 3
   multi-part multiple-choice exam, 5–6
   multiple graders, 5
   public education, 35–6
   summary, 176–7
testing history, fundamental changes
   cognitive ability, 4

item response theory (IRT), 4
objective scoring, 3–4
Texas miracle, 41–2
TOEFL (Test of English as a Foreign Language) 2000, 10

United States Medical License Examination (USMLE), 54, 58, 59–60
US Census example, 98–100

validity, test, 19
value-added models (VAM)
   background, 90–1
   A Nation at Risk, 90
   Nation's Report Card, 90
value-added models (VAM), problems
   causal inference and, 92
   missing data, 94–5
   test comparison, 92–4
Vineland Committee, 5

Wheeling shooting, 51

zombie ideas, testing
   definition, 159
   SAT test coaching value, 159–65
   Strivers, 165–71
   summary, 185–6
   test-optional admission application, 171–5

For EU product safety concerns, contact us at Calle de José Abascal, 56–1°,
28003 Madrid, Spain or eugpsr@cambridge.org.

www.ingramcontent.com/pod-product-compliance
Lightning Source LLC
LaVergne TN
LVHW010257260326
834688LV00044B/1330